CW00550121

Class Inequality in Austerity Britain

Also by Will Atkinson
CLASS, INDIVIDUALIZATION AND LATE MODERNITY

Also by Mike Savage
CLASS ANALYSIS AND SOCIAL TRANSFORMATION

CULTURE, CLASS DISTINCTION (*with Tony Bennett, Elizabeth Silva, Alan Warde, Modesto Gayo-Cal, David Wright*)

GENDER AND BUREAUCRACY (*ed. with Anne Witz*)

GENDER, ORGANISATIONS AND CAREERS (*with Susan Halford and Anne Witz*)

GLOBALISATION AND BELONGING (*with Gaynor Bagnall and Brian Longhurst*)

IDENTITIES AND SOCIAL CHANGE IN BRITAIN SINCE 1940

LOCALITIES, CLASS AND GENDER (*with Linda Murgatroyd, Dan Shapiro, John Urry, Sylvia Walby and Alan Warde*)

NETWORKED URBANISM (*ed. with Talja Blokland*)

PROPERTY, BUREAUCRACY AND CULTURE (*with James Barlow, Peter Dickens and Tony Fielding*)

REMEMBERING ELITES (*ed. with Karel Williams*)

RENEWING CLASS ANALYSIS (*ed. with Rosemary Crompton, Fiona Devine and John Scott*)

RETHINKING CLASS (*ed. with Fiona Devine, Rosemary Crompton and John Scott*)

SOCIAL CHANGE AND THE MIDDLE CLASSES (*ed. with Tim Butler*)

THE DYNAMICS OF WORKING CLASS POLITICS

THE REMAKING OF THE BRITISH WORKING CLASS 1840–1940 (*with Andrew Miles*)

URBAN SOCIOLOGY, CAPITALISM AND MODERNITY (*with Alan Warde*)

Class Inequality in Austerity Britain

Power, Difference and Suffering

Edited by

Will Atkinson
University of Bristol, UK

Steven Roberts
University of Kent, UK

and

Mike Savage
London School of Economics and Political Science, UK

First published 2012 by
PALGRAVE MACMILLAN

Palgrave Macmillan in the UK is an imprint of Macmillan Publishers Limited, registered in England, company number 785998, of Houndmills, Basingstoke, Hampshire RG21 6XS.

Palgrave Macmillan in the US is a division of St Martin's Press LLC, 175 Fifth Avenue, New York, NY 10010.

Palgrave Macmillan is the global academic imprint of the above companies and has companies and representatives throughout the world.

Palgrave® and Macmillan® are registered trademarks in the United States, the United Kingdom, Europe and other countries

ISBN 978-1-137-01637-9

This book is printed on paper suitable for recycling and made from fully managed and sustained forest sources. Logging, pulping and manufacturing processes are expected to conform to the environmental regulations of the country of origin.

A catalogue record for this book is available from the British Library.

A catalog record for this book is available from the Library of Congress.

10   9   8   7   6   5   4   3   2   1
21   20   19   18   17   16   15   14   13   12

Printed and bound in Great Britain by
CPI Antony Rowe, Chippenham and Eastbourne

Contents

v

List of Figures and Tables

Figures

Tables

List of Contributors

Will Atkinson is a British Academy Postdoctoral Fellow in the School of Sociology, Politics and International Studies at the University of Bristol.

Harriet Bradley is Professor Emeritus of Sociology and Senior Research Fellow in the School of Sociology, Politics and International Studies at the University of Bristol.

Matt Clement is Associate Lecturer in the Department of Health and Applied Social Science at the University of the West of England.

Sarah Evans is Engagement Manager for the Social Sciences at the British Library.

Val Gillies is Research Professor within the Weeks Centre for Social and Policy Research and the Families & Social Capital Research Group at London South Bank University.

Nicola Ingram is a Research Assistant in the School of Sociology, Politics and International Studies at the University of Bristol.

Lisa McKenzie is a Leverhulme Research Fellow in the Faculty of Social Sciences at the University of Nottingham.

Diane Reay is Professor of Education at the University of Cambridge.

Steven Roberts is Lecturer in Social Policy and Sociology at the University of Kent.

Mike Savage is Professor of Sociology at the London School of Economics and Political Science, Visiting Professor at the Universities of Bergen and York and Visiting Research Fellow at the University of Manchester.

Andrew Sayer is Professor of Sociology in the Department of Sociology at the University of Lancaster.

1

Introduction: A Critical Sociology of the Age of Austerity

Will Atkinson, Steven Roberts and Mike Savage

The last 15 years or so have witnessed an extraordinary revitalisation of sociological research on social class in Britain. For some time in the doldrums, under attack from within and without academia, it is now back high on the agenda thanks in large part to a progressive deepening of the theoretical scope of its core concept to grasp themes generally excluded from previous programmes of research. Class is not just about exploitation and economic inequalities, it is now established, but cultural and symbolic domination too; it is not just about life chances and 'equality of opportunity', but about self-worth, suffering and denigration as well; and it is tied not only to a politics of redistribution, as crucial as that is, but also, at the same time, a politics of *recognition*. In pursuing these themes the key source of inspiration for researchers has not been Karl Marx or Max Weber, the opposing couple at the heart of the sociology of class through most of the twentieth century, but the ideas of Pierre Bourdieu.[1] For this Frenchman, social class is defined not by relation to the means of production, nor by possession of particular skills and capacities in the labour market, but by the possession of all forms of economic capital (wealth and income), cultural capital (education and 'good taste') and social capital (contacts, networks, names, club membership, etc.) which together shape the kinds of experience it is possible to have, the kinds of goods and opportunities it is possible to attain and the kinds of people one is likely to have regular contact with, and, in turn, the expectations, values, desires, tastes and lifestyles developed in adaptation. Far from all being bestowed with equal value, however, those possessing the most resources, and the most power, impose their own way of life – educational or economic accomplishment, being 'cultivated', 'well-mannered', self-interested and so on – as the legitimate, worthy and

1

ultimately *right* way to do things, denigrating those not possessing the material conditions necessary for their achievement. This process Bourdieu famously dubbed 'symbolic violence'.

For all its advances, however, this new direction in class analysis has been accused by some hanging on to older frameworks, less taken by Bourdieu's ideas, of unjustifiably sidelining – not simply through choice of research object but in theoretical principle – economic inequalities, differences in life chances, the machinations of the business and political elite and the convulsions of capitalism.[2] It may well be supposed, therefore, that it is essentially powerless to understand or effectively critique the causes and consequences of not only the severe economic downturn of the late 2000s and the pervasive political climate of austerity that has followed in the UK but the larger global neoliberal movement from which they both spring. This volume aims to resolutely refute this claim and make the case that frameworks inspired to greater and lesser degrees by Bourdieu – including those developed by Loic Wacquant and Beverley Skeggs – not only *can* grasp and censure the current political-economic juncture but *must*. They *can* because differences in economic capital and power have always been fundamental to Bourdieu's conceptualisation of conditions of life, the formation of tastes and lifestyles, likely trajectories through the class structure and possibilities of action, as have the forces of the capitalist economic field in producing them, it is just that they remain inextricably entwined with the fundamental human quest for recognition and, with that, symbolic power. Consider, for example, the fact that – contrary to Bourdieu's critics who chastise him for presuming 'high culture' is necessarily the legitimated form of culture – symbolic domination is always a question of the precise balance of power between the dominant (economic) and dominated (cultural) fraction of the dominant class. In twenty-first century Britain, could it be that the economic fraction – comprised not only of business owners but of a fusion of higher managers and top-level professional too[3] – has succeeded in asserting its dominance more than ever and thus further (though not entirely) imposed its hedonistic, materialistic lifestyle as the legitimate one, a move which yields a *double victory* insofar as they attain greater symbolic recognition at the same time as efforts by others to approximate them by purchasing the goods and services they produce or administer return evermore economic capital to them (profits, bonuses, shares)?

Moreover, a Bourdieusian strand of research dedicated to mapping the structure and practices of the 'elite' – or the 'field of power' containing individuals from the economic field *as well* as from the intellectual field, political field and so on, all contending to impose their definition of the world, and the policies necessary to achieve it, as legitimate – is beginning to flourish.[4]

They *must*, on the other hand, because sociology is, as Norbert Elias[5] claimed, a *myth buster*, tearing down prevailing misconceptions and folk beliefs, not least, as Bourdieu[6] added, the myths wielded by the dominant and perpetuating the reproduction of inequality. Sociology is thus a means of *defence against symbolic domination* (which, among other things, sustains *material domination*) and the current tropes mobilised by the Conservative/Liberal Democrat coalition government of 'fairness' and compulsory austerity, as extensions of neoliberal orthodoxy, should be no exception. The ideas underpinning government rhetoric must, therefore, be scrutinised, the real effects of the 2008 recession and coalition policy must be demonstrated through rigorous empirical research and the true winners of the current political-economic moment must be unmasked. In short, Marxism, for all its insights, does not have a monopoly on the study of the economic dimension of class, nor does it, as Erik Olin Wright[7] seems to imply in his categorisation of versions of class analysis, possess a monopoly on critique of the current order in the service of bringing a better tomorrow.

In this volume, then, we have brought together a range of rigorous yet engaged interventions, in the form of original research pieces or critical overviews of policy or evidence, from scholars united by their guiding interest in exposing the operations of class domination with reference to Bourdieusian themes yet covering a wide assortment of specialist areas. Broad concerns with the economic and symbolic violence inflicted on and through education, family life and community in the present and recent past weave through more or less every chapter, but the precise themes explored include the stratified impact of the late 2000s recession and austerity on family life and consumption (Atkinson), the deleterious effects of schools policy and cuts (Reay), the likely impact of the hike in higher education tuition fees given the disadvantages already suffered by working-class university students (Bradley and Ingram), the barriers to and denigration of working-class aspirations (Roberts and Evans), the myopic construction of parenting policy (Gillies), the economic and symbolic marginalisation of the most deprived sections of the working class and its role in the genesis of proscribed activity and the summer riots of 2011 (Clement, McKenzie) and the ignorance and hypocrisy of claims that communities in the UK are 'broken' (Savage), with Andrew Sayer offering an analysis of the rise of the new rentier class as a salutary reminder not to take our sociological gaze off those at the top in examining the suffering of those at the bottom. Ultimately, by pooling our expertise and acting as something more like the 'collective intellectual' of which Bourdieu spoke, we hope to offer a more thoroughgoing and comprehensive assessment and, with that, more effective critique of the bearing of current political practice on both conditions of existence and ways of seeing the world. This is robust scholarship, in other words, but in service of the commitment to contributing to political and popular debate to the best of our abilities.[8]

In the rest of this introductory chapter we want to sketch out the socio-historical context for the contributions and, in doing so, follow through on our claim that a Bourdieusian sociology of class possesses the means to make sense of not only the consequences of the current nexus of relations of domination but its genesis too. Specifically, and though constraints of space mean the overview will be suggestive rather than exhaustive, the hope being that it might spur further analysis, we seek to embed the economic crisis and its political fallout within an account of the rise and persistence in Britain of neoliberalism, not as simply an economic model easily imposed by a capitalist elite to serve their interests, as for Marxism, nor – for all its useful insights on the diffusion and reworking of neoliberal categories of thought in multiple contexts – as the overly fluid and decentralised cluster of 'techniques' examined by advocates of governmentality.[9] Instead, the birth of the neoliberal creed and its various articulations, it will be shown, are anchored in the complex struggles and strategies (in Bourdieu's sense) within and across a specific cluster of *fields* diffusing their effects into everyday life via multitudinous circuits of symbolic power.

The neoliberal revolution

On the 11th of May 2010, David Cameron, leader of the Conservative Party since 2005, was invited by Queen Elizabeth II to form a new government, ending thereby 13 years of New Labour power. Within weeks an 'emergency budget' was put together seeking, it was said, to rein in the excessive spending recklessly pursued by Gordon Brown's short-lived administration, slash the bloated budget deficit and steadily navigate the choppy tides whipped up by worldwide recession. At the same time, however, this new government, incorporating an electorally-battered Liberal Democrat Party, sought to couple the new atmosphere of austerity with a determined rhetoric of *fairness*. Indeed, the official 'coalition agreement' penned by a small cabal of like-minded leading lights of both parties has the word boldly emblazoned on its third page in large type alongside 'freedom' and 'responsibility', presenting it as a cornerstone of joint governance, and is crammed with warm words to the effect that the Prime Minister and his Deputy, Nick Clegg, will 'ensure fairness is at the heart of those decisions' on how to cut spending 'so that those most in need are protected' and 'everyone, regardless of background, has the chance to rise as high as their talents and ambition allow them'.[10] Despite this rhetoric, however, in the emergency budget and beyond the coalition have scrapped or whittled down those existing programmes which, however meagre and superficial, were aimed at reducing economic and educational inequalities, such as the Educational Maintenance Allowance – the payment to pupils entering post-compulsory schooling as a means of lessening the demands of economic necessity – and the Future Jobs Fund – the programme of subsidised youth employment. Notable too that, as new means of raising revenue, they have pushed up tax on consumption (VAT) rather than tax on income, which is known to hit those earning less disproportionately, allowed universities to triple tuition fees and sought to 'reform' the welfare system by reducing payments and imposing tougher criteria for receipt. Who exactly this is supposed to be 'fair' for is far from clear.

The shift from prosperity to austerity, however, and from New Labour to the coalition government, whilst offering so many ruptures and transformations in political practice to everyday perception, are in fact relatively small, though not insignificant, details in a much longer-running articulation of state, economy and society sustaining and deepening domination – an articulation best grasped in terms of the ascent of *neoliberalism*, the economic-cum-political doctrine extolling the virtues of unfettered market forces and rapid state shrinkage. Before the 1970s it was confined, albeit obstreperously, to a marginal corner of the field of academic and political economics, overshadowed in all respects by Keynesianism, the economic model advocating active state regulation of markets and a robust public sector in the pursuit of growth and prosperity, but by the end of the decade a dramatic revolution in a multitude of national economic and political fields – those of the UK being first among them – had installed it as the orienting principle of statecraft and set the course for global diffusion. Fundamental to this upheaval, of course, was the shattering anomie in political-economics induced by mounting unemployment and surging inflation (together known as 'stagflation') in the early seventies. The products of a steady intensification of global economic transactions undermining assumptions born decades earlier – brought to a head with the collapse of the consensual system of international exchange controls (the Bretton Woods agreement) and the subsequent Arab oil embargo of 1973 following pro-Israeli US intervention in the Yom Kippur war – from a Keynesian point of view it was believed that these two phenomena simply could not occur together and required completely contradictory solutions (i.e. government spending *and* saving).

Yet neoliberalism eventually succeeded in this climate not thanks to simple rational progress – after all, a whole batch of 'neo-Keynesians' were desperately trying to rework the master's model in order to conserve their position – but, instead, as a consequence of three interlinked strategies of subversion tenaciously pursued by its proponents to counter their domination in the field of economics.[11] First of all, they pushed a progressive *mathematicisation*, soon succeeding, through relentless one-upmanship against econometricians, in imposing statistical prowess as a novel criterion of intellectual credibility within the field with which to discredit the 'gentleman scholars' of Keynesianism. Secondly, academic advocates of neoliberal thought ardently engaged in *vulgarisation*, that is to say, the persistent courting of the sympathetic sectors of the media and political fields, manifest in the endless editorials, newspaper columns, debates and meetings, which forced them to hone their capacities in ideological debate and package their credo in 'common sense' ways. Thirdly, and most importantly, there was the drive toward *internationalisation*, or the constant determination to overcome marginalisation within one national context by fostering homologies in manifold nations across the globe through specific networks of individuals (e.g. the Mont Pelerin Society, the Chilean 'Chicago Boys') and the founding of think-tanks such as, in the UK, the Institute of Economic Affairs, the Centre for Policy Studies and the Adam Smith Institute.

Indeed, it was from these quasi-academic bases that the advocates of neoliberalism endeavoured to impose their construction of the world on the British political field, particularly through the Conservative Party. However, the latter being itself a fractious system of difference and division, while neoliberal economists certainly appealed to the interests of and thus forged concrete links with particular members (e.g. future kingmaker Keith Joseph), the dominant fraction led by Ted Heath, Prime Minister in the early seventies, generally upheld the rapidly crumbling Keynesian orthodoxy. Only with his electoral defeat in 1974, and the inflation and unemployment of the later seventies following the crises already mentioned, did the moment come for the

UK's neoliberal revolution. In fact it entered the political field, in a pincer movement, from two directions: on the one hand, via the budgetary constraints imposed on a reluctant Labour government by the International Monetary Fund (by this time hijacked and steered by neoliberal principles) as a condition of assistance with the financial chaos of the seventies, and on the other hand, and in the long run more consequentially, through the upheavals within the Conservative party in opposition wherein the perceptual schemes of the future Prime Minister, Margaret Thatcher, were fashioned and eventually triumphant. The latter is no simple tale of a single charismatic visionary, nor is it the typical Marxist story of captains of industry 'capturing' political parties in a bid to restore flagging power;[12] it is, rather, a question of complex and shifting struggles, homologies, alliances and networks of interest and influence forged and sustained between multiple individuals (Samuel Britten, Gordon Pepper, Keith Joseph, etc.) situated in multiple fields within the field of power (the think-tanks, the City, the media, the bureaucratic field etc.), some of whom shifted between or stood within more than one field at a time. Nevertheless, none of that would have had the effect it did had it not synchronised with the provincial, petit-bourgeois individualism and anti-'establishment' views of a woman born of a Grantham shopkeeper who, not without serious struggles and strategising within her own party, came to dominate the Conservatives and, through the presentation of herself and her categories of thought as on the side of 'the people', distributed an image and idiom appealing in different ways to political dispositions across the class structure.[13]

The eventual effects of the nascent neoliberal state were threefold. First of all, the economic policies of the Conservative government through the 1980s bore severe and long-lasting *material* and *structural* consequences. In the cause of unleashing market competitiveness and exhorting individuals to work, income tax was cut, the notoriously regressive value added tax was pushed up, wage councils were abolished and the value of welfare benefits dropped relative to earnings,[14] while relentless deindustrialisation, privatisation and flexibilisation of the labour market in the name of 'efficiency' mixed with eager nurturance of financial services quickly delivered devastating levels of unemployment and insecure, precarious labour to the workforce but ever higher returns to the elite within the economic universe. Soon enough a gigantic chasm between the apex and the nadir of the class structure stretched open with disturbing speed and ferocity,[15] with those at the bottom turning to illicit activity and violence as a means of attaining some form of recognition being swept up in the expanding penal wing of the state.[16] This was accompanied, secondly, by intense *symbolic* work aimed at discrediting and vanquishing the category of 'class' once and for all and replacing it with alternative tropes conforming to, and perpetuating, the neoliberal worldview. This battle was waged on several fronts: in the explicit rejection of the category as a politically malignant fiction ('class is a communist concept', said Thatcher), in the invention of new categories to distinguish the poorest (the 'underclass') from everyone else ('taxpayers'), in the moral discourse fostering the image of agents as free-choosing responsible individuals unfettered by fantastical societal forces, but also, critically, in the demolition of trade union power through incessant regulation and restriction, thus relegating to the side lines of the symbolic struggle the chief exponents of the construction of 'the working class' as a unified group with a legitimate political purpose. Finally, Thatcherism succeeded in leaving its enduring residue in the political field, such that when the eponym fell out of favour, the 'common sense' ways of viewing and governing the world – the doxa – it had established remained more or less unchallenged. Witness the steady transformation of the Labour Party, first under Neil Kinnock and John Smith and then most radically under Tony Blair – an individual whose position and trajectory in the class structure and the space of political position-takings aligned him with Conservatives rather than progressives – from democratic socialist party to bastion of unconstrained neoliberalism. Rather than try to challenge the damaging doxic categories and manipulations of conditions of existence pushed on individuals as legitimate, they aped them instead, albeit eventually contained within the superficial discursive shell of a 'third way', in a strategy to gain electoral support.[17]

Thus, when 'New' Labour finally came to office in 1997, accompanied by the strategic language of rupture and renewal – a 'new dawn' no less – the material, symbolic and political landscapes changed very little. Economic growth was, as under Thatcher, valued over economic equality, and so while the (low) minimum wage and (workfare) measures to reduce poverty unquestionably had some effect on conditions of existence, the reluctance to redistribute wealth from the top down on the grounds that 'talented individuals' would then seek reward elsewhere in the global labour market, plus the so-called 'light touch' approach to regulation of the financial sector aimed at attracting those pursuing economic reward, ensured that the rates of inequality, and so the dispersion of the class structure, continued to be as stark as under Thatcher.[18] Moreover, New Labour took over, but revamped, the construction of the social world as divided into two camps – the problematic 'socially excluded' versus the rest – and, though the bare individualism of the Conservatives was replaced by a vague and ineffectual focus on 'communities', the language of 'class', on which the party was founded, was thoroughly expunged from the legitimate lexicon.[19] Not only that, but the 'included' bulk of the populace were, in policy and practice, increasingly conceived as 'customers' and 'clients', and indeed a consumerist mentality, in which the legitimate route to recognition is via ownership and display of exclusive goods and practices, was diffused more widely.[20] One consequence of this, of course, was an increased desire for *credit*, and the deregulated and globally interlinked banks were quick to exploit this by handing out lucrative loans and mortgages to those lacking the capital to pay them back. Indeed, in the US, where economic and political struggles and strategies bore remarkable parallels (and indeed synergies) with those of the UK – staunchly conservative 1980s, the later nineties dominated by a right-wing social democrat claiming a bogus 'third way', neoliberalism and consumerism run rife as a result – the upshot was, of course, the subprime mortgage bubble and its catastrophic eruption, the fallout from which reached deep into the UK banking sector and generated worldwide recession.

New discourse, old ideas

Like the economic crisis of the seventies, the global financial meltdown of the late 2000s threw into question the doxic categories of political-economic thought that had produced it.[21] Neoliberalism and its core tenets were forced out into the open and scrutinised, up to a point, whilst progressive and Keynesian opponents became more numerous and strident in their calls for overthrow. Ironically, however, in the UK the Labour Party, widely (and rightly) held at least partially responsible for providing the conditions of possibility of the nation's experience of the economic crisis, was subsequently replaced in government by a party that had, at the time of New Labour's disastrous programme of deregulation, pushed for them to go even further. Yet the Conservative Party had, in the meantime, been undergoing its own mutations. After battling unsuccessfully against Tony Blair's encroachment on their political turf by lurching further toward the right in the early 2000s, an apparent *emulation strategy* was launched instead in which, essentially, the party was presented by the leading faction as 'modernised', socially liberal, 'fair' and, ultimately, in agreement with Labour on many policies (City Academies, gay rights, etc.). The presentation of a closing down of political difference through mimicry, in other words, was now being pushed in from the right, and reached its apogee when David Cameron joined forces with the Liberal Democrats – themselves led by the so-called 'Orange Book' faction supportive of neoliberal measures – to present their coalition as 'liberal conservatism' in action. However, unlike the steady rightwards shift of the Labour Party a political generation earlier, all the signs indicate that this emulation is, in reality, better described as *dissimulation*.

Take, for example, the flagship discourse of the 'Big Society' which promotes volunteering, social enterprise and charity as the ideal vehicles for fostering the community cohesion and solidarity apparently absent in deprived areas yet key to solving their ills. Seemingly breaking with the individualism of Margaret Thatcher in which there was 'no such thing as society', in reality this is nothing but a giant Trojan horse for precisely the kind of individualism Britain's first female Prime Minister espoused – that is, it is not for the state to provide support, care or education for people; it is up to individuals themselves to look after their own interests, their family's interests, and (if they are so inclined) their neighbours' interests by founding and running their own programmes, whether a 'Free School' or community group.[22] Similarly, though members of the Conservative Party (especially Iain Duncan Smith) have endeavoured to appropriate tropes of 'fairness' and 'compassion' and project an earnest desire to reduce poverty, especially through bestowing such deeply ironic names on their think-tanks as 'The Centre for Social Justice', this is merely a thin recasting of the same old obsession with 'family breakdown', immorality and self-responsibility that marked the underclass debates of the early nineties without the slightest interest in referring to the established sociological causes of poverty and, for that matter, family hardship. Finally, under the banner of 'austerity' the Conservative-led government has essentially declared a 'state of exception', in Giorgio Agamben's[23] words, using the discourse as an excuse to engineer a fundamental restructuring of the public sector in which as much as possible is opened up and sold off to the players, and the fundamental interests, of the economic field. Indeed, as they themselves gleefully admit, the coalition has moved 'faster and further' toward the right-wing paradise of privatisation and self-responsibilisation in a few short years than Thatcher managed in a torturous decade.[24] This time, moreover, it would seem to be oriented less by petit-bourgeois individualism and moral authoritarianism than the worldview of the dominant class – as both the Prime Minister and his Chancellor are millionaire progeny of masters of the economy who successfully converted aristocratic resources into financial and educational ones – meaning that neoliberal governance in the UK has finally come to be executed by its most obvious beneficiaries.

Such is the landscape of political-economic-symbolic power characterising contemporary Britain. What, then, has been and is its bearing on contemporary Britons, on families struggling with shopping bills, school pupils, university students, young workers, parents, excluded teenagers and local communities? We hope the following contributions go some way toward making that clear.

Notes

1 Particularly P. Bourdieu (1984) *Distinction*. London: Routledge, but also P. Bourdieu and J.-C. Passeron (1990) *Reproduction in Education, Society and Culture* (2nd Ed.). London: Sage.

2 R. Crompton and J. Scott (2005) 'Class Analysis: Beyond the Cultural Turn' in F. Devine, M. Savage, J. Scott and R. Crompton (eds) *Rethinking Class*. Basingstoke: Palgrave Macmillan. Cf. also Sayer, this volume.

3 Cf. T. Bennett, M. Savage, E. Silva, M. Gayo-Cal and D. Wright (2009) *Culture, Class, Distinction*. London: Routledge.

4 See M. Savage and K. Williams (eds) (2008) *Remembering Elites*. Oxford: Blackwell. Bourdieu's own key work on the field of power is P. Bourdieu (1996) *The State Nobility*. Cambridge: Polity Press.

5 N. Elias (1990) *What is Sociology?* Columbia: Columbia University Press.

6 P. Bourdieu (2003) *Firing Back*. New York: The New Press.

7 E. O. Wright (2005) 'Conclusion: If Class is the Answer, What is the Question?' in E. O. Wright (ed.) *Approaches to Class Analysis*. Cambridge: Cambridge University Press, pp. 180–92.

8 On scholarship with commitment, see Bourdieu (2003) *op. cit.*, p. 24. For further reflections on the barriers to this, see the Conclusion at the end of this volume.

9 See L. Wacquant (2012) 'Three Steps to a Historical Anthropology of Actually Existing Neoliberalism', *Social Anthropology*, 20(1): 66–79.

10 HM Government (2010) *The Coalition: Our Programme for Government*. London: Cabinet Office, p. 7. Notice the pernicious promulgation of meritocracy is exactly the same as that under New Labour and the previous Conservative government discussed in W. Atkinson (2010) *Class, Individualization and Late Modernity*. Basingstoke: Palgrave Macmillan, pp. 192–5.

11 See Y. Dezalay and B. Garth (1998) 'Le "Washington Consensus"', *Actes de la Recherche en Sciences Sociales*, 121(22): 3–22; J. Peck (2010) *Constructions of Neoliberal Reason*. Oxford: Oxford University Press.

12 D. Harvey (2005) *A Brief History of Neoliberalism*. Oxford: Oxford University Press, p. 48.

13 For details see D. Cannadine (1998) *Class in Britain*. London: Penguin; S. Hall (1989) 'The Great Moving Right Show' in S. Hall and M. Jacques (eds) *The Politics of Thatcherism*. London: Lawrence and Wishart; M. Fourcade-Gourinchas and S. Babb (2002) 'The Rebirth of the Liberal Creed', *American*

Journal of Sociology, 108(3): 533–79; M. Prassad (2006) *The Politics of Free Markets*. Chicago: University of Chicago Press. This is not to argue that Thatcher herself possessed a coherent and self-conscious worldview stead-fastly applied to subsequent events, only that she had an orienting set of schemes of perception – even if highly contradictory ones, as Cannadine shows – that, in conjunction and contestation with others within the field, guided her projects and practice from situation to situation.

14   See A. Atkinson and J. Micklewright (1989) 'Turning the Screw' in A. Dilnot and I. Walker (eds) *The Economics of Social Security*. Oxford: Oxford University Press.

15   See the data in A. Atkinson (2000) 'Distribution of Income and Wealth' in A. H. Halsey and J. Webb (eds) *Twentieth-Century British Social Trends*. Oxford: Oxford University Press.

16   L. Wacquant (2009) *Punishing the Poor*. Durham: Duke University Press.

17   On the vagueness and vacuity of the 'third way' notion, see G. McLennan (2004) 'Travelling with Vehicular Ideas: The Case of the Third Way', *Economy and Society*, 33(4): 484–99. Much academic sociology, however, was increasingly caught looking the other way as it was battered by the 'audit culture' imposed on academia through the 1980s and 1990s, on which see the Conclusion to this volume.

18   For figures see D. Dorling (2010) 'New Labour and Inequality', *Local Economy*, 25(5–6): 406–23.

19   R. Levitas (2005) *The Inclusive Society?* (2nd ed.). Basingstoke: Palgrave Macmillan; N. Fairclough (2000) *New Labour, New Language?* London: Routledge.

20   This began before New Labour, but they certainly accelerated it. The classic analysis, though some conclusions are overdrawn, is Z. Bauman (2005) *Work, Consumerism and the New Poor*. Milton Keynes: Open University Press.

21   Cf. L. Adkins (2011) 'Practice as Temporalisation: Bourdieu and Economic Crisis' in B. Turner and S. Susen (eds) *The Legacy of Pierre Bourdieu*. London: Anthem Press, pp. 347–65.

22   For a telling investigation into the schemes of perception underlying the 'Big Society' discourse, see A. Bednarek (2011) 'Responsibility and the Big Society', *Sociological Research Online*, 16(2): www.socresonline.org.uk/16/2/17.html.

23   G. Agamben (2005) *State of Exception*. Chicago: University of Chicago Press.

24   M. Fallon (2011) 'Look at What the Conservatives are Achieving', *The Telegraph*, 2nd March.

2
Economic Crisis and Classed Everyday Life: Hysteresis, Positional Suffering and Symbolic Violence

Will Atkinson

Economic crises, according to Marx's fundamental law of capital accumulation, undermine the condition of existence of the dominated class – the proletariat – that is to say, their capacity to sell their labour, by relegating ever greater numbers to the impoverished reserve army of industrial labour.[1] From a Bourdieusian point of view, however, the classed consequences of the 'business cycle', as it is euphemistically dubbed, are somewhat different. For if class is indeed defined by shared conditions of existence, then these are constituted not merely by ownership or not of the means of production, even if, as economic capital returning economic capital, that undoubtedly contributes to them, but by *relative distance from material necessity* given by possession of *multiple* forms of capital – economic but also cultural and social capital.[2] This relative distance from necessity, yielding probabilities of access to particular goods, services, powers, experiences and regions of the class structure, produces a habitus, or system of dispositions attuned to those probabilities which, making a virtue of necessity – as all humans seek to find a principle of recognition in the lifeworld into which they are thrown – translates them into *tastes*. The differential distribution of resources, however, endows differential capacity to impose one's own tastes as *legitimate* – as what all should strive to be and do – through the fields of cultural and ideological production, meaning that, far from being considered 'different but equal', classed tastes are hierarchised and venerated or vilified depending on which position one is looking at and from.

Yet conditions of existence are not static. Any one individual's conditions may morph through investment and conversion of capital, and, more generally, the relative values and distribution to different sections of the social space of capitals are determined in the struggles

13

within the political and state (or bureaucratic) fields, witnessed in the steady vertical stretching of the UK social space since the neoliberal revolution as relative proximity to necessity increased at the bottom following diminutions in welfare payments while relative distance yawned ever wider at the top. But here we also see the effect of economic crises, as mismatches between the fields of production and demand within social space, and, moreover, of the political programmes of austerity that follow them. To put it simply, conditions of existence are not undermined but *exacerbated*, as escalating inflation, stagnant remuneration and regressive taxes reconfigure the value of one's capital, the range of possibles open and, ultimately, the degree to which economic necessity presses on the senses. The more deeply and rapidly this takes hold the more the disjunction between objective probabilities and the habitus – which Bourdieu called *hysteresis* – is felt as shocking and disorientating, engendering a shift in the perception of what is possible, a readjustment of daily practice and, with that, a sense of loss.

The dominant, just as in Marx's formulation, are not entirely exempt from this scenario, but contrary to the popular spontaneous sociology of downtrodden 'consumers', 'taxpayers', 'the British public' or, worse, the 'squeezed middle' perpetuated by the political and media fields, the hysteresis induced by the economic cataclysm of 2007/8 onwards has not been evenly distributed through the social space of classes, nor have 'those with the broadest shoulders' – a noticeable equation of economic capital with physical capital, masculinity, virility, symbolic value – subsequently borne the heaviest weight, as the current government likes to say.[3] Instead, everything would seem to indicate that relative proximity to necessity has intensified exponentially the lower in social space one goes, as have the modifications of mundane practices of consumption furnishing one's place within the imposed hierarchy of symbolic value and the distress and emotional pain that go with it.

Transformations in conditions of existence

The broad parameters of this general trend can be traced statistically, though to adequately explore differential shifts in relative distance from necessity by class one must go beyond the official bulletins focussing on income groups and Gini coefficients, however useful they may be for indicating general declines in 'spending power', or the value of economic capital, and, thus, the range of goods and services objectively, and thus perceived to be, accessible.[4] Instead we can usefully turn to analysis of the Office for National Statistics' *Living Costs and Food Survey*, an annual sweep of spending practices in a representative sample of UK households, and, in particular, the figures from 2005/6, comfortably before the economic downturn had begun, and those from 2009/10, at the end of the official recession. Figures 2.1 and 2.2, charting the breakdown of family expenditure in 2009/10, provide a basic illustration of the 'generalised Engel's law'[5] that underpins

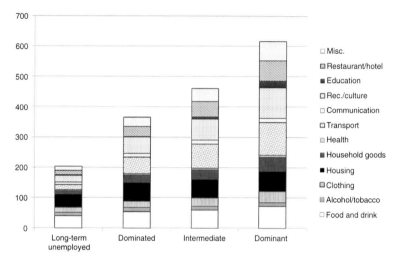

Figure 2.1   Weekly expenditure by class, 2009–10 (£)

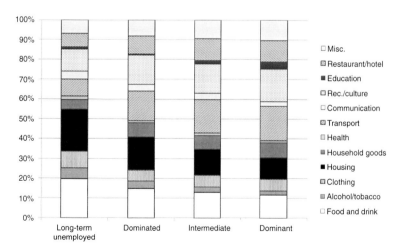

Figure 2.2   Proportion of average weekly spend by class, 2009–10

Table 2.1   Proportion of weekly expenditure by class (%)

	Housing and food		Restaurants/hotels, education, recreation and culture	
	2005/6	2009/10	2005/6	2009/10
Dominant	19	22	29	31
Intermediate	22	26	27	28
Dominated	26	32	27	24
Long-term unemployed	35	41	20	19

Source: *Living Costs and Food Survey* for 2005/6 and 2009/10.

differentiation of class practices, that is, the fact that the greatest disparities in spending appear to concern those goods and services more clearly removed from material necessity – eating out in restaurants, hotel accommodation, culture and recreation and education (which covers fees for private education and tuition) – which, in turn, means that proportion of spend on necessity varies inversely with height in social space.[6] Of course this should not be read as simply a case of the dominant having *more* holidays, meals out etc., for it just as well indicates the *expense* or *style* of holiday, meal etc. consumed by members of each class, which is, of course, adjusted to the possible (long-haul getaway versus local caravanning, lavish bistro versus the fast-food eatery, etc.). In any case, shifting to a diachronic perspective and honing in on the less ambiguous indicators of expenditure on material necessity (housing and food costs), and on those categories signifying, albeit imperfectly, distance from necessity, renders the uneven impact of the recession clear (Table 2.1). As a proportion of household expenditure, the costs of meeting the demands of material necessity, due to rising rents, mortgage interest rates, food prices and fuel costs, have increased for all, but the degree to which necessity demands a greater proportion of family expenditure follows a clear class pattern. The less one has, the less it takes to intensify necessity. Conversely, examining the core facets of distance from necessity, it is evident that whereas the dominant and intermediate *increased* spending here (perhaps because such practices have become more expensive), the fractions of the dominated class have *cut back* on these costs, albeit moderately, to balance out the enlarged spend on the essentials.[7]

The economic crisis in everyday life

This differential distribution of alterations in degrees of necessity, as an index of hysteresis, manifests in the warp and weft of everyday life in two ways: first, through the frequency and force with which changes in capital values, objective possibles and demands of necessity enter the attentive core of the stream of consciousness – or impose themselves as 'relevant', as Schutz might say; and, secondly, the extent to which households have had to readjust their mundane practices in order to consume that which their habitus continues to orient them toward. In order to explore these, qualitative research undertaken between 2010 and 2011, the broader objective of which was to document the ways in which position in social space is lived and reproduced – or resisted – in the most everyday activities and interactions between family members, will be drawn on.[8] Twenty-nine families were recruited by way of mailout to three areas of Bristol with starkly contrasting socio-economic profiles, names being picked *au hasard* from the relevant electoral registers, and took part in a range of activities aimed at building the fullest picture possible of individual lifeworlds and the cross-cutting structures of difference and domination determining their physiognomy. These included multiple stretches of observation, self-completion time diaries, guided tours of the home and routine journeys and an interview, all (usually) within eight consecutive days. Around this nucleus of participants, furthermore, supplementary data was gathered in order to rectify the imbalance toward higher-paid and higher-educated participants. This comprised interviews with two families contacted through a debt advice agency sited within the most deprived of the three areas and a more affluent family who could not take part in the full programme of activities due to time pressures.

Initiated at a time when the lingering effects of the recession on prices and, thus, households, were the subject of rancorous contention in the media and political fields, and when the coalition government's first austerity budget was beginning to bite, the degree to which conditions of existence had mutated, and dispositions adapted to them, was always a guiding interest and, therefore, built into the interviews, from which much of the data that follows is derived, from the start. In turn, three more or less coherent categories of experience and practice emerged which, insofar as they tended to correspond to evident differences in possession of capital (economic but also cultural and social capital), would appear to reveal differences of *class habitus* produced by distinct conditions of existence as well as a differential degree of desynchronisation between dispositions and degree of distance from necessity.[9]

Peace in our time

The first orientation, present amongst those possessing high levels of economic and cultural capital, confirms that, as the above figures suggest, the recession impinged on the consciousness and practice of even the most well-resourced. There is, for instance, a tangible perception of rocketing prices ('food's gone up massively now') and thus a sense that 'life has definitely become more expensive' (Mrs Carlisle, part-time secretary, nursing qualifications, £102k)[10] for them – something which impresses on awareness when either 'filling up the car' or totting up the weekly food bills. In some households where mortgage repayments are particularly high in proportion to household income, furthermore, there is some 'worry' and a keen eye kept on interest rates:

> I tend to watch that first Thursday of every month very carefully to see what's going to happen when they set the interest rates. I couldn't believe they kept it at 0.5% this week actually, I really thought it would go up this time.
>
> (Mrs Samuels, publishing manager, degree, £68k)

Consequently, many of these families reported the reluctant postponement or abandonment of specific large-scale projects of recognition or self-realisation born of distance from necessity, including foreign holidays (Smiths) and a child's gap year to Madagascar (Carlisles), and many more described such curtailments in everyday practice as using the car a little less (Patricks), dining out less frequently (Smiths), turning the heating lower than they would normally (Newcombe/Oliver) and, as Mrs Samuels illustrates, altering shopping practices to include more 'value' products at their usual supermarket or even the occasional trip to so-called 'value' stores:

> So [we've] thought we should start doing more shopping at Aldi and places like that, and that has really helped, because our Tesco food shops are about £130 sometimes.

Yet, as other families indicate, this latter practice is conducted within tightly circumscribed limits of what is and is not acceptable to compromise on given what is still objectively accessible and, with that, subjectively desirable ('quality'). They do not abandon completely their favoured 'mainstream' supermarkets such as Sainsbury's or Waitrose, nor do they switch wholesale to value products:

> I don't buy sort of all the value products if I don't think that they're good quality, but I'll buy things like – I've got these value bin bags because I think 'actually they'll do' and they're like half the price of other stuff.
>
> (Mrs Yates, physiotherapist, postgraduate studies, £64k)

The fact is, even if, as Mrs Yates puts it, 'there are times when we are feeling a bit more strapped for cash and think "oh no I'll just buy something cheaper"', on the whole the families displaying this first orientation, as witnessed in the course of the observations, still opt by default for organic and low-fat meats, hand-delivered vegetable boxes, fresh cuts of meat from the butcher, Fair Trade chocolate, ingredients from pricy local shops in the principled quest to support local businesses or 'finest' supermarket ranges in service of creating their 'nutritious' and cosmopolitan dishes (seafood risotto, squash pasta, black bean bake, kedgeree...). There is, as more than one representative of this first group put it, no doubting they still 'eat very well'.

Moreover, if alimentary practices have altered little in the face of economic crisis, then routines and undertakings oriented toward fostering children's cultural capital stocks have changed even less. These privileged parents still put their children through multiple clubs, pay private tutors and encourage extra-curricular activities, from tennis and French to piano and ballet, and they still insist on buying laptops for their children to do their schoolwork (even, in the Samuels family's case, when they are as young as 11). If there were restrictions on activities, it was usually because they did not want to 'overburden' their children, not because of finances, and even in one case where there had been a sizeable drop in income due to shifting employment circumstances, and all manner of readjustments to the new field of possibles, maintaining capital transmission was prioritised over vacations and ensured through skilled and confident negotiation with the educator of a new payment plan following the common familial doxa that 'the kids come first' (Mr Smith, architect, degree, £38k).[11]

Ultimately, even if the abandonment of those projects of recognition and realisation recounted earlier has undeniably generated a feeling of unjust loss ('I'm a bit cross', 'I want my extension!', 'it's a shame'), the prevailing perception amongst this section of the sample was that the downturn had reoriented the range of possibles, and, thus, the sense of what is attainable and desirable, very little. 'I don't think it's really impacted', admitted Mr Patrick (barrister, postgraduate studies), at least not 'in any major way', principally because, he acknowledged, his family is 'comfortably off' and thus 'don't feel it'. Likewise, Mr Tanner (housing manager, degree, £67k), indicating an undisturbed harmony between objective conditions and subjective dispositions, recognises that 'we really haven't changed our lifestyles much at all' because 'if we want something we can usually afford to buy it'. Overall, as Mr Carlisle (GP, degree, £102k) summarises, the dominant appear to be perfectly 'at peace' with the so-called Great Recession.[12]

The art of conservation and its limits

A second cluster of participating families, possessing, on the whole, slightly less in the way of economic and valued cultural resources – their capital often being more technical in character (BTECs, HNDs, etc.) – than the last group, also mobilised several strategies as a means of preserving or accumulating additional economic capital. They too varied their shopping between 'budget' and conventional supermarkets, though, unlike the previous group, they appeared to do this less discriminatively – splitting, for example, their spend 50/50 between the two – and with less attachment to the high-end stores (as demonstrated in Ms Braithwaite's triumphant 'up yours Sainsbury's!'); and they too looked to transportation strategies as a means of 'saving', though, in at least one case, this involved foregoing a car altogether rather than simply reducing usage (Geoffreys). Moreover, evincing a mode of foresight attuned to the forthcoming, as given by the embodied rhythms and volume of capital receipt, some of these families reported a tendency to 'buy in bulk' when goods were discounted or on 'special offer' (Daniels), packing storage spaces and freezers full of 'two for one' offers (Kings), or when money was more ample at the beginning of the month, as a way to save money both in the longer run and in the shorter term, as Mrs King (project analyst, BTEC, £68k) indicates:

> your last weekly shop you're thinking 'oh can't spend so much this week' you know, so just curtail what you buy. Or what I tend to do is buy quite a lot of your washing powder and stuff like that at the

beginning of the month so that then you haven't got that big bill at the end of the month.

Finally, several of the families had taken in lodgers. Now some of the more privileged families did that too, but the difference here is that, whereas they had welcomed others into their homes not due to a yearning for additional money but simply to repopulate large houses after adolescent children had departed for university, for these families in the intermediate zone of social space it was a strategy specifically aimed at bringing in extra revenue. As Ms Floyd (a former language teacher, degree, £32k) states, it allows her family to 'sustain a mortgage', while Mr Geoffrey (a Detective Constable, A levels, £44k) sees the rent as a 'formal wage' for his wife, replacing the earnings lost from her exit from the labour market to tend to their young children (as they cannot afford childcare). Moreover, insofar as houses were only of relatively modest size, unlike the multi-roomed and extended abodes of those in higher reaches of social space, opening the home to boarders is an acknowledged burden or sacrifice, obliterating privacy and closing down lived space. To take our two participants again, Ms Floyd was 'pleased to get her [the second lodger] out' to make space for her children's shared bedroom – they could afford it because she had taken on evening bar work – as it 'feels like the house is a lot bigger', whereas the Geoffreys, who have to share their own bedroom with their three children in order to make enough space for their several lodgers, admit that 'sometimes you just want to be on your own with the family' and regret that 'it's not our home so much', even if they claim they have gotten 'used to it' and extoll the added potential pedagogic effect of their children coming into contact with dissimilar others.

Beyond their more extreme character, however, there is a fundamental difference between these strategies and the tweaks to daily practice undertaken by the first cluster of participants: the lines of action, tactics and sacrifices of these families are not, in fact, adaptations to the recession at all – they are not efforts to readjust practice to the newly possible or rebalance shifting conditions of existence – for they all either predate or were conceived separately from the change in economic climate. Instead they would appear to be long-standing *petit-bourgeois conservation strategies*, that is to say, efforts of saving, economising, 'going without' and so on, an *ars conservandi* orienting a whole *modus vivendi*, in order to maintain the commitment to expenditure on the food, clothes, housing, holidays and such like that they aspire to. Buffered thus – as Mr Geoffrey noted, foregoing a car has 'saved us hundreds of pounds a month' compared to others during the recession not least because petrol costs 'don't really affect us', while Ms Floyd reports that her family countered rising fuel prices by putting up their lodgers' rents – they can, in the words of Mr Hughes (copywriter, HND, £57k):

> have a standard of living where we feel that we can do most of the things we would want to do. Maybe at this point in life it would be nice if we could do a bit more, have a bit more spare time and a bit more money to do things like go travelling, go on nice holidays. But we still manage to do that to a certain extent.

In other words, he and his spouse can still generally afford that which their dispositions, attuned to their long-standing material conditions, lead them to desire.

None of this means that those occupying the intermediate belt of social space are not aware of rising food prices or do not develop a disquiet over having 'not as many pennies in the pot as there were before' (Mr Hughes), but, in general, any concern over the increase in everyday costs is somewhat overshadowed by pervasive anxieties over employment and income insecurity, particularly for the self-employed in fields hit hard by the latest recession or workers in the bureaucratic field due to be axed by spending cuts.[13] Amongst the latter, for example, Mr Michaels (degree, £51k), a mental health and addiction support worker, describes the 'uncertainty' and 'insecurity' at his work, where everyone is thinking 'how much are we going to be cut by?', which is 'a bit worrying' and 'something that's at the back of your mind all the time', while Mr Geoffrey states:

> obviously there's concerns about work. They always think in these times 'let's hit the public sector', it's the first thing to get hit. All the teachers, nurses I know are worried [...] we find out what the cuts are going to be for the police force after Christmas, so just waiting to see, thinking about that.

As to the self-employed, Mr Buchanan (HND, £62k), an electrical engineer struggling to sustain his self-employment as contracts become scarce, and whose wife has had to take on work in a bid to hold on to their old income level, described his situation as 'hard financially', and Mr Hughes, a freelance copywriter, notes that the recession has 'chipped away' at the regularity of his work: 'the phone doesn't ring anymore', he says, so he has 'effectively been made redundant', which has 'not exactly been easy', though his availability to help his wife with her childcare business has given some 'certainty'. Indeed, on closer inspection it would seem that, due to stored or proxy (i.e. household) resources, in all these cases the insecurity is more apparent than real. Mr Michaels is reassured by the fact that his wife has secured permanent work as a social worker, bringing a sizeable increase to their disposable household income; Mr Geoffrey is comforted by the fact that full redundancy is 'unheard of' in the police force; and Mr Buchanan is still bringing in enough income to ride out the drier patches – or keep the family 'ticking over', as he says – and is thus not 'majorly stressed'. In fact he is quite enjoying the new 'autonomy' in his work day, just as Mr Hughes appreciates the new balance between his home and professional life – both permitted only by a threshold of economic security.

Necessity multiplied

But what of those already closest to necessity, for whom the devaluation of economic capital and cuts in welfare expenditure have withered what distance there was at a disproportionate rate, widening the relative difference from those in the higher sectors of social space? Well first of all there are those who, so attuned to the possibles previously open to them ('you get used to a certain lifestyle'), have undertaken several courses of action in a struggle to make up the shortfall in capital value. Some, for instance, have taken to selling their possessions on the internet auction site eBay in a bid to gain 'a few quid' on the grounds that 'it helps' (Mrs Duncan, cleaner, GCSEs, £19k) or 'pays for "a something", you know, it pays for your food or your shopping' (Ms Jeffers, CSEs, £65k). However, the prime tactic in this regard is simply to work more, either by 'putting in the hours', when waged or self-employed, or, if overtime is not available, by taking on more than one job. Mr Nash (no qualifications, £20k), a delivery driver now working 12-hour days, states:

> if at the moment if I don't work those hours we struggle, and in this current climate…we had a bill this morning about our gas and electric going up, so you've got to keep on it. […] if I can afford to go and reduce my hours I will, but at the moment we've just got to stay [as we are].

But Ms Jeffers, clearly from the upper fraction of the dominated class and currently working five separate part-time jobs, puts it clearest of all:

> I've had to take on more jobs, which is why I've increased my hours at [employer] because money's…the food's gone up, our kids are getting older, they want more [...] the bills have gone up about forty percent so my hours I work have gone up forty percent. Because Mr Arnold [her partner] can't earn any more, what he gets paid is what he gets paid, he don't get overtime. So the only way of increasing our income is by me doing more hours and finding more jobs [...] It's not like we've cut back, we're doing exactly what we did before but just having to do more hours and earn more money to get there.

None of this, however, is without negative consequences, whether in the form of tensions and quarrels between partners ('we had rows about it', said Ms Kent, housewife, degree, £39k), a sense of abandonment for the ones (usually women) left at home alone for long stretches with the children ('I was feeling sorry for myself' said Ms Kent again) or interference with the 'family life' so highly valued ('I don't see as much of the kids as I'd like', said Mr Nash).

Not only that, but for many of these families such strategies bear little fruit insofar as they, like other families in similar circumstances who, for whatever reason, do not bring in extra capital to compensate its declining worth, still have to make deep cutbacks in expenditure. Inevitably the first goods and practices to go are those furthest removed from the demands of material necessity – plasma-screen TVs, children's costly social activities, lengthy Christmas gift lists and family jaunts away:

> We don't go on half as many day trips as what we used to. Like before now we'd take them camping for a couple of nights or we would go to Weston for the day, or we'd take them to the zoo, and we just haven't got the spare money to do that since things have gone up and money's gone down. Like our tax credits has like been cut and this and that's gone up, so I don't know.
>
> (Mrs Green, housewife, GCSEs, £15k)

> It seems that wages haven't gone up but everything else is going up so you're having to worry more. Have more heating bills, money's got to go somewhere else. Like at Christmas time, we had to cut the

Christmas present list. Didn't want to but had to. Cutting corners, juggling. It is, it's basics, all your money is just spent on food and heating.

(Ms Kent)

Furthermore, many of the families struggled to reconcile the ballooning costs of food with their interpretation of the political discourse, framed by dominant dispositions toward the body and (mis)recognised as legitimate, for self-responsible 'healthy eating', especially concerning children. Ms Kent, for instance, was determined to feed her children lean chicken, but now, instead of buying chicken fillets, which are 'really expensive', she roasts a whole chicken in order to 'get three meals out of it', something which is, she says, 'more effort' as 'you have to think ahead'. Fresh fruit too is, according to Mr Duncan (unemployed, former lorry driver, GCEs, £19k), 'a luxury now, we can't even afford it', and the nourishment they can access – chicken strips, pasta, etc – is 'rubbish', 'not the sort of stuff I like to give 'em', 'but we gotta have it cos it's the cheapest thing'. Healthy eating, adds his wife, is a 'nice ideal' – demonstrating the acceptance of this dominant trope as legitimate – 'if you can afford it'.

Of course while the dominated (especially its upper fractions) may recognise the discourse of 'healthiness' they twist and blend it with the orientations grounded in proximity to necessity for sugary and salty, 'filling' and 'substantial' food which ameliorates the pressures of life and satiates hungry children, and this has taken a hit too. There has, accordingly, been a foregoing of many of the 'treats' and 'nice things', as Mrs Green put it, the families once enjoyed – ice cream, confectionary, biscuits, crisps, beef burgers etc – or, more often, a determination to sustain spend on them only by buying special offers or items that are reduced in price because of damage or short shelf life.[14] Moreover, while the dominant and intermediate can compensate for food prices with the odd shop at value stores or by buying own-brand products, this option is not open to many of the dominated simply because they *already* shop at value stores or buy own-brand products as a *matter of course*. Instead, the only way to maintain the consumption of that which they desire is to now shop between multiple supermarkets and keep a note of where the *absolute lowest price* for each particular item is. 'I know what's cheapest where', said Mrs Green, as 'every penny counts', while the Lyon family talked bluntly about it being a 'pain in the ass' to 'shop between various supermarkets where I know I can get things at a reasonable price [...but] I have to think what's cheaper and be careful'. In fact, as Ms Taylor (Access course student, £13k) indicates, this principle can extend to cover all consumption, whether of holidays, televisions sets, beds or clothes. 'I can't just go and buy something without knowing that I can't get it cheaper somewhere else', she states, and so has to 'really research it' to ensure she is 'getting the best deal'. This was not, of course, a completely new disposition induced by economic crisis, but the creeping necessity it has wrought has meant that she is now forever 'trying to find the cheapest price for everything'.[15]

Such practices indicate that increased necessity, in all its manifestations, impresses upon attentive consciousness in one form or another almost constantly, which is to say that the thoughts of the dominated class, their concerns, their projects, their interactions, the range of conduct entering the mind as 'what must be done', are incessantly oriented toward meeting urgent material demands. Not only that, but if all being-in-the-world exists, as Heidegger would have it, under moods which manifest 'how one is and how one is faring',[16] then the worsening of material conditions serves to aggravate an extant *positional suffering*:[17] words like 'anxious', 'stressed', 'worried', 'unhappy' or 'feel a failure' speckled the participants' accounts like a cruel virus – sensations triggered by the perception that one cannot access goods and services, especially those one *used to* be able to, which are defined as symbols of success and recognition to be sought or done by all, as measures of one's value as a social being, by those who already possess success and recognition thanks to their privileged conditions of existence. To take some examples:

> Mr Duncan: So yeah, we do try to look at things that we can do to save money, and where we can save we'll save, we're always thinking of different ways ain't we of how to save money?
> WA: is it something that's in your mind all the time?
> Mrs Duncan: oh god yeah
> Mr Duncan: oh never goes out, never goes out. We never row over it do we? But we're always trying to negotiate what we're gonna do. Just this morning, that was one letter we had this morning [he picks a letter up off the floor], we've had a letter come through this morning from a store card which my wife pays for, [it's] another reminder.[18]

> The pressure of everyday life knocks your happiness down a little bit I think. Worrying about the fact that I've got no petrol in the car and where am I going to get the money for that.
>
> (Ms Jeffers)

Yeah we're always trying to think 'how can we save?' [...] Get very unhappy every time I've shopped. The prices have gone up and up. We spend £30 extra on food a week, we've had to go without other things to pay for food [...] You're always aware of turning the heating up. I walk around in a scarf and jumper. The winters are getting so cold these days as well. It does worry you.

(Ms Kent)

Omnipresence of necessity and the distress it engenders are especially clear in the case of 'auntie', as she was called by local residents, an unemployed single mother with four dependent children whose struggles with bills, food prices and school expenses have been intensified by rampant inflation. Each morning, she recounts, she now has to check there is enough money on her electricity meter for the day; and each morning she telephones her bank to check her balance so that she knows what she can and cannot spend in the day. Furthermore, during the course of the interview at her home the post is delivered – at the sound of the letters hitting the floor she places her head in her hands and groans 'I bet that's a bill. I'm not even picking it up'. A little later, the telephone rings and she again drops her head into her hands and grimaces, sighing 'It'll be some bill. I hate answering the phone'. She then goes on:

[it's coming from] all different angles. But it's not just me that's going through it. If you go up to the school, like all the mums are sitting down and talking about – it's the same thing. It's quite depressing actually, it is quite depressing [...] we all talk up the school, yeah, all 'go to that shop, this shop, this one's having a good deal, go down'. If it's sports day, 'go down Primark'. Everybody's on – I can remember years ago Primark, oh my god, you could never go there, 'can't go there, too cheap, too cheap'. Everybody's in there now. [...] I'm not afraid to take charity. Before I said 'nah, I don't want that, sorry love', now you ain't got no choice. You either take it or you suffer. [...] I'm not proud, I don't care. Before, I used to, now I don't care.

Ever greater necessity thus pervades her lifeworld insofar as her contact with others – whether similarly-situated individuals sharing tips or bearers of symbolic power, meeting her senses through mediated contact, enforcing the demands of necessity – are oriented around it. It pervades her consciousness almost constantly, insofar as her daily rhythms and routines are structured by awareness, and a need to be aware, of how much she has. It pervades her categories of perception, her typifications, her associations and her sense of the upcoming loaded in the present – in short, the meaning of the social world – insofar as specific stimuli (the squeak of the letterbox, the chime of the telephone) induce fear and loathing. And it pervades her sense of self-worth, tears down her pride and depresses her humour insofar as tightened economic limits necess-itate visitation of outlets and acceptance of charity the rejection of which once furnished some degree of 'independence' or 'respectability' – in other words, symbolic recognition.

As to the future, few of the these families perceived that the forth-coming political plan of action would ameliorate their situation. On the contrary, projection of the time to come was laden with expecta-tions of further hardship and adjustments. 'There's going to be less money', said Mr Arnold (construction engineer), 'we're going to have to cut back', while Mr Nash anticipated 'we'll feel the pinch, but then we'll have to look at something else and cut our other things back, probably turn Sky [satellite television] off – I mean that could be one of the things'. And yet, at the same time, many of the dominated simply asserted that one has 'got to do it', 'do what one can' and 'see it as it comes' (Mr Nash), that they will have to 'work harder' but 'that's what life's about' (Mrs Green) and that one has 'just got to get on with it, there's no point moaning about it. You just have to make things...just have to deal with what you've got' (Mr Duncan).[19] This sort of *amor fati* – not in the usual sense of desiring that which one can have, but as acceptance of that which befalls one – is, as Bourdieu noted, bitterly paradoxical.[20] Having the stream of consciousness constantly directed toward solving upcoming and ongoing problems of necessity, of how to hold on to what little one has, in the service of putting 'first things first', is part and parcel of the logic of practice, of doing 'what must be done', and yet, forever focussing attention on the present and forth-coming, it forestalls the projection of alternative futures and realisable courses of action bearing the possibility of challenging the structural sources of those problems.[21]

Conclusion

Hysteresis, the disjunction between the objectively possible and the subjectively desired induced by rapidly changing social conditions, is not diffused evenly through the social space in the wake of economic crisis and political austerity. To be sure, those from the dominant and the intermediate classes have made their sacrifices and savings, and they have their worries and their concerns, but it is those within the dominated class who are jolted closer to necessity at a disproportionate rate by inflation, wage freezes, welfare 'reform' and regressive taxes, who struggle hardest to maintain the tastes adapted to their previous conditions of existences and who have their stream of consciousness relentlessly filled with the thoughts and fears of making ends meet. In short, it is they who suffer most from both the *economic* violence born of neoliberal capitalist orthodoxy and the *symbolic* violence that accompanies the surrendering of the means of attaining, in however limited a way, the forms of recognition legitimated by those with the power to legitimate. Yet this particular round of hysteresis does not seem to have prompted a critical reflection or breaking of fundamental doxai, as Bourdieu sometimes suggested it can. People do perceive their situation as, in their words, 'shit' (auntie), there is a direction of liability toward a new constructed group from within the field of power – 'the bankers' – and there is a clear awareness, contrary to the current political rhetoric, that 'we're not all in it together at all. Anyone can see that' (Mr Duncan). But the pressure to feed, clothe, house and heat oneself and one's family, and to struggle after the goods and services still valued in capitalist Western societies, forecloses, for many, the likelihood of resisting.

Conditions of existence are unlikely to improve in the near future.[22] With a patently regressive programme for the remainder of the current parliament and constant uncertainty over the probability of further crippling economic crises yet to come, the fatalistic futurity of the dominated is, unfortunately, well founded. Given that the political agents gelled together under the banner of the Labour Party still, for the most part, sustain the toxic neoliberal orthodoxy saturating the political field and remain blinded by the blatantly strategic discourse of the 'squeezed middle', furthermore, no easing of economic and symbolic violence can be expected from them if they supplant the current incumbents of government in the years ahead. Instead, only *a truly progressive revolution in the political field*, one which either overhauls or replaces the confused and adrift Labour Party as the recognised representative of true egalitarianism and batters down the fallacies of neoliberalism, can ease the suffering of the dominated, but this will only be possible if the current heterodoxy espoused by activists and intellectuals, so disparate and so marginal for so long, can consolidate, organise, attract trade union support and succeed in communicating that their struggles are undertaken in the interests not just of disgruntled possessors of cultural capital but of the dominated class, the 'ordinary person' with no time and few resources to rally, too.

Notes

1 K. Marx (1954) *Capital, Vol. I.* London: Lawrence and Wishart, chapter 25.
2 P. Bourdieu (1984) *Distinction.* London: Routledge.
3 E.g. H. Mulholland (2011) 'Cameron Hints that Top Rate of Income Tax will Stay', *The Guardian*, 11th November 2011.
4 See e.g. M. Myers (2011) *The Impact of the Recession on Household Income, Expenditure and Saving.* London: ONS; A. Barnard, S. Howell and R. Smith (2011) *The Effects of Taxes and Benefits on Household Income, 2009/10.* London: ONS.
5 Bourdieu (1984), *op. cit.*, p. 247.
6 Class categories have been recoded from the Socio-Economic Group variable to maximise internal homogeneity of resources. In practice this three-class categorisation is not dissimilar to the aggregated ONS-SEC scheme, the official classification of classes in the UK, except that a few subcategories have been reallocated, namely, the lower professional and higher technical occupations and lower managers, the average possession of economic capital, as approximated by total disposable weekly household income in 2009, of which (£659) was closer to the rest of the 'intermediate' class (£597) than the professionals, owners and managers making up the dominant class (£921). Analysis of the *Labour Force Survey* for the second quarter of 2009 (as the *Living Costs and Food Survey* does not measure educational attainment) also reveals that the, admittedly rough and ready, proxy indicators of cultural capital for these groups (e.g. 33 per cent possessing HE) are closer to the other 'intermediate' categories (22 per cent with HE), excluding the self-employed economic fraction of the petite bourgeoisie (14 per cent with HE), than the higher professional-managerial categories (61 per cent with HE). Names of the classes have also been altered to reflect the underlying principle of capital possession rather than employment contracts, and it should be noted that assignment to a class is based on the position of the 'household reference person' in the ONS survey, i.e. the highest earner in the household, and has to be taken as a crude measure of the social capital of the other household members. Finally, though the long-term unemployed have been distinguished due to homogeneity of resources, in reality – as the qualitative analysis that follows will suggest – their orientations indicate they are best thought of as a fraction of the dominated class rather than a class unto themselves.
7 Logically the dominant and intermediate have cut back on *something* to balance the increased spend on the other categories, and in fact the greatest shrinkage would appear to be in the ambiguous 'travel' category.
8 The research was funded by the ESRC (ref. RES-062-23-2477) and conducted in collaboration with Harriet Bradley and Adam Sales. My thanks to the latter for discussions of the data.
9 A not dissimilar categorisation can be found in A. MacLean, J. Harden and K. Backett-Milburn (2010) 'Financial Trajectories: How Parents and Children Discussed the Impact of the Recession', *Twenty-First Century Societies*, 5(2): 159–70. However, the focus on income categories rather than classes and the interest in the impact of particular family events obscures the classed response to the recession and the underlying habitus.

10 All family names are pseudonyms. Occupation, highest qualification and annual household income are given for context, though it must be borne in mind that the precise balance of resources (including the social capital provided by partners) is crucial to class membership, such that, for example, an apparently high household income or a degree do not alone signify membership of the dominated or even intermediate class. On this see W. Atkinson (2010) *Class, Individualization and Late Modernity*. Basingstoke: Palgrave Macmillan, pp. 199–211.

11 Cf. J. Ribbens McCarthy, R. Edwards and V. Gillies (2003) *Making Families*. Durham: Sociology Press, chap. 3.

12 For the idea that the 'Great Recession' is better thought of as a 'Second Great Contraction' (after the first, the Depression), see C. Reinhart and K. Rogoff (2009) *This Time is Different: Eight Centuries of Financial Folly*. Princeton: Princeton University Press.

13 This is not to say that job and income insecurity were confined to this cluster of participants alone – on the contrary, as will be detailed on another occasion, those with fewest resources suffered greatest uncertainty over their occupational future – but that it was of greater relative weight in producing hysteresis than price rises, benefit cuts etc. compared to others because of their conservation strategies.

14 The 20 per cent VAT rate introduced in the 2010 Budget (an increase of 2.5 per cent) was defended against the charge of being regressive by the government on the grounds that food, as a necessity, is exempt. Yet not all food is exempt from VAT: items defined as 'luxuries' (crisps, ice cream etc) are taxed at the current standard rate. Insofar as the dominated consume such items at a disproportionate rate – an established phenomenon in epidemiology – they will have been hit hardest by the VAT hike.

15 Some of the practices described in the foregoing have also been found by others, notably, for just before the recession, T. Green, J. Owen, P. Curtis, G. Smith, P. Ward and P. Fisher (2009) 'Making Healthy Families?' in P. Jackson (ed.) *Changing Families, Changing Food*. Basingstoke: Palgrave Macmillan, pp. 205–25; and, on their exacerbation through the recession, A. Finney and S. Davies (2011) *Facing the Squeeze 2011*. London: Money Advice Trust. The latter report, however, suffers from the same shortcomings as the MacLean et al piece cited in note nine.

16 M. Heidegger (1967) *Being and Time*. Oxford: Blackwell, p. 173.

17 On this notion see P. Bourdieu et al (1999) *The Weight of the World*. Cambridge: Polity.

18 Mr Duncan was particularly burdened by the fact that the government had, as part of its cuts programme, stopped paying the interest on his mortgage to compensate his inability to work due to his fragile mental health.

19 Cf. R. Hoggart (1957) *The Uses of Literacy*. Harmondsworth: Penguin, pp. 91ff.

20 P. Bourdieu (1998) *Acts of Resistance*. Cambridge: Polity.

21 The reader will no doubt have noticed that the overviews of each orientation got progressively longer. This reflects the amount the research participants spoke on the effects of the recession and austerity, despite the fact that those with greater capital are slightly more numerous in the sample and generally gave longer, fuller answers in the interviews. Clearly on this specific topic they had so little to say because so little had changed, whereas

as the degree of hysteresis increases down the social space so too does the amount to tell.

22 For a rigorous assessment of the likely outcomes of the coalition government's policy programme, see P. Taylor-Gooby (2012) 'Root and Branch Restructuring to Achieve Major Cuts: The Social Policy Programme of the 2010 UK Coalition Government', *Social Policy & Administration*, 46(1): 61–82.

3

'We never get a fair chance': Working-Class Experiences of Education in the Twenty-First Century

Diane Reay

Introduction: The growing landscape of inequality

Definitive evidence is emerging from the wider economy that we are by no means 'all in it together' in relation to the current recession.[1] Rather, austerity is primarily for those who already have the least while the secure upper echelons of the middle class and our political and economic elites remain largely untouched.[2] Instead of cushioning those who are already disadvantaged, a recent Institute for Fiscal Studies (IFS) report[3] confirmed that in relation to government cuts announced in December 2011 it is lower-income groups who would bear the brunt. Furthermore, the economic struggle between capital and labour has increasingly been resolved to the growing benefit of capital, with profits now taking 47 per cent of GDP, up from 35 per cent in 1973.[4] Since then there has been a continuing decline in real wage growth.[5] This growing imbalance between capital and labour was starkly revealed in the *Daily Mail*'s front page headline of 20th December 2011. It blazoned 'As families are chased for every penny corporate giants dodge massive bills as they are let off £25 billion in taxes'. The rising share of profits and falling share of wages have had significant consequences for the economy, in particular, leading to a growing concentration of income and wealth among the top 40 per cent of society and the relative impoverishment of the bottom 60 per cent.[6]

When Margaret Thatcher took power in 1979 the Gini coefficient (the measure of inequality in society) was 0.27; by 2009 it had risen to 0.36, the highest level of inequality in Europe. Since the 1970s, income inequality has been growing faster in the UK than in any other rich country.[7] This wider troubling economic context, largely disregarded by educationalists when they focus on educational attainment, is at the core of working-class educational underachievement and provides the backdrop to working-class experiences of schooling. In contemporary under-resourced state schooling the assets and resources that families can invest in their children's education both in the home and at school make the difference between success and failure. The new century has seen the advent of the 'scholarisation of childhood',[8] or what Annette Lareau in the US terms 'the concerted cultivation of children in middle-class families'.[9] This is not simply an issue of material resources, the number of books, enrichment activities or private tuition sessions that middle- and upper-class parents can afford to pay for; it is also an issue of other, less visible benefits of affluence – confidence, entitlement, a sense of belonging within education – that come with a family history of privilege.

But class inequalities in education are not just about what students bring to the classroom; they are also about the very unequal educations students receive once they are there. The much-trumpeted diversity of schooling within England, introduced over the last 20 years, has simultaneously intensified and attenuated an existing hierarchy. We now have a system of crudely hierarchised schools, organised along the lines of class, with the public schools at the pinnacle and working class, ethnically diverse comprehensives at the base. In between lies a plethora of different school types with widely differing funding regimes, different degrees of selection and a range of levels of privatisation.

City Academies and Free Schools, alongside the policies to implement them, have been allocated disproportionate amounts of the education budget at a time of education cuts and further squeezes to the income of comprehensive schools. In particular, the coalition government's ideological fervor for new variants of privatised schooling has resulted in a concerted pressure campaign to persuade existing comprehensives to convert (and more recently a policy of enforced conversion for those schools deemed to be performing unsatisfactorily).[10] But the associated inequalities do not end with differential levels of funding. The new Academies and Free Schools are, with a few exceptions, both more white and middle class than the comprehensives they share the same locality with.[11] While, nationally, 16.7 per cent of children are entitled to claim free school meals (FSM) because their household income is below £16,000, in Free Schools the percentage is 10 per cent.[12] And the most recent research shows that the few FSM students who attend Academies underperform compared with their counterparts in comprehensive schools.[13]

The climate of austerity in the wider economy has affected resources within the state educational system. An IFS report[14] on spending on education in England stated that it was falling at the fastest rate since the 1950s. They predicted spending will fall by 13 per cent in real terms between 2010–11 and 2014–15 with the deepest cuts in school buildings, 16-to-19 provision and early years. This would represent the largest cut in education spending over any four-year period for 60 years and would return education spending as a share of national income back to 4.6 per cent by 2014–15. And it is working-class students who are most affected by underfunded state provision. In particular, the axing of Educational Maintenance Allowances for poorer students and their replacement by lower discretionary bursaries has reduced financial support to young people on free school meals by £370 per annum and appears likely to have an invidious impact on working-class staying-on rates.[15] And despite the introduction of a pupil premium for disadvantaged students, even schools in deprived areas are having to make swingeing cuts, affecting a wide range of services from careers advice to individual support for students falling behind in literacy, as well as school building repairs.[16]

As Bourdieu succinctly argued, the few working-class survivors in education owe everything to the education system – they are totally reliant on it for their success. In contrast, middle- and upper-class students, if they use the state system, can guarantee educational success by recourse to a wide range of resources both inside and outside of schooling, including acceleration courses, top sets, enrichment activities and private tuition. They, unlike their working-class peers, are not totally reliant on what the school provides. Processes of 'class racism'[17] are evident when we focus on the different types of schools different social classes attend, and the differing levels of regard in which they are held and resources they have access to. But, as touched on earlier, it is also revealed in intra-school processes of segregation. The OECD Report on *Economic Policy Reforms: Going for Growth*[18] found that school practices or systems that start grouping or setting students early on in their education are associated with larger social class inequalities in secondary educational performance without any gains in average performance (pages 14–15), while Brook[19] argues that the growing emphasis on competition between schools based on test results has encouraged both setting practices and 'game playing' as schools channel lower achieving students into non-academic subjects at GCSE. Such practices have been growing exponentially across the state sector over the last decade and have been accompanied by a fall in England's international position in league tables of educational performance. The OECD's latest PISA (Progress in Student Achievement) league tables show that in the last decade England has plummeted in the rankings: from 4th to 16th for science, 7th to 25th for literacy and 8th to 28th for maths. Exacerbating this decline is the growing gap in educational opportunities for the rich and poor. The latest DfE statistics showing only 30.9 per cent of pupils eligible for free school meals are achieving five or more A*–C grades at GCSE or equivalent, compared to 58.5 per cent of non-FSM students. Growing practices of setting, streaming and academic differentiation fix failure in the working classes, who are disproportionately allocated to the bottom sets.[20] This is an extremely perverse form of the 'fair chance and fair play for all' that is traditionally viewed as underpinning the UK's education system.

This is not to contend that there has ever been a time when working-class students had equal opportunities in education. They have never had 'a fair chance'. Instead, I am arguing that their relative disadvantage has increased in the twenty-first century from what was already a low base. For those of us prepared to look at what Bourdieu called 'difficult spots',[21] what becomes apparent is how painfully the educational world is experienced by those who occupy an inferior, devalued position in a privileged universe. Working-class relationships to education have always been deeply problematic and emotionally charged, inscribing academic failure rather than success. As Bourdieu goes on to point out, for working-class young people and their families: 'The school system increasingly seems like a mirage, the source of an immense, collective disappointment, a promised land which, like the horizon, recedes as one moves towards it.'[22]

In the research described in the following section we see signs of disappointment, and at times a critical reflexivity with regard to 'the way things are', but also evident are processes of what Bourdieu calls symbolic violence, an internalisation of dominant classifications and meanings as legitimate.[23] Bourdieu defines symbolic violence as 'a gentle violence, imperceptible and invisible, even to its victims, exerted for the most part through the purely symbolic channels of communication and cognition (more precisely, misrecognition), recognition, or even feeling'.[24] In contemporary England, neoliberalism has become an extremely powerful and effective form of symbolic violence, and the research studies show how it increasingly dominates working-class young people's thinking and feeling. It is there in their strong sense of individual responsibility for learning, but it is also there in the poignant sense of shame and personal responsibility some young working-class people feel in relation to circumstances that are beyond their control.

Researching working-class educational experiences in the twenty-first century

The routine everyday humiliations and slights of social class in classrooms

There has been a long history of research that investigates the depth of the psychic damage which class inequalities inflict on the working classes,[25] but little since the turn of the century. My own research on a number of projects conducted over the last decade reveals many mundane humiliations and slights of social class that regularly infuse both inter-actions between teachers and pupils and those between pupils. Class recognitions, visceral aversions and feelings of inferiority and abjection are routine, everyday aspects of school life for working-class young people in England. The examples that follow, drawn from an ESRC study on pupils' perspectives on their teaching and learning carried out from 2000 to 2002, are particularly stark, but there were many similar examples across the data. The wider study focused on students from both middle- and working-class backgrounds but the students quoted here had parents employed in manual or low-status service occupa-tions who had left school at either 16 or 18 years of age, although one mother had recently returned to study at an FE college. In these two focus group extracts, a group of ethnically-mixed working-class stu-dents talk about their teachers:

> David: Some teachers are a bit snobby, sort of. And some teachers act as if the child is stupid. Because they've got a posh accent. Like they talk without 'innits' and 'mans', like they talk proper English. And they say 'that isn't the way you talk', like putting you down. Like I think telling you a different way is sort of good, but I think the way they do it isn't good because they correct you and make you look stupid.
> Matthew: Those teachers look down on you.
> David: Yeah, like they think you're dumb.
> Candice: I'm not really comfortable asking for help from the teacher. I don't know why. But it's because they don't listen to you. I just prefer to talk to my mum and dad and my brother.
> Carlene: With your parents, because with your parents you've got a special bond. You can tell them stuff. With the teacher you don't

have anything. You can't exactly tell them how you feel, that you're stuck on something, can't actually speak to them.
Candice: They look down on you.

In both extracts the working-class secondary school students' sense of unfairness was palpable as they poignantly talk about being 'looked down on' by their teachers. But many other working-class students in the study talked about a sense of educational worthlessness and feeling that they were not really valued and respected within education. As MacDonald and Marsh[26] found, there was a widespread perception of not being an educational priority, but it was particularly in the bottom sets that working-class young people expressed the greatest levels of despair and antipathy towards school-based learning. The extract below epitomises the alienation, disaffection and dis-engagement from learning we found among working-class young people in the bottom sets:

Diane: If you had a choice what would you choose to learn?
Jason: Nothing
George: Nothing
Andy: No idea
Paul: Definitely nothing!

The Council of Europe's Report on Social Mobility and Social Cohesion[27] found that the educational policies that best promote equal opportunities are social mixing in schools and delayed setting and streaming. Yet these young people share in common with the students I discuss in the next section negative experiences of segregation both within schools and between them.

The damaging consequences of choice for the 'choice-less'

A market driven, privatised educational system that operates with a crude test-led system of attributing value has resulted in the devaluation and pathologisation of many working-class students, particularly those who are not predicted the 'gold-standard' of five A* to Cs at GCSE. It has also resulted in the devaluing and demonisation of the schools, mostly comprehensives, which these working-class students attend. We do not need to scrutinise research reports to recognise the low esteem and contempt with which such schools and their pupils are widely regarded. Reading national and local press, but also spending any concerted time with groups of middle-class parents, will reveal a litany of failures and lacks in which words like 'rubbish', 'bad', 'sink' and 'rough' proliferate.[28] Much has been written about middle-class choice-making,[29] including middle-class avoidance strategies of so-called 'sink' schools, but there is far less work on the repercussions for working-class students of this stigmatisation of themselves and the schools they attend.

In an ESRC project conducted with Helen Lucey from 1999 until 2001 that looked at 450 children making the move from primary to secondary school, we found that the lack of access to representations through which positive identifications can develop generated negatively framed and defensive identities among the working-class students which were expressed through shame, disavowal and dis-identification.[30] But at the same time there were also examples of working-class white and ethnic-minority children, moving on to what were widely viewed as 'sink' schools, expressing a complex mixture of pride, hopefulness and ambivalent defensiveness. These children were striving to escape the damaging process of implicating the self that seems inevitable in our current judgemental and regulatory educational system.

Shaun and Lindsey both went to 'sink' inner city secondary schools. Lindsey to a school that was deemed to be so bad it was closed down and reopened under another guise, while Shaun attended a school under special measures described in the local press as 'a haven for drug dealers'. However, both children managed to sustain an optimism of the will despite their circumstances. In the two excerpts below they dispute dominant representations of inner-city schooling which are powerfully classed and, by association, invidious and judgemental understandings of children like them:

> Everyone said Sutton Boys was a rubbish school full of tramps and low-lifes but they were wrong. I've done really well here and so have a lot of the kids. (Shaun)

While Lindsey has a similar positive tale to tell of Phoenix Academy:

> Diane: So how would you describe the average child in your school?
> Lindsey: A mixture of a lot of things, a bit loud but sometimes a bit quiet and successful, maybe, I hope.
> Diane: Do you remember Jordan saying it had lots of rough kids?
> Lindsey: Yes, but I don't think that's right because I'm not from a very good background because around my area there's always police up there and there's lots of violence and drugs but we've got a nice flat. We live in a block of flats that's very unhygienic and scruffy but

inside we've got a nice flat so you can't say rough just from the outside.

Both children challenged hegemonic representations of the working classes and their schooling. While they are miles away from Hebdige's subcultural working class, they too are trying to 'recognise and rise above a subordinate position that is not of their own choosing'.[31] However, in doing so they confronted the difficult task of psychic reparative work: a making good of what is uniformly depicted as bad. Despite their efforts, there is no getting away from the consequences, both psychic and material, of being positioned at the bottom of the secondary schools market. While we can see in their narratives a compelling drive towards a useful integration, connection and reparation, these children are still the losers in the educational game.[32]

Earlier work has identified a working-class proclivity to focus on the individual rather than the institution as instrumental in academic success.[33] Certainly for those children in this sample with no option than to go to one of the demonised schools, the discourse of individual volition makes attending low-achieving 'rough' schools a far more manageable proposition than subscribing to a discourse that views the culture of the school as impacting on individual subjectivity.

However, surges of individualisation, whilst ameliorating the situation for the individual, do not cancel out the experiences of a collective fate.[34] As current research demonstrates, inequalities in education remain as great as they were 40 years ago, while both class and racial segregation in inner-city schooling is increasing, not diminishing.[35] A lot of the working-class young people talked in terms of trying to stay 'normal' in the pathologised schools they were moving to. So Maria said 'I'll try and stay normal even though Chiltern is a bad school'. However, it is Lewis' tale that exemplifies the psychological repercussions of the struggle to remain normal and avoid pathologisation. Lewis, working class and Black British, had put down Westbury as his first 'choice' but, as he lives on the edge of the catchment area, realised he is likely to be allocated a place in one of the borough's three demonised schools:

> Lewis: My mum doesn't want me to go to Chiltern, she says it's a rubbish school with bad results but I can't get into the other schools we wanted so I'm probably going to Chiltern. I don't want to go there but there's this boy I know called Taylor, he's in Year 8

and he hasn't got into any fights. He hasn't done anything wrong yet so I'm just hoping I can be like him and stay as I normally am.

Diane: So has Taylor done well at secondary school?

Lewis: Yes, his mum told my mum his results are good so there is one kid who is doing well at Chiltern so if I try and be like him, not like all the other kids that muck around I should do ok.

Lewis' narrative brings together a number of strands in the analysis of working-class survival in demonised schools. He exemplifies working-class children's need to know about the prospects for survival and the possibilities of success for 'someone like them' in secondary schooling, although, in relation to the demonised schools, the emphasis is more often on survival than success. And he has clearly taken refuge in an individualistic understanding of academic success and survival. Lewis is hoping to stand out against the collective influences that threaten to 'pervert' his normal self. This acceptance of, 'the buying into', individualistic discourses is part of an array of recuperative strategies in which to deny the power of the collective provides hope for the individual. As Bourdieu asserts:

> The logic of stigma reminds us that social identity is the stake in a struggle in which the stigmatized individual or group, and, more generally, any individual or group insofar as he or it is a potential object of categorization, can only retaliate against the partial perception which limits it to one of its characteristics by highlighting, in its self-definition, the best of its characteristics, and, more generally, by struggling to impose the taxonomy most favourable to its characteristics, or at least to give to the dominant taxonomy the content most flattering to what it has and what it is.[36]

However, we need to set against the individualistic discourses of children confronting demonised schools the informing character of the 'with' relationship in our society. As Goffman[37] asserts, to be 'with' a particular group, in this case the 'rough' children who attend Chiltern, often leads to the assumption that one is what the others are:

> If I went to Chiltern I would probably get a bit, uhm, I'm not saying everyone that goes there is bad, but I might get a bit argumentative

with everyone and get into fights, starting fights and all that. But in Westbury I think I'll just be normal, stay the same. (Joe)

The shameful silence in both Joe's and Lewis' text is the pathology that represents normality's other. Unlike the middle-class children who often have actual 'choices' and can demonise at a distance, working-class children are frequently caught up in self-betraying processes of stratification – self-betraying because they utilise classificatory systems which position themselves as inferior, 'at the bottom' of any hierarchy. Half-concealed between the lines of children's accounts were associations, links that were particularly painful for these children. Yet they provide insights, the glimmer of a recognition of these schools as sites of regulation, as schools for the poor:

> all I know is that sometimes people sit and ask for 10p in Sutton Boys, because I've been finding out quite a lot about Sutton Boys because I am going there. So I am going to try and find out as much as I can about it, because if I don't and I go into school and people go – have you seen something or so and so? And then they are going to pull you into the toilets and beat you up. So if I find out all about it I'll know how to protect myself from the rough kids (Shaun, Irish, working class).

However, black, working-class Mustafa is more explicit about the link between 'sink' schools and poverty: 'pupils in Sutton Boys beg for 10p like, and they sit down on the floor and go "have you got 10p, so I can get some lunch?"'. In a twenty-first century Britain where a taste for the working classes has long disappeared, being poor is increasingly demonised. Many of the working-class children in the study spent enormous effort separating themselves out from a group they were desperate not to be seen to belong to. As a consequence, the poor were always a group who were even worse off than they were. So Steph, whose mother was a single parent living on benefits, commented: 'on the estate there are real poor families not like my family.... We're not poor'. And Jamie, one of five children in a single-parent family living on the same council estate, said: 'There's loads of poor living on our estate but we live at the rich end'. These children are constantly trying to hold on to a conceptualisation of the poor that stops short of their own experience. As Daniel rationalised, 'of course I'm middle class, I'm not poor, no way man. I'm not a dosser'. One of the children's main mechanisms of defence against pathologisation is transforming the negative into a positive, as Lindsey, quoted earlier, had attempted to do. In her account and that of other young working-class students we glimpse the workings of symbolic violence as these young people, in large part, accept responsibility for structural conditions they and their families have no power to control.

Those children for whom school 'choice' constitutes being left with the unwanted choices of more privileged others are caught up in oscillations of identification, veering from hopeful acceptance to depressed antipathy. One result is a kind of concentrated ambivalence. The nature of ambivalence is to hold opposing affective orientations towards the same object.[38] Unsurprisingly, then, ambivalence tends to be unstable, expressing itself in different and sometimes contradictory ways as individuals cope with it.[39] However, the children going to demonised schools continue to be bombarded by negative evaluations both among the peer group and the wider public, generating what Helen Lucey and I termed 'a concentrated ambivalence' in which their defence mechanisms are constantly under threat of breaking down. These children are caught up in the dynamics of shameful different-ness and have to struggle with 'invidious expressive valuations based on a virtual middle-class ideal'.[40] Although they buy into a discourse of individualisation as part of an array of self-protective tactics, they are the casualties of neoliberalism, not its beneficiaries.

Since the research was conducted, both Labour and now the coalition government have exacerbated and exaggerated the negativity with which both the working classes and the schools they attend are regarded. Their choice policies focus not simply on providing more diversity of school types, but also the creation of a hierarchy of school worth (and implicitly a hierarchy of student worth). In this hierarchy those who have neither the resources nor the inclination to play 'the choice game' are deemed to be inadequate neoliberal subjects, lacking both initiative and enterprise. The opening up of the education sector to markets and choice is centrally about rewarding the strategic, those who can operate as good neoliberal subjects. It has little to do with raising working-class levels of achieve-ment, and, as the PISA data quoted earlier reveals, the extension and deepening of such policies has been accompanied by steady falls in edu-cational attainment in England, particularly among the working class, compared to other OECD countries.

'Hard Times': Working-class schooling in a period of austerity

In the most recent research project I am involved in, conducted from 2010 to 2012, the constraints and difficulties surrounding working-class educational experiences are still ever present. The research is taking place in a large multiethnic, predominantly working-class comprehensive school in a town in South East England, and focuses specifically on working-class young people at risk of educational failure – those at the borderlines of academic 'achievement'.[41] The data comprises five focus group interviews (with between eight and 12 young people) and repeat in-depth interviews with 11 students aged 14 and 15. The students were unambiguously working class. None had parents who had been to university. Two of the young people lived in lone-parent households dependent on benefits, a young man was looked after by the local authority. Other young people lived in families with fathers working in jobs such as security guard, taxi driver, builder and car paint sprayer. Five of the 11 were in receipt of free school meals and a further young woman was eligible but had not claimed her entitlement.

These young people, perhaps more than those in the earlier two studies, are good neoliberal subjects, buying heavily into process of individualisation and free choice. Neoliberal influences are particularly evident in the young people's espousal of aspirational discourses of 'having it all' – so Hasim dreams of owning houses across the globe and having a fleet of cars, including an Aston Martin; Cerise wants to be rich and marry a footballer; while Jide dreams of living next door to Wayne Rooney in a mansion with a games room for his children and cars like Ferraris. Neoliberal attitudes also permeate their attitudes to their learning and, in particular, their powerful sense of individual responsibility for learning (and in a majority of cases their failure to achieve educational success). Students told us 'it's down to the individual how well you do at school', 'you have to make yourself stand out compared to all the other people doing the same exams', and 'if you want to do well you just have to work really hard. You can't blame the school or your teachers'. These young people were heavily invested in notions of the autonomous, self-reliant individual, primarily responsible for any future outcomes – so we glimpse one of the ways in which symbolic domination works through individualisation processes.

Yet their strong sense of individual responsibility for learning was coupled with weak, often disengaged, learner identities, evident in the other two research projects. A lot of the time they fail to see the relevance of, in particular, the academic subjects they are studying. Learning out of school was seen to be both more rewarding and relevant than school-based learning. As a consequence, a significant number of the young people specified that the most enjoyable thing about school was being with friends rather than any aspect of learning. So when Maya, when asked what she most enjoyed about school, responded 'my friends', and Satvinder asserted 'the best thing about coming to school is meeting my friends'. The damaging impact on learner identities of being allocated to bottom sets was also just as prevalent:

> Joe: The behaviour's bad. You don't learn unless you're in the first set.
>
> Shulah: The behaviour, it gets worse in the bottom set when like teachers don't pay attention to you. And they pay attention to like the higher ability students and like you get bored because there's nothing for you to do if you don't understand the work.

And:

> Atik: I was completely failed. I think I failed proper badly in the tests and that's why I'm in a proper bad set now...I can just answer the questions really easy because there's like no really smart people and they behave quite bad as well and they influence me.

In all three quotes, low sets are clearly perceived to be coterminous with educational failure.

However, it was Satvinder, who, in her lamentation about being 'a bottom set student', makes an explicit link between educational success and 'having it all':

> Right now, because I'm in the bottom set for everything I don't actually like it, because I'm only doing the foundation paper, and I don't...I really don't want to do that. Because from Year 6 when I left I went to myself I'm going to put my head down, and do my work, but I never did. And then it...like every year I say it, but I never do it. [...] I haven't even done it this year either. [...] Yeah, I could have like gone to a better higher place, and then I could have done everything.

The themes of aspirational individualism and weak learner identities were evident across all three research projects. However, in the current study, for the first time, nearly all the students made unsolicited criticisms of the physical environment they were learning in. The school and its resources were variously described as 'crap', 'rubbish' and 'trampy'. Carly even specifies 'this place is poor'. Overcrowding, in particular, was seen to be a major problem:

> Atik: Sometimes you go in the corridor and it's just crowded, people are pushing and you can't get through.
> Shakira: It's not made for like the amount of children in the school.

Also lamented was the old fashioned and decrepit nature of many of the resources:

> Michael: The school just needs to be up-to-date. Like the computers that they've got. Like now all of the computers are flat screens and some of the computer rooms are just like, I don't know, they don't have the newer versions of things. Like they've got Powerpoint 2003 and it's like really old.
> Shakira: Like one of the computer rooms, like half the computers don't have like mice and half the keys are missing, like people pull the keys off and you can't log on to half of them. The projector doesn't work, the printer doesn't work, and it's really like useless…I'd prefer to work in a classroom where like everything like works, it's so much easier.

The scrapping of the Building Schools for the Future Programme has clearly had a major impact on the material conditions in which these students were being educated. Almost all the students commented on deteriorating aspects of either the school buildings or the educational resources they had access to. In particular, the impoverished physical environment was perceived to be detrimental to their learning. The school buildings were generally seen to be too old and too small:

> Richie: I don't think the building's good for the amount of people in the school. They're too old and they're for like smaller people. People are a lot taller now than they used to be.
> Cassie: They need to get it rebuilt.

Shulah makes an explicit link between the poor physical conditions and a sense of demoralisation among the students:

> I think sometimes it's the building because like we don't have a lot… like of stuff…we need more stuff. But because we don't have enough money it just makes some people want to mess around.

While Michael compares the facilities in other schools which he feels are much better than those in his comprehensive school:

> like you go into other schools, like I went in one like the other week in London because that's where I train for football and you went in there and they have like a swipe card to go through and you don't have to pay for lunch, you do a swipe card and at the end of the year you get a bill for your food, and it's just like really modern compared to this school. Like laminated floors and just a lot better.

Overall, there was a righteous sense of indignation at the poor physical conditions and inadequate level of resourcing in which they were expected to learn. This may be far from resistance in the classic Willis mode,[42] but, like the earlier quote from David in which he protests against teachers who try to humiliate working-class students, it points to a sense of unfairness and should be viewed positively. The more working-class students who question the unequal conditions governing their learning, the harder it will be for systems of symbolic domination to maintain their hold.

Conclusion

Processes of symbolic violence are endemic in the contemporary English educational system. Bourdieu argues that the dominant only 'let the system they dominate take its own course, in order to exercise their domination'.[43] But our current political elite are engaged in a restructuring of the educational system, a re-traditionalising of the curriculum, and the reintroduction of policies that work to re-inscribe the working classes as educational losers. Under the current performativity regime, schools in England are encouraged to fetishise the sort of attainment that can be easily quantified for national and international comparison and there is a growing preoccupation with distinguishing between those who make the grade and those who do not. English working-class students learn alongside the official curriculum that their failure to perform well academically and achieve success is the result of their own inadequacies; that it is the direct result of their own lack of effort and ability. The suffering this gives rise to is evident in the working-class young people's words as they seek, with only partial success, to reinvent themselves and their schools as 'good enough' and struggle to reclaim some personal value.

The working classes have never had 'a fair chance' in education, and they certainly do not have one in a twenty-first century Britain scarred by growing inequalities. The rhetoric of equality, fairness and freedom in education has intensified since the beginning of the century but it has done so against a backdrop of ever-increasing inequality, the entrenchment of neoliberalism and class domination. It is predominantly babble, or what Stephan Collini[44] calls 'blahspeak', signifying little, and certainly nothing that will make any contribution to a fairer, more equal educational system. In the aspirational society contemporary Britain has become, there is intense competition for 'fair chances' as middle- and upper-class parents strategise and invest in order to ensure their own children have a better chance of having a fair chance than other people's children. As Collini concludes, this is about transmitting and entrenching advantage and works against, rather than promoting, equal opportunities. Within the field of education the working classes have increasingly become what are to be avoided, and as economic austerity has grown and the poor have become poorer, working-class exclusions within education have both deepened and extended.

Young working-class people are suffering from the heavy contradictions of an elitist hierarchical educational system articulated with a meritocratic neoliberal imaginary. Individualism has always worked better for the middle and upper classes than for the working classes, for whom the individualising of experiences has come to result in viewing set-backs, crises, and now increasing economic disadvantage and educational failure as personal failures, even though they are largely connected to processes, structures and levels of resources far beyond their personal control. When it comes to the working classes, as Ball et al point out, 'individualism all too readily collapses into individual pathology'.[45] While the inequitable operations of social class damage all of us, regardless of where we are positioned in the social field, it is the most vulnerable and powerless, the working classes, who are made to bear the greatest psychological burdens and economic deprivations of an unequal society.

Notes

1 R. Ramesh (2011) 'Income Gap Rising Faster in UK than Any Other Wealthy Nation', *The Guardian*, Tuesday 6th December, p. 2.
2 K. Hopkins (2011) 'Britain Leads the World as Pay Gap Between Rich and Poor Widens', *The Times,* Monday 5th December, p. 42.
3 H. Chowdry and L. Sibieta (2011) *Trends in Education and Schools Spending.* London: IFS.

4 M. Offord (2009) *Bankrupt Britain*. London: Centre for Social Justice.

5 Office for National Statistics (2011) International Comparisons of Productivity – New Estimates for 2009. Available at http://www.ons.gov.uk/ons/taxonomy/ index.html?nscl=International+Comparison+of+Productivity.

6 S. Lansley (2009) *Unfair to Middling: How Middle Income Britain's Shrinking Wages Fuelled the Crash and Threaten Recovery*. London: TUC Touchstone Pamphlet.

7 M. Forster (2011) *Divided We Stand: Why Inequality Keeps Rising*. OECD.

8 The Primary Review (2007) *Children's Lives and Voices: Research on Children at Home and School*. Primary Review Research Briefings, Esmée Fairbairn and the University of Cambridge.

9 A. Lareau (2003) *Unequal Childhoods*. Berkeley: University of California Press.

10 S. Milne (2012) 'Crony Capitalism Feeds the Corporate Plan for Schools', *The Guardian*, 15th February, p. 28.

11 M. Benn (2011) 'Education – The Current Political Landscape', speech to the Comprehensive Future AGM, 15th November 2011.

12 Free Schools and disadvantaged children: the data November 14, 2011, available at Schoolduggery's Blog: http://schoolduggery.wordpress.com/2011/ …/14/ free-schools-and-disadvantaged- children-the-data/.

13 F. Millar (2012) 'We Must Have an Open Debate about Privatisation', *The Guardian*, 14th February, p. 37.

14 Chowdry and Sibieta, *op. cit.*

15 Ibid.

16 J. Shepherd (2011) 'A Dampener on Aspirations: How Pupils are Paying Price of Austerity', *The Guardian*, 27th December, pp. 12–13.

17 P. Bourdieu (1993) *Sociology in Question*. London: Sage.

18 OECD (2010) *Economic Policy Reforms: Going for Growth*. Available at: http://www.oecd.org/document/51/0,3343,en_2649_34325_44566259_1_1_1_1,00.html.

19 A. Brook (2008) *Raising Education Achievement and Breaking the Cycle of Inequality in the UK*. OECD working paper 41.

20 D. Gillborn and D. Youndell (2000) *Rationing Education: Policy, Practice, Reform and Equity*. Buckingham: Open University Press.

21 P. Bourdieu (1999) 'The Space of Points of View' in P. Bourdieu et al, *The Weight of the World*. Cambridge: Polity, p. 3.

22 P. Bourdieu and P. Champagne (1999) 'Outcasts on the Inside' in P. Bourdieu et al, *The Weight of the World*. Cambridge: Polity, p. 423.

23 P. Bourdieu (1990) *In Other Words*. Cambridge: Polity, p. 138.

24 P. Bourdieu (2001) *Masculine Domination*. Cambridge: Polity, pp. 1–2.

25 L. Rubin (1976) *Worlds of Pain*. New York: Basic Books; R. Sennett and J. Cobb (1972) *The Hidden Injuries of Class*. New York: Random House.

26 R. MacDonald and J. Marsh (2005) *Disconnected Youth? Growing Up in Britain's Poor Neighbourhoods*. London: Palgrave Macmillan.

27 A. Nunn (2011) *Draft Report on Fostering Social Mobility as a Contribution to Social Cohesion*. Strasbourg: Council of Europe.

28 D. Reay, G. Crozier and D. James (2011) *White Middle Class Identities and Urban Schooling* Basingstoke: Palgrave.

29 S. Ball (2003) *Class Strategies and the Education Market*. London: Routledge-Falmer; T. Butler and G. Robsen (2003) *London Calling: The Middle Classes and the Remaking of Inner London*. Oxford: Berg; C. Vincent and S. Ball (2006)

Childcare Choice and Class Practices: Middle Class Parents and Their Children. London: Routledge.

30 This study was carried out with Helen Lucey from 1999 until 2001. Phase one took place in eight primary schools in two London boroughs and data was collected using focus group and individual interviews. We chose to use focus as against group interviews because of our specific research interest in interaction between participants. We wanted to ensure a forum in which children could both build on, and challenge, each others' perspectives. Our main sample included every child in the Year 6 of these primary schools, totalling 454 children between ten and 11 years old; a total of 77 focus groups in all. In phase two a group of 45 was selected to constitute a target group to be followed through their move into Year 7 of secondary schooling. These 45 were individually interviewed either three or four times over the course of the two years, as were a subsample of their parents. Year 6 primary school teachers and the Year 7 tutors were also interviewed. All interviews were taped and transcribed in full.

31 D. Hebdige (1979) *Subculture: The Meaning of Style.* London: Methuen, p. 139.

32 D. Reay (2004) '"Mostly Roughs and Toughs": Social Class, Race and Representation in Inner City Schooling', *Sociology*, 38(4): 1005–23, p. 1012.

33 D. Reay and S. Ball (1997) 'Spoilt for "Choice": The Working Classes and Education Markets', *Oxford Review of Education*, 23: 89–101.

34 U. Beck (1992) *Risk Society.* London: Sage.

35 R. Lupton and A. Sullivan (2007) 'The London Context', in T. Brighouse and L. Fullick (eds) *Education in a Global City: Essays from London.* London: Bedford Way Publishing.

36 P. Bourdieu (1984) *Distinction.* London: Routledge, pp. 476–7.

37 E. Goffman (1968) *Stigma.* London: Pelican Books.

38 R. Merton (1976) *Sociological Ambivalence and Other Essays.* New York: The Free Press.

39 N. Smesler (1999) *The Social Edges of Psychoanalysis.* Berkeley: University of California Press.

40 Goffman (1968) *op. cit.*, p. 173.

41 C. Oliver, D. Reay, N. Singhal, K. Black-Hawkins and R. Byers (2011) 'Who Do You Think You Are? Eliciting Young People's Identities at the Intersections of Disability, Ethnicity and Class', paper presented at the British Sociological Association annual conference, Leeds, April 2011.

42 P. Willis (1977) *Learning to Labour.* Farnborough: Saxon House.

43 P. Bourdieu (1977) *Outline of a Theory of Practice.* Cambridge: Cambridge University Press, p. 190.

44 Stephan Collini (2010) 'Blahspeak', *London Review of Books*, 32 (April): 7.

45 S. Ball, M. Maguire and S. MacRae (2000) *Choice, Pathways, and Transitions Post-16: New Youth, New Economies in the Global City.* London: Routledge.

4

Banking on the Future: Choices, Aspirations and Economic Hardship in Working-Class Student Experience

Harriet Bradley and Nicola Ingram

'Education, education, education'. The Blairite slogan appears on the face of it uncontroversial and designed to attract universal electoral support. We all 'know' that education is important as a means to success in a meritocratic society, that qualifications are increasingly crucial for accessing a good career and that university education continues to be rewarded with higher incomes over the course of a working life. We assume, probably rightly, that all parents want to see their children do well at school and that increasing numbers of working-class parents are joining the middle class in aspiring to a university education for their children.

Yet behind this picture lies a reality of conflict and contradiction. Yes, we value university education, but what for? Is it a consumer good purchased to ensure individual prosperity or a social good designed to promote an enlightened and creative modern society? Is it a means to a job or a tool for personal fulfilment and enrichment? Should it follow the demands of the 'free market' in its provision of courses or should it seek to structure the market in the interests of a flourishing economy and culture? Should it be open to all or confined to those who can best utilise what it offers? Who should pay: the state or parents and students? Who should control the curriculum: the academics, central government, quasi-governmental agencies or students as active consumers? These conflicts over meaning have infused debates over higher education policy since the Blairite period when New Labour first introduced university fees but have reached a crescendo under the Conservative-Liberal Democrat coalition, with the raising of fees and the allowing of private providers to enter the HE arena.

While the Conservative-dominated coalition affirms its commitment to open participation and fair access, using the rhetoric of 'free at the point of delivery' to justify the massive hike in fees to up to £27,000

51

over three years for many universities, a cynic or conspiracy theorist might argue that the coalition have in fact deliberately sought to restructure post-compulsory education to mirror the existing hierarchy and create a system of at least two tiers. The dominant class, to use Bourdieusian terms, possess the necessary capitals, cultural and social as well as economic, to secure their children places in the research-led Russell Group universities.[1] Private education is often a key tool in this process. Meanwhile different segments of the dominated classes are likely to make their way into the lower tiers: the upper segment into the post-1992s, while the lower levels will either remain excluded from higher education or find their way in through foundation degrees, further education colleges and possibly private providers. The proposed raising of the participation age (RPA) to 18 by 2015 is likely to encourage more vocational strands in schools and colleges, but also to combine these with new types of partnership provision involving some universities.

Of course, the channeling process outlined above is neither new nor absolute.[2] In this chapter we will be examining the experiences of those young people from the dominated classes who do make it through to the top-tier universities, focusing on the role of economic capital. How do economic decisions frame their choices? How have they garnered economic resources to get through their student years? How does their relative lack of economic capital, compared to their middle-class peers, impact upon their study experience? And how much of a disincentive might the incoming fees regime prove for people from a similar class background, given the attempt of the coalition to shift the 'less academic' into vocational types of training?

Methodology: The 'Paired Peers' project

The data which we use to explore these questions is taken from a project funded by the Leverhulme Trust and carried out by a team of researchers from the University of Bristol (UoB) and the University of the West of England (UWE). It is a longitudinal qualitative study, using various methods to explore the progress of a cohort of students through the three years of their degree (that is up to bachelor's level, as some of our participants are on four year courses which include a master's). Ideally, we would have liked a fourth year to observe 'what happened next' but Leverhulme limit their funding to three years.

Our aim was to compare systematically the experiences of pairs of students from different classes, in two universities (the traditional 'elite' UoB and the 'new' more teaching-focused UWE), doing the same subjects. Pairs were thus matched in three ways: by class, by institution and by discipline. Our objectives were to note the various kinds of capital the students of different classes brought into their university experience (economic, social, cultural, technical, bodily and so forth), and to explore the various types of capital they acquired over the three years. In this way we can begin an exploration of the potential offered by university attendance as a vehicle of social mobility, which we hope to explore more fully in a follow-up study.

Our target was to recruit a sample of 80 students from ten disciplines (eight from each), involving 40 students from UWE and 40 students from UoB. We aimed to cover a range of disciplines, although we were limited to those taught in both universities. Our recruitment strategy involved short presentations about the research at introductory lectures during induction week. Questionnaires and information leaflets were distributed and from the students who volunteered to participate in the research we selected middle-class and working-class individuals who represented a good 'match'. Expecting that some students would drop out of university or opt to leave the research study, we 'over-recruited' and carried out a total of 90 initial biographical interviews from 11 disciplines. Second interviews were conducted with 76 students, including 30 pairs. At the end of the first year of this research, three of the selected students left university and a further five had dropped out of the study.

With the study now in its second year, a further two interviews have been conducted with the cohort. Interviews have been varied, one unstructured, three semi-structured. Some quantitative data have been collected, for example a questionnaire on study skills. We have also collected some visual data (photos of students' rooms, Christmas holiday photos, etc.), constructed weekly timetable data and solicited some 'day in the life' diaries. Through this range of methods, our aim is to develop an in-depth understanding of student choices and pathways through university, the problems they face and the benefits they accrue.

A note on 'class'

At the core of this research is the comparison of the experiences of students from differing class backgrounds. This, of course, presented both theoretical and operational problems. How did we as social scientists define class? And how could we ascertain the class of our student population and sample, especially in view of the fact the students could be viewed as to some extent removed from the class nexus, in a moratorium between their class of origin and their class of destination?[3] Such problems are not easy to solve. Our predominant issue was the need to operationalise class in finding our pairs of students. This necessitated a simplification of the complexities of class; we sought to classify students using a number of indicators: type of school attended, location, parents' occupations, whether parents had been to university and self-reported class. On the basis of this we divided the cohort into three groups: clearly working class, clearly middle class and 'in the middle' – a division which might correspond to the three-class model employed by Bourdieu of dominated, dominant and intermediate.[4] We picked our sample of pairs on this basis, but inevitably as we interviewed them and got to know them some of our original placings appeared inaccurate. It seemed to us eventually that our students' backgrounds fell into four clusters: unambiguously middle class (what in common parlance would be referred to as upper middle class and even upper class); ambiguously middle class (might include some self-employed people, teachers, nurses and so forth, people with degrees but working in low-paid work); ambiguously working class (the same sorts of occupations, but lacking qualifications or having climbed up from lower echelons) and unambiguously working class (manual and unskilled occupations).[5] Because of our constituency we were able to find 40 people who pretty clearly belonged to the dominant classes, as defined by Bourdieu, but the paucity of unambiguously working-class students in some disciplines led us to draw from the intermediate groupings. We would argue, however, that, in Bourdieusian terms, those students we designate as working class do originate in the dominated groupings, not the dominant, and they do clearly display differentiated patterns of attitudes, experiences and behaviours, as the following sections will show.

Investing in education? The choices of working-class students

Why go to university? *The Guardian* newspaper and IT company Campus Management recently organised a roundtable with representatives from HE (including the director of marketing from UoB) to explore student recruitment and retention under the new regime. They concluded that student behaviour was significantly changing. Their needs were more diverse but also more focused, and they were becoming much more sophisticated in exploring what was on offer, utilising the internet, social media and their own networks to make informed choices. Framing this debate was the idea of university as a long-term investment: 'students want to know that they are going to get satisfactory, well-paid jobs'.[6]

Data from our project certainly lent some support for this set of arguments. Our participants were questioned on several occasions about how and why their choices were made. In both the first and the second interviews we talked to the students about their reasons for going to university, their reasons for choosing (or ending up at) UoB or UWE and why they had selected their particular courses. Clearly, we received a wide variety of answers , but among them we were able to discern some repeated patterns of response, and on the basis of these we distinguished three sets of orientations towards university which had structured the transitions of these young people. First was the *normative* approach among young people who took university for granted, seeing at as the 'normal' thing to do (echoing the findings of others);[7] those we called '*determined planners*' who had made a series of rationally considered choices over a period of time; and the '*drifters*' who had stumbled into university almost by default and who expressed no strong reasons or motivations.

In a minority of cases, a chaotic or disrupted transition had been caused by reverses of fortune or upheavals. Among these we distinguished three different 'pathways' into university. *Derailment* referred to those students who had set out with plans or expectations but had been disappointed or suffered setbacks. A second group of people had been drifting and heading towards non-attendance at university, but had been as it were '*rescued*' by some intervention, normally by a parent or teacher. Finally we can define a group whose transitions are highly *disorganised*, whereby a young person may start a degree, leave it, return to another course later in life, or enter into employment for a time before entering HE. This pattern is quite common with mature students, who, however, were not included in our sample. Two students from the sample who quit during their first year fitted into this category.

The 'determined planners' were clearly the group displaying the mindset of 'professional consumers' as *The Guardian* characterised them. Interestingly, students from working-class backgrounds were rather more likely to display this kind of orientation. Table 4.1 shows how these orientations were displayed in relation to the participants' class background and the university they were attending. In a number of cases, students expressed attitudes relating to two of the orientations we had distinguished, and this is shown in the table. The most striking finding is that working-class students at both universities display the

Table 4.1 Passages to university: Motivations and pathways

	Taken for Granted (TFG)	Planned	Planned/ TFG	Drifting	Drifting/ TFG	Derailed	Rescue	Disorganised
UoB Middle class (24)	8	7	5	–	1	1	1	1
UoB Working class (19)	4	8	1	2	1	2	1	–
UWE Middle class (18)	2	2	2	3	2	4	2	1
UWE Working class (20)	1	9	–	6	–	–	2	2

highest level of planning in their decision-making. This determination has propelled them on the first stage of a journey towards possible upward social mobility. In contrast, middle-class students are also more likely to follow the default pathway. Working-class students are more likely than middle class to drift or suffer a disrupted pathway. However, the most disrupted pathways are those of the middle-class students who have ended up at UWE. This suggests that post-1992 universities may have a crucial role in catering for middle-class students who don't perform as well as they had anticipated. Although some of our middle-class students were disappointed in having ended up at, as one of them termed it, an 'ex-poly', they can use their cultural capital to shine in an environment less academically competitive than that at Bristol – for example, one of them has become a student union officer.

We need to explore the reason the young working-class people in our sample chose to pursue their path to university. We should expect, particularly at the current conjuncture , that financial reasons played a major part, and so they did. There was a strong awareness across the whole sample that higher education was a necessity if one aspired to some kind of career path, rather than a job. This was expressed very clearly by Garry, studying history at Bristol, and supports findings by Roberts whose participants did not find fulfillment through training within the retail sector:[8]

> Prospects aren't that great…if you don't have a degree, in retail, because a few of my friends at Sainsbury's I know are trying to work their way up…one of my friends, he's been there five years and he's only just become a team leader, the next step, and…yeah, it's not worth the effort you put in I don't think. The rewards you get back from that career structure isn't brilliant. Whereas conversely, my old store manager, he had an economics degree, he was 29 and he's been promoted again; now he's left, he's become personal assistant to the regional manager I think he's on really good money.

Some working-class participants described how their aspirations to an economically rewarding career were derived from observing the struggles of their parents. Thus Kyle, a law student at UWE, told us:

> Well none of my mum or dad have gone to university and through my life I've sort of seen the impacts of that, like financially through-out my whole life my mum's never had any money, and neither has my dad really. …my whole life has just seen them struggling

through debts and I just thought 'well I can't be bothered to handle that', I'm going to work like hard and get a job hopefully that will earn me loads of money, which is why I want to be a barrister.

Zoe had also selected to do law, but chose UoB for its prestige. She, too, talked about seeing her parents struggle and knew that university was a necessity to escape from the poverty trap of a depressed South Walian township:

> I had the ability to do it and so I didn't want to waste my potential. I'm from an area where I see a lot of deprivation and I see the loons just wandering around jobless and I didn't want to fall into that bracket. There's no big opportunities and I've always felt I was meant for bigger things. So I thought, I can do this, I may as well utilize what I've got, go to university and get a degree. I hope that while I'm here I will find out where I am going to be in life.

Arthur, studying biology at UWE was one of those who had experienced a rescue transition. He had got in with a 'bad crowd' and found himself in trouble in and out of school. Firm intervention by his mother (a nurse) got him back into school compliance, but it was a friend who finally steered him into university

> I didn't think about university until half way through my GCSEs…at one point I was going to do a sporting qualification, probably full time sport, and I thought I'd do that until about six months before I did my decisions. And I thought like 'what's the point in doing a sporting degree, it won't get me anywhere, a sporting qualification'. One of my friends said to me 'sporting qualifications don't work, you won't get a job or anything like that' and I was like 'yeah that's a fair point' so I changed my ideas to do A levels instead. Yeah, I wasn't going to do A levels at all.

While there were other working-class students – especially women – who spoke more about their interest in a particular subject, or a desire for self-development, it is clear that the economic factors will weigh heavily on those from disadvantaged backgrounds. So it is not surprising that working-class young people are drawn particularly to the subjects that they believe will lead to a career (in our study law, economics and engineering). It proved harder to find working-class recruits at Bristol University in subjects such as drama, geography and history.

Reading the accounts of Garry, Kyle and Arthur, it is apparent that their choices are firmly grounded in their own specific classed experiences of struggle and limited opportunities, making, as it were, a kind of resource out of their knowledge of the realities of everyday life. They are able to utilise this resource, which we might term experiential capital, as a fuel for motivation and decision-making, which can work alongside habitus transformation through pedagogic effort and institutional influences to engender a strong desire for university education.[9] Furthermore, they are able to use their grounded knowledge as an asset to negotiate a degree of prestige and respect with their peers and with their tutors. By contrast, the motivations of the middle-class students are more generalised and less grounded. Adrian, an economics student, is fairly typical:

> If you don't have a good degree and you want to earn a lot of money in the future, which I do, there are very few avenues open to you...I like the idea of sort of management consultancy, you know, maybe investment banking, something in the City, something that would pay very, very well...a sort of multinational company would maybe give me the opportunities in the future of being able to work abroad for a few years...get an MBA which you need sort of five years in business.

We suggest we can discern a type of class-based aspirationalism grounded in local everyday knowledge of the limitations experienced by their parents and within the localities they have inhabited which guides these young people towards upward mobility. To do so, though, comes at a cost as it means moving out of your 'comfort zone' and breaking away from family and old friends. Samantha, a geography student at Bristol, for example, was making this break deliberately, though she told us how all her friends had remained working or studying in her northern home town:

> I wanted to get a higher level of qualification as well as meet new people, do something, not just go straight out into work and stay in the same northern bubble that I was in, but to remove myself and like go to a completely different environment.

The investment such young people make, then, are both economic and psychological,[10] and further costs ensue as they enter student life.

Saving to survive: Strategies for funding

Not surprisingly we found that many working-class students at both universities struggle financially, both in terms of the basic cost of living away from home and in terms of having an experience of studenthood beyond the acquisition of a degree. The much vaunted 'student experience' is understood by many (both the working and middle classes) to be a crucial component of undergraduate life. However, the financial cost of this experience is often taken for granted by students from wealthier backgrounds whose parents foot the bill for their accommodation, pay sums of money into their accounts on a monthly basis and send them a Tesco food delivery once a week to ensure that they need not worry about necessities. The less affluent students, on the other hand, employ various strategies in order to survive and participate in student life. For some these strategies began before they started university, taking jobs to save for their first year as an undergraduate, either in the summer prior to enrolment on their course or during what many term their gap year. It is important to note that this 'gap year' is distinguishable from the culturally enriching travelling to far-flung parts of the globe variety and involves working long hours in retail or catering. The need to work during term-time is an imperative that restricts many working-class young people's quality of life as a student.[11] Both term-time and pre-term employment have their disadvantages when it comes to university experience in terms of the investment of time that could be used for studying and/or in the acquisition of the 'right' sort of capitals that will enhance employability (not to mention the health and social gains of leisure activities).

Pre-term or holiday employment was not exclusively limited to the working-class student. It was, however, more likely to be seen by working-class students as a necessity to fund university survival rather than for added luxuries, fun or travel (as was more likely the case for middle-class students). The following two examples illustrate this contrast:

> Well I had a gap year last year and just pretty much worked the whole time, saved my money for the accommodation here so I didn't have to sort of pay it back on the loan. I worked at a theme park and a restaurant and sort of cleaned and loads of different things really. (Alfie)

> Yeah, I didn't really do much actually. Because my plan was to get a job, work, earn some money and then go away, but it was really

hard to find a job because I didn't have really any qualifications or anything, eventually I just kind of gave up, sat around til February not doing much really. And then I went and worked for my company until July, having done a couple of re-sits in January. Then came back and then I guess summer was just spent with old school friends who had been at uni for a year, or the ones that had been away on gap years, to other countries, and just spent doing summer stuff I guess, BBQs, lazing by pools etc, that's about it. So that was my gap year in a nutshell. (Joel)

While many of the working-class students must use their money to fund their undergraduate life the more affluent of the middle classes can either afford not to work or to use their earnings to enhance their social and cultural capital through travel or meaningful (i.e. related to future career) employment either before or during university. Thus, the dominant can 'appropriate the stakes' before the game even begins.[12] Term-time employment was a further restriction on many working-class students' experience of university. Zoe works 20 hours a week as a waitress while studying for her law degree. Not only does this significantly impact on her available time for study but it causes her to re-evaluate her social activities, in particular socialising in clubs. She says:

But then I get really drunk, go home early because I think it's rubbish, and then suffer for two days because I get the worst hangovers in the world. During those days I have to work, I have to do uni work – it's not worth it. And it's money that I've worked so hard for... how hard I have to work for £4.92 an hour. Like some hours I think I'm going to die, like a crazy, busy hour where you've got like so many tables and so much going on, I just think 'wow that drink was that hour that I absolutely like hated life for' and it's just not worth it.

Throughout her interviews Zoe talks of the exhaustion she feels because of trying to both study and earn money. Although a very bubbly and outgoing person, Zoe (as discussed further in the next section) experiences a degree of social isolation at university, a situation that is not helped by the lack of time and economic capital to resource her social self.

Struggling to compete: Expenditure, class and difference

The gains from university are not just in terms of acquisition of symbolic capital, in the form of qualifications and of elite types of knowledge which will, it is hoped, lead to the securing of high levels of economic capital by the acquirers. As the adage has it, 'it's not what you know, it's who you know'. Social networks formed at universities, 'old boys' networks' and membership of the Bullingdon Club which will help propel rich young men into positions of national power-holding, are also crucial to the reproduction of dominant class positions. At a less exalted level, university networks can provide useful links for accessing jobs and providing know-how of the professional world; moreover the social and cultural activities available at university are a valuable resource for 'CV building'. How do our working-class students fare in that respect?

Some students are quick to grasp the differences between their previous experiences and those of their middle-class colleagues. Adele at UWE told us she had not joined any clubs because of her lack of relevant skills. Her mother had not been able to propel her through the typical intensive regime of enrichment or 'concerted cultivation' with which middle-class parents seek to secure a middle-class future for their children.[13]

> My mum didn't push me, she didn't have the money, and a lot of people I know have 'oh yeah when we were little we were sent to ballet', we were sent to this, we were sent to that – I wasn't. I kind of wish I could get into something, maybe to do with sport, athletics, netball, something like that, now, but I haven't got the confidence to do that just because that was just not in my radar when I was younger. (Adele)

> My mum and dad do have money saved but they don't like have enough to each year just give me like three grand for my tuition fees and stuff, it just would be too expensive...because like no-one from Stoke...well obviously people do (have enough money) but there's not many that are on like a Bristol type.. you know what I mean. Different places, but yeah it's two totally different places. (Lizzie)

Joining in with the cultural and social activities of their more advantaged peers can be an expensive business, as a number of students told us:

> I'm on a lower budget than most of my flat-mates, so, they still want to go out two times a week and like 'no I can't afford to go out two

times a week'. I'm on about £500 a term, which is £50 a week, which I'm managing quite well because I limit myself. (Samantha)

Their choices of social activities are therefore limited in a way those of their richer colleagues are not. Alfie explains why he took up rock climbing:

> The only problem is with quite a lot of them is that they're quite expensive to go into and I can't afford really to go into them. Snow sports looks quite good but you have to pay to go to the dry slope every weekend. They have about five holidays or something and they're like £500 each so it's a bit too much…rock climbing is the best one really because…I think it was £20 to join and £6 for the induction…and yeah after that they go to the Lake District for two nights for £20 for the whole trip, you know, travel there, two nights there, rock climbing and then back and it just seems really cheap…but all the other ones are quite a lot. I think gliding is about £80 a lesson, which is good compared to normal, you know going to an actual airfield, but it's still a bit too much. I think a lot of it's sort of aimed for richer students really. (Alfie)

Megan, an English student at Bristol, feels bitterly her exclusion from the activities of her richer friends, especially the music at which she is talented:

> My boyfriend is able to do all these musical instruments and they have horses and I love riding and just like things that are all around him all the time I can never keep up with financially. And my other friend, his parents will just give him their credit card like any time and he was always wearing like ridiculously expensive clothing.

The working-class students were realistic about their situations and had learned to operate within them. Yet this does mean that they may be excluded from developing the kind of social assets open to their richer peers:

> I don't go out an awful lot. I'm not stupid, if I haven't got the money I won't go out. But you can't stay in all the time because you're missing the whole aspect of socialising with your friends. You get lonely if you do that. (Adele)

In some cases students responded to the constraints by seeking friendships among their own kind, although this was not a universal pattern.

Zoe, however, exemplified it. She told us from the beginning how isolated she felt from those who surrounded her:

> I'm the only person in my hall from a state school…there's ten people on my law course of 250 who have been to a state school & the majority of them are like 'oh I could have gone to boarding school but my parents thought it was a waste of money'. I know no-one from my background, that's why I find it so difficult to adjust, when no-one can relate to me.

In her second year she moved in with a group of UWE students whose background she found compatible with hers. Hugely ambitious, she has yet failed to make the contacts that might help her to the wealthy future she aspires too. Such are the hurdles to joining the dominant class.[14]

Banking on the future: The £27k deterrent

And the hurdles are set to heighten. Working-class students already encounter significant obstacles in getting to and getting on in higher education and they have recently done so to the tune of around ten thousand pounds in tuition fees. With the expectation that they will earn more than non-graduates when they leave university this fee has become an acceptable price to many who have not known the pre-Blairite era of free university education. However, with the almost tripling of fees to £27,000, the cost of a degree is perhaps too high for many working-class students. However, government ministers are complacent on this issue, even arrogantly insinuating that what students will have to pay is not actually a debt. David Willetts, the minister for universities and science, for example, is dismissive of the reality of university debt, saying: 'We're trapped in this language of debt. It's not like leaving university with £25,000 worth of debt on your credit card or anything…it is a graduate repayment scheme that has many of the features of income tax. It's not like some debt around their necks'.[15] This demonstrates an extraordinary lack of understanding about the experience of ordinary working-class people for whom debts of £27,000 are significant. Families who are likely to be particularly affected by the fees are those whose household income is above the threshold for widening participation grants and bursaries. Arguably, the grants and bursaries do not go far enough in assisting all working-class students to access higher education. Indeed many of what we have identified as working-class students in our sample are from households that are not eligible for additional financial support. Although not the poorest of the working classes, these students are often the first generation in their families to go to university and do not have the privileged know-ledge of the higher education system that their middle-class peers have absorbed through familial cultural capital, let alone the economic capital to finance their education. For these families university edu-cation is a significant financial burden leaving many students feeling guilty about putting financial pressure on their families. Although their income is above the threshold they do not have the disposable income to comfortably support their children's university education. Zoe, for example, highlights this issue.

> Me being at uni, I feel slightly guilty because they're under a lot of pressure because although they earn on paper enough for the gov-ernment, well for my local authority, to say 'we're not going to give you any help, we're not going to give you a grant, you are just going to get the standard amount of loan' so that's how they get around that. But then my parents are literally struggling. So they can't afford to give me any money, hence why I've just got this crazy job with crazy hours just trying to support myself, because my loan like barely covers my accommodation.

Many working-class students feel the financial squeeze at university under the initial three-and-a-half grand tuition fees. Given the sharp increase in fees, which these students feel lucky to have escaped, would the working-class cohort still consider going to university? The simple, and perhaps surprising, answer is mostly yes. It appears that many stu-dents have bought into the government rhetoric of 'free at the point of delivery'. Moreover, these students do not think about their student debt because they 'don't see the money' exchange hands. The debt is an almost invisible and certainly intangible entity that they need not worry about until a later date. And as nearly all of our students are optimistic about their future earning potential, despite the recognition that there is currently considerable graduate unemployment, this future debt is considered entirely manageable. Both Harvey and Tony, for example, exemplify this conceptualisation of student debt as an investment in the future.

> As I say, it's an investment. I would have paid , whatever. And at the end of the day, it's nine grand a year but you still only pay about

9 per cent and you still only pay it after 20 grand is it, or 21 now I think. And I mean I've worked it out, if you're earning about 24 grand a year and you're paying 9 per cent, that's about £45 a week you're paying back. (Harvey)

I judge it as pay this much to the university now, I have a better chance of getting a higher paid job further on in life. So right now I'm paying a lot of money to be taught my subject but later on it will pay for itself, so that's really how I view it. (Tony)

However, in light of the reality of the graduate job market, it is unlikely that the future will be quite as manageable as they expect. In their recent book, and associated publications, Brown et al refer to the 'opportunity trap' where the expectation of graduate careers and a good life cannot be realised by all because of the 'inherent tension, if not contradiction, in the relationship between capitalism and democracy'.[16] The expansion of higher education and the uncertainties of the job market increase the competition for the elusive well-paid career and the middle classes are better positioned to arm themselves for this struggle. It would therefore seem appropriate to claim that the government is capitalising on working-class young people's aspirations by mis-selling the dream of a better life for the not insignificant risky investment of £27,000. Burdening the aspiring working classes with a crippling debt increases the likely outcome of inequality in terms of quality of life. Not only do the middle classes still have the odds stacked in their favour when it comes to coming out on top in the graduate market, but they are better positioned to manage their debt through family support and inheritances, and it is perhaps people in these circumstances that David Willetts has in mind when he brushes off the significance of student debt.

But what choice do students have? Gaining a university degree, despite the increase in competition for graduate jobs and record rates of graduate unemployment, is for many of today's youth the only hope they have of escaping a life of poverty and exclusion, despite the fact that the £100,000 graduate lifetime premium offers only about two to three thousand pounds extra per annum of their working lives. The opportunities for school leavers who do not go to university are few and far between, and many of our students recognised this lack of alternative opportunity. In fact many students could not conceptualise another route to desirable employment and saw the likely (non-graduate) alternative future as one in routine, insecure, poorly-paid employment within the service industry as the following three UWE students illustrate:

> I moved out of my parents' house when I was 18 and then I just did full-time work in an office doing debt collection on the phones. And then while I was doing that I just applied for uni because I didn't really want to do phones all my life. (Tracey)

> Well I did like try going to work…because when I finished college I didn't want to go to uni, and then I started working full time at the place where I was working and I was like 'oh I can't hack this for like indefinitely'. (Shane)

> Because I was working already I thought 'if I don't go to university I'll be stuck in these types of jobs in shops and stuff' and I didn't really want to do that. (Sophie)

This experience of the mundaneness of low-paid work is another example of how working-class choices are grounded in everyday reality. Higher education becomes the only imaginable alternative, so they have no choice but to pay. Megan is resigned to the lack of choice in the matter of paying fees regardless of how high they are:

> I think £3,000, I'd feel like I'm getting my money for it, but if it was triple that amount I would be like 'no this is awful', but I'd have no choice, I'd have to do it anyway.

The students may be banking on the future, but it is a high-risk investment and government and university funding provide inadequate financial support to off-set this risk. Unfortunately, they have no viable alternative.

Conclusion

Becoming and being a student are highly differentiated by class, as we have shown through our discussion of students' university decision-making processes, funding strategies, and struggles to compete with middle-class peers. The economic constraints faced by many working-class students can cut them off from various aspects of university experience. In terms of social networking, as well as simply socialising, working-class students are more likely to face serious budgetary and time restrictions. They are more likely to need to work in order to meet the basic costs of living, which not only has a knock-on effect on their studies but precludes them from enjoying many of the social freedoms that university life offers their more privileged counterparts. Furthermore, students from working-class backgrounds struggle to become involved in culturally (and CV) enriching extra-curricular activities because of the prohibitive costs both in terms of finances and time – a situation that will potentially lead to disadvantages in the graduate job market.

On other hand, they show resilience in overcoming these obstacles and a strong resolve to do well educationally, building on the personal resources they developed in order even to get to university with the odds stacked against them. Although we focus here on their instrumental approaches to higher education as a means to a better future, many of our students also expressed a love of learning and knowledge. It is our contention that these aspirational working-class students need to be supported in their endeavours, since high aspirations are not enough in themselves to lead to success. The current government's apparent liberalism needs to be realised through better financial support for working-class young people. Financial backing is needed to alleviate the economic difficulties they experience at university, giving them a proper chance of a decent future. Instead they are being hampered with unprecedented levels of debt which will not enhance future prospects. The government should not one-handedly encourage aspiration and on the other hand erect barriers impeding the realisation of such aspirations.

Perhaps this contradiction betrays the lack of genuine conviction in the Widening Participation agenda and the equalisation of both opportunity *and* outcome, as David Cameron exposed through his unfortunate comment to factory workers: 'Do you think it's right that your taxes are going to educate my children and your boss's children?'.[17] It is clear from this comment that Cameron assumes that university education is not for the children of working-class factory workers. This kind of thinking lies behind the push to channel 'less academic' (i.e. deprived of cultural capital) children into vocational training. Leaving this prejudiced thinking aside, it is important to ask a question back to the Prime Minister – why should not your taxes, and those of your privileged ilk, pay for the university education of the children of the economically deprived working classes? If the government is genuine about its desire for social equality, then logically they should do so.

Notes

1   Cf. P. Bourdieu (1996) *The State Nobility*. Cambridge: Polity Press.
2   I. Bates and G. Riseborough (1993) *Youth and Inequality*. Milton Keynes: Open University Press; F. Devine (2004) *Class Practices: How Parents Help Their Children Get Good Jobs*. Cambridge: Cambridge University Press.
3   M. Brake (1980) *The Sociology of Youth Culture and Youth Subcultures*. London: Routledge and Kegan Paul.
4   P. Bourdieu (1984) *Distinction: A Social Critique of the Judgement of Taste*. London: Routledge.
5   For more detail on the issue of ascribing class in the project see A-M. Bathmaker, N. Ingram and R. Waller (2011) 'Higher Education, Social Class and the Mobilization of Capital', BERA conference, Institute of Education, London.
6   H. Swain (2012) 'Rules of Student Attraction', *The Guardian*, 28th February.
7   D. Reay, M. David and S. Ball (2005) *Degrees of Choice: Class, Race, Gender and Higher Education*. Stoke-on-Trent: Trentham; W. Atkinson (2010) *Class, Individualization and Late Modernity: In Search of the Reflexive Worker*. Basingstoke: Palgrave Macmillan.
8   S. Roberts (2012) 'Gaining Skills or Just Paying the Bills? Workplace Learning in Low-Level Retail Employment', *Journal of Education and Work*, iFirst article. All student names used in this chapter are pseudonyms to protect the anonymity of participants.
9   P. Bourdieu (2002) 'Habitus' in J. Hillier and E. Rooksby (eds) *Habitus: A Sense of Place*. Aldershot: Ashgate, pp. 27–34.; N. Ingram (2011) 'Within School and Beyond the Gate: The Difficulties of Being Educationally Successful and Working-Class', *Sociology*, 45(7): 287–302.
10 D. Reay (2001) 'Finding or Losing Yourself? Working-Class Relationships to Education', *Journal of Education Policy*, 16: 333–46.
11 J. Mellor, R. Waller and A. Hoare (2012) 'UK University Students and Paid Work', paper presented at the British Sociological Association annual conference, Leeds; C. Callender (2008) 'The Impact of Term-Time Employment on Higher Education Students' Academic Attainment and Achievement', *Journal of Education Policy*, 23(4): 359–77.
12 P. Bourdieu (1990) *In Other Words*. Cambridge: Polity Press, p. 64.
13 A. Lareau (2003) *Unequal Childhoods: Class, Race and Family Life*. Los Angeles: University of California Press.
14 This resonates with experience of the young women experiencing the strangeness of the 'Hogwarts' institutional culture of Oxbridge discussed in Roberts and Evans, this volume.
15 Quoted in D. Atkinhead (2011) 'David Willetts: "Many More Will Go to University Than in My Generation – We Must Not Reverse That"', *The Guardian*, 20th November.
16 P. Brown (2003) 'The Opportunity Trap: Education and Employment in a Global Economy', *European Educational Research Journal*, 2(1): 141–79, p. 141; P. Brown, H. Lauder and D. Ashton (2010) *The Global Auction: The Broken Promises of Education, Jobs and Incomes*. Oxford: Oxford University Press.
17 J. Hari (2011) 'The Plan to Save Ed Milliband', *The Independent*, 1st April.

5

'Aspirations' and Imagined Futures: The Im/possibilities for Britain's Young Working Class

Steven Roberts and Sarah Evans

Introduction

Since the 1970s, successive governments have overseen a retrenchment of the welfare state alongside a concomitant lowering and alteration of individuals' expectations of entitlement and the relationship with the state more broadly. Davidson explains that this is in line with the ways in which 'neo-liberal governance aims to ensure that the state's goals become synonymous with individual goals'.[1] Building on Bourdieu's notion of pseudo-concepts,[2] Raco theorises that this approach has given rise to 'existential politics', whereby:

> governments actively define, categorise, and institutionalise the *essential characteristics* of human nature, well-being, responsibility, and virtue...by defining some of the fundamentals of human condition such as: what it means to be happy, fulfilled, and contented; what constitutes essential and non-essential human needs; what processes shape the ways in which the social and cultural status of individuals and groups is defined... More broadly an existential politics is also about the processes through which dominant social *values* are defined and institutionalised.[3]

Accordingly, individuals' aspirations are a central priority for policymakers, being at once the potential Achilles' heel and the potential saviour of national economies. 'Low aspirations', policymakers feel, are in part the cause of contemporary social and economic ills; the remedy, according to the broad political consensus outlined in the following quotes, is to raise these aspirations:

> Aspiration is not about class, background or position. Everybody dreams of rising up in the world, and everybody dreams of giving their children a better life. I don't care where you started out in life; my mission is to help you rise higher.
>
> (David Cameron, speech to Chance UK, 2007)

> The poverty of aspiration is as damaging as the poverty of opportunity and it is time to replace a culture of low expectations for too many with a culture of high standards for all.
>
> (Gordon Brown, speech at the University of Greenwich, 2007)

> We can become an aspiration nation once more...
>
> (Michael Gove, oral statement on the Schools White paper, House of Commons, February 2011)

> Nobody from whatever school they come from, whatever background they come from, should be discouraged from trying to do good things with their lives. Aspiration, ambition, hope, optimism is always important, but it's especially important in the teenage years.
>
> (Nick Clegg, speech at Charles Edward Brooke School for Girls, Camberwell, October 2011)

'Low aspirations', as defined by this rhetoric are those which do not comply with middle-class norms and ideals. For example: pregnancy during the teenage years (and indeed, it could be argued, early twenties); beginning a family before completing further or higher education; single-parenthood; prioritising sexual and intimate relationships above the pursuit of educational 'success'; and the pursuit of full-time employment rather than further or higher education. It is worth highlighting that with the exception of single-parenthood, most of these outcomes for young people (working class or not) would have been considered to be quite respectable 20 or so years ago. 'High' or 'appropriate' aspirations are those recognised and defined as legitimate by the dominant parts of society that have the power to do so.[4] These include, for example, the pursuit of a university degree and professional vocation, and, for women, deferring pregnancy until a professional career and heterosexual relationship have been 'achieved'. This discourse of 'aspiration' is a powerful and apparently persuasive rhetoric, but it represents more than simply orthodox thinking; orthodoxy exists only in as much as it is a choice, indeed the accepted choice amongst *competing possibilities*.[5] Instead the discourse of 'aspiration' amounts to what Bourdieu calls doxa – a taken for granted assumption, the common sense approach; one which is seemingly embraced and understood by political parties of all persuasions (and probably ingrained into wider public consciousness) as being an incontrovertible, self-evident truth.

Bourdieu explains that 'crisis is a necessary condition for the questioning of doxa but is not in itself a sufficient condition for the production of a critical discourse'.[6] There is no doubt that the fall-out of the global economic downturn represents a crisis, but sociologists have yet to fully and successfully challenge the integrity of this doxa and expose the discourse of aspirations for what it really is: an art of government, which, consistent with the dominant neoliberal approach the last four decades, aims to link economic governance to individual behaviour, choices and responsibilities for these choices. In other words, the politics of aspiration 'seeks to individualise responsibility for personal wellbeing by promoting a self-reliant, entrepreneurial citizenship that is counterposed to the expectation that the state will provide a welfare safety net to support those who lose out from persistent social inequalities'.[7] This dominant view therefore takes as a central premise the idea that it is 'low aspirations' which are a causal factor in the reproduction of social inequality. Despite enormous evidence to the contrary, the 'aspirations' discourse espouses that it is low aspirations themselves which limit social mobility for working-class people, rather than multiple cultural, social and economic factors which reproduce social inequality across generations.

This chapter therefore contributes to the emerging body of work aiming to develop 'the critique which brings the undiscussed into discussion'[8] and explicitly reveal how, contrary to David Cameron's comments above, harbouring legitimate or 'appropriate aspiration' cannot be so easily disentangled from *class background and position*. Drawing on two pieces of research with young people, we examine the various desires for the future held by young working-class men and women, tracing the gaps between the fantasy work which constructs their hopes for the future, and the symbolic and material attacks (in rhetoric and in social policy), on these desires by both the previous and present British governments. As indicated above, what is central to our argument is that, in discussing 'aspiration', policymakers are in fact promoting a very particular set of aspirations associated with the *active rational individual agent* with explicit links to national economic competitiveness. As the evidence presented here demonstrates, the 'aspirations' which young working-class people hold for their future are not necessarily 'active decisions'. Their hopes and dreams are influenced by the realities lived by family members and friends with reference to what they understand about the wider social and political context. Not only does the rhetoric of aspiration *not take the realities of social inequality* into account, but it implies that the responsibility for continuing inequality lies with those who are in fact the victims of policies which have increased social differentiation.

On the surface, when someone does not share the aspirations built on middle-class cultural values, there ostensibly appears to be two outcomes. The first is that an individual is perceived as somehow lacking, patho-logised and constructed as the incorrect, illegitimate 'other'. An example of this can be seen in the ways in which some young middle-class people have positioned others as being 'chavs' when they do not share their proclivity for educational engagement.[9] The second outcome is that young people might engage in what Elias refers to as the 'civilising process': this entails a form of self-regulation (itself a distinguishing feature of the appropriate neoliberal subject) stimulated by fear of the particular kinds of stigma outlined in the last example and/or a wish for the status that is accorded to those already deemed 'civilised'.[10] Such a transformation of self-conduct frames the idea and the act of *becoming* middle class as a choice, a choice which is promulgated by policymakers because the acqui-sition of certain values and skills is framed as means to overcome social problems and/or an 'at risk' status.

Methods

The data used in the chapter is drawn from two separate projects which explored the lives and perceived futures of young people in the South East of England through a combination of qualitative methods, including ethnography and in-depth biographical interviews. In both projects the respondents were defined as working class, (located in the dominated sections of social space, to use Bourdieu's terms),[11] using a number of measures, including the occupation of their head of household,[12] as well as by their housing type and highest level of education within the immediate family.

While the two pieces of research explored some common themes around imagined futures and the realms of the im/possible, they took place in dif-ferent landscapes of young people's lives. One analysed the lives and expe-riences of 24 'moderately' qualified,[13] white, working-class young men (aged 18–24) employed in entry-level service-sector jobs in their efforts to engage with the labour market on a permanent basis. These young men were all based in the east part of the county of Kent, where, with the exception of one participant, they had been brought up and resided their entire life. The other project examined the educational progress and aspirations for higher education among 21 working-class young women who were in the process of studying for their A level qualifications and were considering following these qualifications with a university degree. The respondents in this project came from a variety of ethnic backgrounds, with seven of the 21 coming from first generation immigrant families from Somalia, China, Vietnam, Bangladesh and India. All of these girls spoke a language other than English at home, but had either been born in the UK or had lived in the UK since pre-school age. The remaining girls were all white and had been born in England. Of these girls all had at least one parent who was from London (for the majority, both were from London); furthermore, 12 of these girls had at least one parent who had been born and raised in the local area.

What sort of 'aspirations' do young working-class people hold?

1. The young men

In the project looking at young men, all were convinced they were unlikely to ever to go into higher education (HE). The aspirations rhetoric therefore positions them as having 'low aspirations'. This is also important to note because it is this very group who have been deemed a threat to the achievement of widening participation targets and lifelong learning strategies in the UK.[14] However, such aspirations need to be carefully considered and critically interrogated. Similar to other research, the idea and the culture of HE were largely positioned as 'foreign fields' and 'unreal' for these young men.[15] However, this was just one layer among a complex web of issues at play found in their reasoning for not applying or not wanting to go into HE. Again consistent with other research, their perceptions of HE were 'unreal' in that these young people largely had very limited direct, inside experience upon which to draw, in contrast to those young people in whose families and communities there is an established tradition of participating in HE. This can be seen in the absolute lack of knowledge among some of the sample about what people do at university:

> Interviewer: Has anyone in your family ever been to university?
> Christian: Not my immediate family, no. Oh no. My dad sorry, my dad was like an electrician or something, so I guess he must have gone to uni for that.

Bobby: I don't think it's for me. Cos I'm not really, I don't know if you can do mechanics and stuff there? But the only reason I would really go to uni is the partying. I don't think they do much else, the fuckers!

Another core issue, and one which is a very timely point of discussion, was the cost. The research was undertaken prior to the Browne review of HE fees and the tripling of course costs passed on to students; yet, the idea and perception of debt was a significant deterrent and an additional important reason for potentially not ever considering HE as a viable option:

> Christian: [On not even considering HE] it was because I didn't think I'd be able to afford to do it to be honest, I wanted to be able to, at the time, I was learning to drive so I wanted to be able to afford, I wanted to be able to work to have money to get a car and things like that. I didn't really think about loans and stuff. I don't know anything about that stuff.

> Tim: Cost didn't [put me off at first] but when you hear of people [lads he play football with] being in 18 grand of debt and loans or something after a three year course...and the thing that pisses me off about university is that you are in about 12 hours or something of lectures a week and the rest of the time, you're nothing. I mean you can go to the library and do your work and things like that, but I mean all you are paying for is 12 hours of study a week. I mean that's not fucking six grand a year. If you are living on campus as well, that's an extra £400 a month as well on top of that so you are gonna be screwed. So it does put me off.

The negative perceptions of debt come across very strongly here, and this came through in many interviews where the burden of debt was described in both terms of constraint (e.g. 'how could you pay your rent if you are having to pay back this massive loan' (Pat)) and stigma (e.g. 'I'm not *that kind* of person, it's not good is it, to have a whopping debt' (Dave, respondent's emphasis)).[16] These kinds of sentiments ensure that recent policy initiatives in relation to HE fees are bedevilled with contradiction: on the one hand the recent and present governments have obsessed at the idea of increasing the supply of qualifications in order to have a highly skilled workforce to remain competitive in the global 'knowledge economy', yet such efforts at 'raising aspiration' are undermined by a fees regime that leaves HE participation increasingly beyond the possible. Thus, 'inspiring aspiration' appears to be the actual goal of government[17] rather than a real commitment to enabling equality in access and outcomes in HE for all of those who hope to pursue it.

At the same time as concerns about debt accumulation and misunderstandings about HE culture prevailed, throughout the sample there was an acute suspicion that it was far from certain that a degree would lead to 'aspirational' labour market outcomes:

> Jake: [A friend] went to uni and he is working down bloody customs now and yet he still, he graduated and that but he didn't get a well paid high earning job. He just got the same kinda job [he'd have gotten anyway]; and his dad probably got for him, too!

> Tim: If people have got the money to blow on it then yeah, fuck it. But if you are gonna go to uni for three years and at the end of the course you can't really go into anything, like you know they have just brought in an exercise science course that you can do at uni but that doesn't lead into anything, so you have got to do more years of uni, and then at the end of the uni course you could go and work in fucking Blockbusters.

This instrumental, quasi-vocational understanding of the value of a university degree provides further evidence of the lack of knowledge about the potential links between qualifications and occupations. But importantly it also shows the lack of relevance that legitimate and recognised (in the Bourdieusian sense) traditional degrees have in the lives of such young people. These kind of sentiments echo Cooke et al.'s commentary on HE participation choices among teenagers from the Midlands, in that 'where families and communities have little experience of HE, or where there are strong traditions of entering the labour market straight from school, knowledge and understanding of the culture, processes and potential benefits of HE are limited. This is not the same as having what are often crudely termed 'low aspirations'.[18] It is this culturally specific and pertinent knowledge embodied in the habitus, rather than a poverty of aspiration, that is critical here, as it is likely to provoke anxieties and antagonism towards the education system among parents and young people. Furthermore, such anxieties about education and labour market outcomes are not entirely unreasonable. While governments can make statements like 'the undeniable truth is that if a young person continues their education post-16 they are more likely to achieve valuable qualifications, earn more, and lead happier, healthier lives',[19] alongside this is another absolute fact: more than 350,000 young people each year end up with vocational qualifications which have absolutely no value in the labour market.[20] This is the context in which young people are encouraged to raise their educational aspirations and it amounts to a situation where the government is selling a dream but young people end up living a nightmare. To be convinced to proceed with a course of action that represents a disjuncture from the familiar young people need to feel that there are likely to be some dividends and realistic chances of success. As Bourdieu notes, 'the level of aspiration of individuals is essentially determined by the probability (judged intuitively by means of previous successes or failures) of achieving the desired goal'.[21]

These kinds of social processes, which are usefully summed up by Bourdieu's concepts of habitus and cultural capital, are equally at play when considering the aspirations of those who are well equipped in terms of educational qualifications who have decided to go to university. In the research project focussing on young women this was indeed the case.

2. The young women

The young female respondents nearly all had, on the surface, aspirations which fit with the 'appropriate aspirations' as defined by the current government and the last. They were all in the process of undertaking their A levels, having achieved suitably high grades at GCSE. All of the young women envisaged that completion of a university degree was the most tangible route towards a professional career. Unlike the young men discussed above, these young women were immersed in a sixth form community (attached to a secondary school) in which university study had, over the past ten years, become increasingly normalised for its students. Reflecting the positive attitude of their sixth form teachers, this group often subscribed to the view that young people with a degree compete for employment on a relatively 'level playing field', and similarly, considered the university system to be more democratic and meritocratic than it once was. As Jennie put it:

It seems like it's become a lot different from what – a lot more open, more different people – different classes, different races [...] It seems like in the past, it used to be a certain class – certain people, to go; only the – well – the most highly educated people with the most money, of the best class: like middle, upper classes. Now I think it's more open to everyone because you've got loans that you can get and it's become like more widely accessible to everyone.

Despite Jennie's optimism about the university system that awaited her, she was also acutely aware that it is only recently that university has opened its doors to 'people like her', and there were certain HE institutions that Jennie and the other young women considered to be neither realistic nor desirable as options.[22] The affects of habitus were certainly significant in the construction of this view, which made the elite institutions of Oxbridge beyond reach. While a number of the young women had visited open-days at Oxford and Cambridge, the historical exclusion of 'people like them' (women, minority ethnic groups and working-class people) from these institutions was quite evident from the architecture and décor of these spaces: from the portraits of 'old white men' hanging on the walls to the 'fancy' dining wear, the demarcation of difference was everywhere. Thus, as has been found in other studies of minority groups and elite spaces,[23] these universities felt entirely foreign and exclusive, as Beth describes:

> Beth: I think, like, it was spectacular, it was really beautiful, but even when we went to have lunch in one of the colleges, I think it was Fitzwilliam College, like all the plates have got gold rim on it with, like, the logo of Cambridge on it, and a dessert is like three-pound-fifty. And everywhere you sit down inside, all the teachers have got chairs with higher backs than the students, and they're on a raised platform.
> Interviewer: Like high-table?
> Beth: [I was like] 'are you mad or what? This ain't Harry Potter!' I mean, you'd expect that that kind of snootiness wouldn't be around by the time you've gone to uni. I thought uni was about finding out who you are, not being repressed anymore.

Overwhelmingly, the young women had instrumental ideas about the purpose of HE. This instrumentality resonates with the earlier work by both Skeggs and Mirza in which the primary purpose of post-compulsory education for working-class and ethnic minority girls was its place in gaining entry to particular forms of gendered work,[24] namely, care and social work or administration. In these studies, the kinds of jobs sought by the young women reflected their knowledge about the kinds of work it was possible for women like them to achieve, and also, as in Skeggs' study, was significantly tied to local expectations of gender performance. The primary research presented here reflects the combined effects of recent changes to employment structure, education reform and cultural narratives about women and work, in that professions which the young women hoped to enter were not explicitly gendered. Furthermore, the fields which this group were interested in were areas in which no family member before them had worked. They aimed for jobs in journalism, medicine, law and the media, hoping to achieve well-paid and stimulating careers, as described by Jo:

> Jo: Yeah, I want a good job. I don't want to be like, I don't want to be like my family like, they've never been like really educated and they've never had professions – and I want a profession. I want a good job.
> Interviewer: You want a profession that's sort of recognised?
> Jo: Yeah, I wanna be like, so I can say 'Yeah, I'm a teacher' or 'Yeah, I'm a lawyer' I want to *be something*. I don't want to be like, just working, I want to have something, to do a job that I enjoy and I want to get money as well! 'Cause you've gotta have money! (Respondent's emphasis)

Jo, like the other young women, wanted financial security and a good job: one which would provide her with some social status and recognition. Jo desired entry to those professions which have traditionally been dominated by the middle classes and hoped to train to be a barrister – an overwhelmingly white, middle-class, male profession. On paper at least, Jo – like the other young women in this study – would appear to be the perfect example of the young working-class person with 'appropriate aspirations'.

Yet the narratives about the transition through higher education and into employment that these girls presented were not imbued with ideas about of 'bettering oneself' which the 'aspirations' discourse promotes.[25] The young women did not want to become 'middle class', as indicated by Beth:

> I feel now that I should do the best that I can within what I am, rather than trying to be something else. Because, I don't know, that's just the way I feel kind of thing. As a working-class person I owe it to my family to make...to prove that a working-class person can do something and they don't have to fake it to prove that.

At the same time, the aspirations of these young women were not individualistic, for many spoke about their desire to bring improvements to the social conditions under which they, and their family, were living. Indeed, this desire to improve the circumstances of existing family and ensure improved living conditions for their future family was a common narrative amongst the young women.[26]

> Keira: The one thing I want to do is just give something back to my family really, that's the most important thing to me, and helping my Nan and all [...] that's the main thing, because my Mum's given me a lot – she's worked hard – I mean, she has two jobs, so she's worked quite hard.

These 'altruistic narratives', which have been described elsewhere,[27] were also entangled with heteronormative desires for children, a stable heterosexual relationship (many spoke of marriage) and a home of one's own in which to raise children and have a 'ordinary' family life. The normative and 'ordinary' futures that the young women described were echoed by the young men seen above, as will be outlined below. As we will go on to demonstrate, these 'ordinary' futures for young working-class people are amongst a set of future possibilities which are under direct attack by the present government.

Heteronormative desires and 'ordinary' futures

As we have described above, all too often discussions about young people's aspirations in the political and wider public/media domain construct the hopes for the future by young working-class people as inferior to those held by their middle-class peers. Moreover, the absence of 'appropriate aspirations' positions working-class young people, and indeed their families, as being essentially irresponsible, 'unmotivated, unambitious and underachieving'.[28] Thus, in order to be upwardly socially mobile, working-class young people must learn to 'aspire' like their middle-class peers.

There are a number of issues with the notion of 'aspiration' as a political construct, which assumes that the desires which young people (of all class backgrounds) hold for the future are constructed via rational processes of decision-making in which there is equality in access to a set of 'choices'. Thus, imagined futures, hopes, desires, dreams and fantasy are all constructed as 'aspiration' rather than as processes which are inherently bound-up with young people's emotional and psychological worlds, which are constructed and developed through the experience of their social realities.[29] For example, where young people do not conform to the 'appropriate aspiration' of higher education and the pursuit of a professional career, political and media rhetoric very often suggests that it is 'celebrity culture' which is to blame. In 2008, for instance, the BBC reported on a piece of research funded by the Association of Teachers and Lecturers which explained that 'pupil's obsession with footballers, pop stars and actors are affecting their progress in school and limiting their career aspirations'. The narrative of the working-class youth who 'want it all and want it now' without 'hard work' is prevalent and, indeed, was frequently described as a key factor in the looting which took place during the riots of August 2011. Indeed, Work and Pensions Secretary Ian Duncan Smith deemed the 'get rich quick' ideals of a generation obsessed with the 'X-Factor culture' to have fuelled the UK riots.[30] Furthermore, highlighting a refusal to give up the pleasures of (real and imagined) consumption, and to live a life of appropriate austerity, Education Minister Nick Gibb insisted in the House of Commons in December 2011 that young people have 'unrealistic expectations about the lifestyle they can afford, fuelled by the glittering trappings of celebrities'.[31]

Both pieces of research discussed in this chapter debunk this as something of a myth. There is a distinct difference between asking young people whether they ever *dream* of being David Beckham or Katie Price (and enjoying the material luxury of wealth) and asking young people to offer realistic descriptions of how they envisage their future and what would make them happy. Far from the ideal of 'wanting it all and wanting it now', the young people in both pieces of research consistently reported grounded, 'modest' imagined futures which were closely tied to heteronormative ideals as they describe below:

Pat: In the future I want a family and that; like kids and a dog and Mrs and nice place to live, you know what I mean? Just the same as everyone wants. It doesn't really matter about having a mortgage or anything – actually I wouldn't know where to start! – but like, serious important thing is to just do your best and have a nice life. But as I just said mate, I've been working part time for donkeys' years and can't get a full time job.

Johnny: God knows. I still live with my mum! I'm not some flashy fuck, I'm not gonna sit here and say I wouldn't like a big house and that, and a Merc or something, but it's not likely to happen. What I want more than anything is to just be able to have my own place eventually, be able to go and see my mates after work sometimes, sometimes stay in on my own... And, um, end up living with a girl

I guess. But I'd wanna live close enough to look after the old dear if she needed it, too, cos she aint got a partner or anything.

Emma: I want to be happy and like stay in a stable job that I like, that I've worked for, and that [...] I'll be daily challenged by it. But then I want the whole, normal life as well, like kids, marriage.

Keira: I don't want to be greedy, I just want to be comfortable, whereas most people are like: 'I'd like this, I'd like that' I just want to be comfortable, without having to say, 'I can't afford this this week, I'll hold back,' – do you know what I mean? I just want to be able to – not afford everything but – be like, well I can pay off the mortgage this week, I can do this, I can do that and I can fill up the fridge and if I have kids, I can buy them stuff, like not all the time, but like I can treat them and if they want to go on school trips I can afford it.

All of these examples conflict with the prevalent myth amongst many widening participation practitioners and policymakers (as well as the media and wider public) that young working-class teenagers are only motivated by dreams of glamour, wealth and celebrity. The responses which our young respondents gave showed similarities to those given by Gavin Brown's respondents who desired emotional wellbeing and financial stability and security:

Rather than aspiring to academic success or professional careers, large numbers of these young people focused their ambitions and definitions of personal success on questions of emotional well-being and security... A significant minority of the young men believed success to be defined in terms of material wealth, while [but many] were motivated by the prospect of earning 'good' money that was enough to get by comfortably, and no more. Again, this speaks to a desire for (financial) security.[32]

It was also the case that in both pieces of research the young people's hopes for the future were structured by powerfully heteronormative expectations. This was consistent with the findings of Henderson et al who identified that young people's aspirations for adult life remain structured by heteronormativity, as demonstrated by expectations about marriage and/or partnership, children and the significance of wider family.[33] In both pieces of research a concerted effort was made to avoid implying heterosexuality in the way that questions were phrased, yet heterosexual relationships were consistently presumed by the respondents in their discussions of future partners. Thus, the possibility of a sexual future which was anything other than heterosexual was never raised by the respondents themselves. Indeed, even where it was difficult for the young women to imagine themselves being married, they couldn't imagine having children without being married, as Gracie described:

> Interviewer: Is marriage something you think is important or do you think it is less important now?
> Gracie: Um, I don't know, you see, I don't think I could actually see myself getting married, but at the end of the day, I'd also want that traditional idea of it, because of…I always…because my Mum and Dad are married and they were married the whole time, so I, I've always grown up with that, so I also think it wouldn't be right not to be…so, it's a really weird idea, I don't see myself getting married, but I also couldn't have a family without being so, because I think I'd have to be stable, and secure before I did.

This ideal was positioned slightly differently by the young men, many of whom suggested marriage was not necessarily important, but that it was something that might happen. However, all the young men were clear in their understanding that their long-term future would be within a committed relationship and if they were to have children this is the only time they'd consider it:

> Gavin: I'd have kids, I want kids, not yet though, far too young. I need to find someone first don't I!? Dunno about marriage. Never been keen on marriage, but I'll probably end up getting married because they [future partner] would wanna get married and you'd be like yeah alright…

Overall, across these two pieces of research there were consistencies in the future desires held by the young people: the majority of the respondents in both pieces of research hoped to achieve (i) a home of their own; (ii) a comfortable and stable financial situation and (iii) a stable heterosexual relationship as the basis in which to have children. The key difference for the two sets of respondents was in the mechanism through which they hoped to achieve these aims. For the young women, these would be achieved through success within education which would also lead to a satisfying, professional career.[34] For the young men, embarking on full-time employment as soon as possible was the most realistic way of achieving these hopes. The below section will examine how realistic these desires are for young people from working-class backgrounds in light of the policies of the previous government and the present one.

Conclusion

The story which emerged from the words of the respondents in both of these studies was contrary to the popular and political discourse of 'low aspirations' that continue to demarcate young working-class youth as lacking and feckless. Both the young men and young women in this study hoped to achieve 'respectability'[35] through full-time employment which they envisaged would lead to a home of their own and the means through which to have a stable family life and financial security. The young women wanted to achieve recognition through higher education and employment in traditionally middle-class spheres. For young working-class women who are rarely accorded status in our society, their desire to achieve recognition through the medium of educational success and professional employment is certainly understandable. The young men were sceptical of the value of HE in achieving full-time work, and drew on the experiences of friends and family to construct their view of the best route into full-time work, in ways which would allow them to maintain friendships and family connections. Both sets of respondents spoke of their desire to improve existing family circumstances and to achieve financial security for their future family. Thus, the investments that were made by these young people were far from the individualised notion of 'aspiration' espoused by the current coalition government and New Labour. This aspect to their narratives served to highlight a failure in public and political rhetoric about education as an 'individualised' activity which continues to cast a veil over both the histories of social actors and the way in which decisions are made with respect to existing (and future) 'significant others'.

It is our view that the 'aspirations' discourse, with its value-laden poles of 'low aspirations' and 'high/appropriate aspirations' is far from helpful in enabling an understanding of the way in which young people imagine their futures and make choices. Not only does this discourse suggest that employees who do not precede their entrance to the labour market with a HE degree have less social value than those who do, but central to it is the unrealistic expectation that 'professional' employment is in high supply and open to everyone who 'aspires' to it. This obviously contributes to questions about the value which we attribute to different forms of work and the way in which different forms of work are remunerated. Furthermore, the limits to such forms of discourse and their attendant policies are inescapable, 'since social mobility can only be enjoyed by a minority and in competition with everyone else'.[36]

Rather than 'aspirations' we prefer to consider young people's imagined futures. Yet, as described above, the relatively modest outcomes which these two groups of young people hoped to achieve are made increasingly more difficult, if not unlikely, by the policies of the present government. In closing, we feel it important to re-emphasise the context in which these young people aim to realise these hopes and plans. The young people described here are within the age group most at risk of unemployment in the UK – those aged between 16 and 24. At the time of writing, there are more than one million young people between the ages of 16–24 looking for work in the UK – the highest rate for this age group since the early 1990s. The rate of graduate unemployment has never been higher and women are disproportionately represented amongst those who are currently unemployed. At times of high unemployment, the cultural and social capitals which accompany a middle-class background are at their most valuable. This has recently been subject to public scrutiny, as unpaid graduate internships in both public and private organisations have been demonstrated to be most accessible to those who have the social connections to gain access to them and the financial support to be able to work without a wage.[37]

These internships are often a valuable way of gaining initial access to an institution and achieving experience in a professional sphere. For the working class however, the government has its 'work experience programme' which has come under recent criticism for effectively pushing young unemployed people into unpaid short-term positions (largely in unskilled work) for large corporations. For those young people in paid employment in the low-pay low-skills sectors of the economy, progression routes to supervisory and junior management positions have become progressively few and far between as graduate intake into jobs re-labelled as 'graduate-level' roles have increased. Even making the move from part-time to full-time employment proves difficult for many young people as they compete for hours with students whose desires for part-time work often fit better with employer preferences for shorter, more flexible contracts over full-time, permanent ones.[38] This influx of over-qualified workers in low-skilled jobs has therefore blunted wage growth at the bottom of the earnings distribution, despite the growth in demand for workers in these jobs.[39]

In December 2010, the coalition government voted to implement an amended version of a recommendation made by Lord Browne in his report on the future funding of higher education.[40] The government voted to raise the basic threshold for degrees to £6,000 per annum with a cap at £9,000 to be implemented from this academic year (2012/2013). The majority of institutions have opted to charge fees at the highest rate following additional cuts to Higher Education by central government, and also citing the negative connotations of charging a lower rate when 'competitors' are charging the higher rate. Thus, the HE system in England and Wales has become increasingly marketised. For young people from working-class backgrounds (as well as many of those from lower-middle and middle-class backgrounds) the prospect of borrowing in the region of £18,000–£28,000 (fees only) for a first degree is an unfathomable financial risk.[41]

Accompanying this is the declining return on degrees. The present government and the last government have been keen to repeat that graduates earn £100K more over their lifetime than non-graduates. Yet, given graduates can expect to have a working-life of 40 to 50 years, this often cited benefit could amount to around £2,000 above the average wage per year. This is hardly a considerable sum. In addition to this is the fact that the policy of 'widening participation' has had the effect of increasing differentiation across the HE sector. With degrees from the most prestigious institution holding more currency than those from less well established institutions.[42] It is no surprise that prestigious institutions such as Oxford and Cambridge continue to be overwhelmingly populated by already privileged, middle-class students.[43]

Finally, let us consider the current prospects for having a home of one's own. In terms of becoming owner occupiers, the young people described here, and millions of others like them, face an uphill struggle. Recent estimates suggest it will take *31 years* for someone on a low to middle income to save up a *deposit* to buy an averagely priced property.[44] Of course, in describing a desire for a home of one's own, young people are not exclusively talking about owning their home. A home of one's own can also be linked to residential independence achieved in the private renting sector or in social housing. Here, too, there are substantial obstacles for young working-class people to overcome. In terms of the private sector, recent evidence shows that while some people navigate this market fairly successfully, such people tend to have had a background in higher education or are very likely to be in the median to higher earning bracket. Meanwhile, those on the lowest incomes, as well as those who are vulnerable or with unmet support needs, are often in no position to exercise any real choice in the market, which leaves them open to exploitation and to living in the worst conditions.[45] Depending on their circumstances, young people have little chance of making the imagined futures a reality in the social housing sector – as of 2010 there were more the 1.7 million households awaiting appropriate social housing,[46] while 7.4 million homes in England fail to meet the government's Decent Homes Standard.[47] Even with suitable availability of such provision, this does not even start to account for the stresses or concerns of having to cope with the stigma of being someone who lives in council dwelling or other social housing.[48]

Ultimately, newly implemented economic measures ensure that the achievement of suitably 'middle-class' aspirations – let alone modest, 'ordinary' ones, such as full-time employment and a house of one's own – remain increasingly out of reach. It is the responsibility of social researchers to do more than simply demonstrate this to government. We need to think of ways to support and empower members of the public in their dialogue with MPs and policymakers, and to consider our own position as both researchers and voting members of the public. The view that academics can remain objective and detached researchers is untenable given the harmful impact of the current government to those whose voices we seek to make heard.

Notes

1 E. Davidson (2011) *The Burdens of Aspiration: Schools, Youth, and Success in the Divided Social Worlds of Silicon Valley*. London: New York University Press, p. 194.
2 This is a concept which is simultaneously prescriptive and descriptive. For details see P. Bourdieu (2003) *Firing Back: Against the Tyranny of the Market 2*. London: Verso.
3 M. Raco (2009) 'From Expectations to Aspirations: State Modernisation, Urban Policy, and the Existential Politics of Welfare in the UK', *Political Geography*, 28: 436–54.
4 See P. Bourdieu (1984) *Distinction*. London: Routledge.
5 P. Bourdieu (1977) *Outline of a Theory of Practice*. Cambridge: Cambridge University Press.
6 Ibid., p. 169.
7 G. Brown (2011) 'Emotional Geographies of Young People's Aspirations for Adult Life', *Children's Geographies*, 9(1): 7–22.
8 Bourdieu (1977) *op. cit.*, p. 168.
9 See S. Hollingworth and K. Williams (2009) 'Constructions of the Working-Class "Other" Among Urban, White, Middle-Class Youth', *Journal of Youth Studies*, 12(5): 467–82.
10 N. Elias (1969) *The Civilizing Process, Vol. I: The History of Manners*. Oxford: Blackwell.
11 P. Bourdieu (1984) *op. cit.*

12 For all the young women, the head of household was a parent. However, a handful of the young men had ventured into independent living and were the head of their own household.

13 This is a heuristic term used to avoid the simplified and polarised vocabulary of 'good' and 'bad' qualifications. Here, the young men had a combination of a broad range of Level Two and Level Three qualifications (using the UK QCF).

14 See J. Quinn, L. Thomas, K. Slack, L. Casey, W. Thexton and J. Noble (2006) 'Lifting the Hood: Lifelong Learning and Young, White, Provincial Working-Class Masculinities', *British Educational Research Journal*, 32(5): 735–50.

15 See S. Ball, J. Davies, M. David and D. Reay (2002) '"Classification" and "Judgement": Social Class and the "Cognitive Structure" of Choice of Higher Education', *British Journal of Sociology of Education*, 23(1): 51–72, and Quinn et al, *op. cit.*

16 Comparable with similar findings among students attending HE prior to the Browne review. See Bradley and Ingram, this volume.

17 Brown (2011) *op. cit.*

18 For similar findings in Glasgow see K. Kintrea, R. St Clair and M. Houston (2011) *The Influence of Parents, Places, and Poverty on Educational Attitudes and Aspirations*. York: Joseph Rowntree Foundation.

19 DfES (2007) *Raising Expectations: Staying in Education and Training Post-16*. London: The Stationary Office, p. 3.

20 A. Wolf (2011) *Review of Vocational Education – The Wolf Report*. London: Department for Education.

21 Bourdieu (1977) *op. cit.*, p. 111; cf. W. Atkinson (2010) *Class, Individualization and Late Modernity*. Basingstoke: Palgrave, pp. 193–4.

22 S. Evans (2009) 'In a Different Place: Working-Class Girls and Higher Education', *Sociology*, 43(2): 340–55.

23 See e.g. D. Reay, G. Crozier and D. Clayton (2010) '"Fitting In" or "Standing Out": Working-Class Students in UK Higher Education', *British Educational Research Journal*, 32(1): 1–19; W. Moore (2008) *Reproducing Racisms*. New York: Rowman and Littlefield.

24 See e.g. B. Skeggs (1997) *Formations of Class and Gender*. London: Sage; H. S. Mirza (1992) *Young, Female and Black*. London: Routledge.

25 L. Archer and M. Hutchings (2000) '"Bettering Yourself": Discourses of Risk, Cost and Benefit in Ethnically Diverse, Young Working-Class Non-Participants' Constructions of Higher Education', *British Journal of Sociology of Education*, 21(4): 555–74.

26 See also Bradley and Ingram, this volume.

27 Evans (2009) *op. cit.*

28 D. Reay (2009) 'Making Sense of White Working-Class Educational Underachievement', in K. Sveinsson (ed.) *Who Cares about the White Working Class?* London: Runnymede Trust, pp. 22–8.

29 A. Nilsen (1999) 'Where is the Future? Time and Space as Categories in Analyses of Young People's Image of the Future', *Innovation*, 12(2): 175–94.

30 *The Guardian*, 9th December 2011.

31 *The Telegraph*, 15th December 2011.

32 Brown (2011) *op. cit.*, p. 18.

33 S. Henderson, J. Holland, S. McGrellis, S. Sharpe and R. Thomson (2007) *Inventing Adulthoods: A Biographical Approach to Youth Transitions.* London: Sage.
34 For the young women, this was a dream in its own right as well as a means to financial security.
35 Skeggs (1997) *op. cit.*
36 C. Crouch (2004) *Post-Democracy.* Cambridge: Polity Press. Cf. also Bourdieu's comments in *Distinction* (p. 144) about the cheating of a generation, who get 'less out of their qualifications than the previous generations would have obtained'.
37 See e.g. F. Furstenberg (2008) 'The Intersections of Social Class and the Transition to Adulthood', *New Directions for Child and Adolescent Development*, 119: 1–10; and S. Jenkins (2011) 'Social Immobility is Built into the Way Britain Lives and Learns', *The Guardian*, April 5th.
38 S. Roberts (2011) 'Beyond NEET and ("Tidy") Pathways: Considering the Missing Middle of Youth Transitions Studies', *Journal of Youth Studies*, 14(1): 21–39.
39 M. Goos and A. Manning (2007) 'Lousy and Lovely Jobs: The Rising Polarization of Work in Britain', *The Review of Economics and Statistics*, 89(1): 118–33.
40 Lord John Browne (2010) *Securing a Sustainable Future for Higher Education: An Independent Review of Higher Education Funding and Student Finance.* Available at http://www.bis.gov.uk/assets/biscore/corporate/docs/s/10-1208-securing-sustainable-higher-education-browne-report.pdf.
41 See also Bradley and Ingram, this volume.
42 S. Power and G. Whitty (2008) *Paper 118: Graduating and Gradations within the Middle Class: The Legacy of an Elite Higher Education.* Cardiff School of Social Sciences.
43 A. Zimdars, A. Sullivan and A. Heath (2009) 'Elite Higher Education Admissions in the Arts and Sciences: Is Cultural Capital the Key?', *Sociology*, 43(4): 648–66.
44 V. Alakeson (2011) *Making a Rented House a Home: Housing Solutions for 'Generation Rent'.* London: Resolution Foundation.
45 J. Rugg (2010) *Young People and Housing: The Need for a New Policy Agenda.* York: JRF.
46 Communities and Local Government (2010) *Housing Strategy Statistical Appendix Data 2010*, available at http://www.communities.gov.uk/housing/housing-research/housingstatistics/housingstatisticsby/localauthorityhousing/dataforms/hssa0910/hssadata200910/.
47 Communities and Local Government (2009) *English House Condition Survey 2007 Headline Report.* London: CLG.
48 B. Rogaly and B. Taylor (2009) *Moving Histories of Class and Community: Identity, Place and Belonging in Contemporary England.* Basingstoke: Palgrave Macmillan.

6

Personalising Poverty: Parental Determinism and the Big Society Agenda

Val Gillies

Recent years have been characterised by government attempts to requisition family as a mechanism for tackling social ills. Everyday parenting practice has been pushed to the centre stage of the social policy curriculum, marking a transgression into an area previously considered private and immune from state intervention in all but the most extreme of cases. Poverty, disadvantage and many of the problems associated with it have become routinely attributed to 'suboptimal' parenting practices and a failure of the working classes to equip their children with appropriate personal resources and social skills. Articulated through a discourse of family competence, this evaluative focus on parenting practices has seen class differences and inequalities increasingly framed as developmental outcomes. In the process, childrearing has been reformulated as a skilled job, with the successes and privileges enjoyed by middle-class offspring credited to the proficiency of their parents.

The election of the Conservative-led coalition government in 2010 has been characterised by an acceleration of this trend towards parental determinism. The flagship Big Society agenda, defining the direction and aims of the new administration, has seen particular emphasis placed on family responsibility, further entrenching and naturalising class distinctions. The Big Society idea dictates that the well-off are to be set free from state interference and encouraged to mobilise all their resources to secure the best outcomes for their children. Meanwhile, the poor are to be incentivised to accept greater responsibility for their children through the withdrawal of state support and subsidies. This chapter will outline the consequences of such thinking in terms of policy initiatives and their impacts. It seeks to deconstruct the Big Society agenda in relation to family policy, trace the long-standing themes it reproduces and consider the implications of directions currently being pursued. More specifically it demonstrates how this political ideology has tied itself to reductionist and heavily biologised understandings of child development to further promote and warrant neoliberal approaches.

Families, communities and the Big Society

The political appropriation of family has a very long history, but the extent to which it has shifted to the heart of government policy-making reflects more contemporary preoccupations, not least with balancing the primacy of individualism and free market choice with social responsibility. During the reign of the previous New Labour government, concern centred on the challenges of globalisation and the potentially corrosive influence of unfettered individualism in undermining the cooperation and reciprocity necessary to sustain families and communities. The notoriously vague concept of the 'third way' was developed in an effort to mediate individual rights and personal obligation through a contingent emphasis on both liberty and responsibility. Alongside claims about the inevitability of change and the democratisation of personal relationships, family remained the symbolic lynchpin of dutiful community, with good parents seen as fostering and transmitting crucial values to their children to protect and reproduce the common good. An active 'enabling state' was posed as necessary to ensure parents live up to their ethical obligations to their children and communities in the context of new threats and pressures.[1] As will be outlined, such arguments formed the basis for a new kind of interventionism characterised by explicit and implicit attempts to control and regulate the conduct of parents.

Despite occupying a distinctly different ideological grounding, the Big Society initiative framing the Conservative-led coalition's policy agenda shares notable parallels with New Labour's 'third way' project. Alongside their common public reception as nebulous, slippery and lacking in credibility, both are predicated on the notion that families and communities have been weakened and damaged by social and economic change. But while New Labour sought to involve the state in strengthening parenting and civic participation, Big Society is sold on the basis that local communities and families are best placed to understand their needs and reclaim their social responsibility. The state is portrayed as encouraging dependency, stifling citizen engagement and eroding agency and responsibility. The solution is presented as a radical shift in power from central government to neighbourhoods, which, bolstered by an austerity drive and accompanying harsh deficit reduction plans, has resulted in an unprecedented assault on public spending.

Beyond political discourse, the implications and consequences of Big Society philosophy are highly class specific, particularly in relation to family policy. While initiatives are characterised by a narrative of deliverance articulated through the notion that families and communities must be facilitated to solve their own problems, the nature of this promised liberation is determined by the resources and capacities of those concerned. Pierre Bourdieu's concept of 'symbolic violence' best encapsulates this imposition of systems of meaning that overwrite and obscure lived experiences of inequality, for such rhetorical frameworks and significations work to buffer and reinforce relations of oppression and exploitation by 'hiding them under the cloak of nature, benevolence and meritocracy'.[2] In the context of Big Society narratives the well-off are enabled to use all their means in pursuing the best interests of their children, while the poor are to be responsibilised through the removal of services and practical and economic support. High profile 'emancipatory' policies have included giving parents the right to start up and run their own 'Free Schools' and enabling communities to take over responsibility for local amenities such as parks and libraries. Such initiatives are presented as opportunities for those who care enough about their children's wellbeing to become more agentic. As Anna Coote notes, this approach ignores prevailing barriers created by money and privilege and encourages the wealthy to flourish at the expense of others.[3] Those unable or unwilling to participate and govern themselves are positioned as corrosively dependant on the state and in need of community-led help to become more active and self-reliant citizens. This has been pursued through a drastic programme of cuts, a renegotiation of welfare systems and a hiving off of remaining interventions and services to private and third sector organisations.

Inevitably, such policies map on to and reinforce existing social divisions and inequalities. The ability to set up and run a 'Free School' requires considerable middle-class capital in the form of time (and associated financial conditions), social connections, confidence and a strong sense of entitlement. Unsurprisingly the vast majority of Free Schools have to date been founded in the most affluent parts of the country.[4] For resource-rich middle-class parents dissatisfied with schools within a catchment area this system offers an opportunity to found their own elite institutions, draining surrounding schools of high attaining pupils and compounding deep divisions in educational attainment. In many ways this approach represents the continuation and logical conclusion of a long-standing emphasis on parental choice and consumerism in state education. Stephen Brown coined the term 'parentocracy' to describe a policy shift away from children's abilities and potential and towards a concern with the 'wealth and wishes of parents'.[5] Introduced by a Conservative government in the 1980s, parental choice in education was promoted as mechanism for better meeting needs and driving up standards, with little consideration given to the deeply uneven territory from which such 'choices' are made.[6] This consumerist framework expanded under the auspices of New Labour, extending deep into the arena of childrearing itself, with model parents expected to choose, access and continuously evaluate services such as those providing childcare and parenting advice.[7]

The rise of 'parentocracy' as an ideology has also promoted a distinct moral agenda generating a new orthodoxy around parental involvement in children's education as a general measure of family competence. Responsible parents seek out and use information and advice to make the right choices for their children, engaging with and prioritising educational development as a route to future success and fulfilment. Those who make ill-informed choices or who demonstrate insufficient commitment or aspiration (most often the poor and disadvantaged) are problematised and positioned outside of the Big Society. Policy measures in this context are focused on building the apparatus through which individuals, families and communities are forced to accept responsibility for themselves and others. Poverty and other social problems are directly attributed to family failings and are portrayed as a wider social malaise typifying sections of what Conservatives have termed 'Broken Britain'. From the perspective of the coalition government disadvantaged families and communities must be repaired as part of the Big Society initiative, but at a grassroots level to avoid the corruptive influence of the state. Charities, local enterprise, the corporate sector and voluntary organisations are accorded a key role in reforming and regulating the family practices of those deemed to be letting their children and their communities down. Such interventions are envisaged as preventative as well as restorative, designed to avert the reproduction of dysfunction and ineptitude.

The cycle of deprivation cycle

At the core of the Big Society pledge to repair and responsiblise families and communities is an enduring narrative which seeks to portray the poor as authors of their own misfortunes. As many have pointed out, the notion that poverty is culturally transmitted through the generations extends right back through time, reflecting deeply held convictions among the wealthy that deprivation is distinct, self-perpetuating and disconnected from mainstream society.[8] Of persistent concern has been the stability of working-class families and their capacity to adequately care for each other in the context of social change and upheaval.

Nikolas Rose has described how a 'moral topography of urban space' emerged in the nineteenth century depicting a dangerous preponderance of criminally-minded children and triggering a new psychologised focus on family relationships and parenting practices.[9] By the twentieth century, explanatory frameworks prioritising evolutionary biology had come to prominence with the rise of the eugenics movement. Parental inefficiency was commonly viewed as a symptom of mental degeneracy passed on through the generations, implicating genetic and environmental factors in the perpetuation of social ills.[10] Despite a post-war retreat from hard-core biological determinism, research, policy and practice literature at the time retained a distinct eugenic flavour describing the pathologies spawned by the poor.

By the 1960s and 70s a new social determinism was gaining in popularity, promulgated through the notion of a 'subculture of poverty'.[11] The poorest in society were regarded as sharing and reproducing lifestyles and values that positioned them at the fringes of society. The conviction that poverty could be separated from household income and understood in terms of a cultural mindset gained particular traction with the Conservative government in the early 1970s. The then Secretary of State, Keith Joseph, drew attention to the way patterns of impoverishment were enduring despite rising living standards and hypothesised that children were inheriting values and lifestyles which locked them into permanent disadvantage. While Joseph's 'cycle of deprivation' theory garnered substantial interest and influence, the concept eventually fell from favour after research, commissioned to prove the theory, instead highlighted the significance of multiple structural factors as opposed to culture or attitude.[12]

As Alan Walker noted, virtually every decade of the twentieth century was marked by a resolute effort to distinguish blameless from self-inflicted poverty.[13] By the 1980s the underclass thesis had gained ground, with theorists such as Charles Murray proposing the existence of a distinct and growing social group set apart from society by their cultural pathology and resulting poverty.[14] Once again root causes were attributed to family, with lone mothers in particular accused of breeding a 'new rabble' of crime-prone sons and promiscuous daughters dependent on welfare handouts. In time, the concept of a distinct underclass was discredited by a wealth of sociological research evidence[15] and the accompanying harsh rhetoric broadly came to be viewed as an unjust attempt to blame the poor for their plight. But while language and political theorising moved on, the core theme of responsibilisation remained a political touchstone.

New Labour, new cycle

Attempts to directly control and regulate the moral behaviour of family members sit uneasily alongside the individualistic ethos underpinning Western culture, not to mention the libertarian instincts of many positioned on the political right.[16] However, the advent of the New Labour government in 1997 was marked by a remarkably aggressive attempt to reposition family life as a public rather than a private concern. This was pursued through a new emphasis on 'post-industrialisation' as a primary focus for concern, with social and economic changes regarded as encouraging individualised lifestyles and mindsets. A new age of modernity was hailed as having replaced the old predictabilities and certainties of industrial society, bringing with it new risks and opportunities. Freedom from the roles and constraints associated with traditional social ties were regarded as enabling new forms of personal development and prosperity, but at the expense of conventional family support systems and cohesive norms. Yet, family was also hailed as the formative site through which 'competent personhood' is cultivated, with well-parented children better able to navigate and capitalise on new post-industrial economic landscapes.[17]

This perceived dilemma subjected family to a whole new level of political scrutiny, resulting in a more intensive and systematic policy of intervention than has ever be seen before.[18] Significantly, this was implemented and justified through a discourse of social justice founded on the claim that children who are parented well will have a better chance of upward social mobility, combined with long-standing assertions that crime and delinquency are rooted in family practices.[19] Policy reforms sought to enforce a normative consensus on 'parenting good practice' across the population as a whole, but political attention predominantly centred on a section of society described by New Labour as the 'deeply excluded'. After a near 30-year lull the specific term 'cycle of deprivation' was resurrected, notably without reference to its previous incarnation and with scarce extra in the way of an evidence base.[20]

New Labour, though, were particularly successful in blurring and reframing the concept of transmitted deprivation as a progressive, liberal concern with tackling inequality and supporting the poor. This was partly achieved through coupling parenting interventions with practical measures to address family hardship and alleviate child poverty. For example, New Labour's flagship nationwide family support initiative, 'Sure Start', provided subsidised childcare, toy libraries, cafes and drop in groups alongside more didactic attempts to regulate parenting practice through classes and explicit advice. Children's wellbeing featured heavily as a moral impetus for family intervention, alongside a much greater appropriation of 'science' in the pursuit of what John Welshman has termed 'policy-based evidence'.[21] Close examination of the claimed 'evidence base' reveals little new in the way of plausible research verification, aside from the uncontested finding that children from disadvantaged families are more likely to experience negative outcomes in the future. Nevertheless, during their time in office, successive New Labour governments presided over a political step-change in the way family and parenting is envisaged and targeted, reshaping public understandings and expectations in the process.

While previous state involvement had been limited to broad-brush policies, and intervention in extreme cases, family policy under New Labour was characterised by the emergence of a whole new workforce charged with monitoring and regulating parenting.[22] For the poorest and most disadvantaged families interventions became increasingly coercive and authoritarian, instigated through ever greater use of compulsion, fines and imprisonment. Political rhetoric, sharing many similarities to 1980s underclass discourse, translated into specific policy interventions. For example, Parenting Orders designed to force parents (usually mothers) to attend classes and adhere to particular childrearing rules were developed and expanded through a range of legislative acts, while record numbers of parents were prosecuted and jailed for failing to prevent their children from truanting.[23]

By the end of New Labour's reign the political and cultural landscape had been transformed, particularly in relation to understandings of family and inequality. Constructions of 'good parenting' were asserted and promoted as central in sustaining a meritocratic society. As a result, political understandings of family have largely shifted away from previous concerns with their composition to embrace a new orthodoxy of 'competence'.[24] More specifically, governments have come to see families more in terms of their practices than structures, with 'what families do' readily translating into a concern with family proficiency. A key feature of this change has been a re-evaluation of childrearing as a job requiring particular know-how and expertise. Once interpreted as an ascribed family relation (like spouse, grandparent or sibling) the word 'parent' is now more commonly viewed a verb. Mothers and fathers 'parent' children and this task is loaded with moral and practical consequence. Contemporary interpretations tightly tie the wellbeing of society (and that of individual children) to the exact family practices and parenting techniques pursued. From this perspective the success and privilege of the middle classes are attributable to competent upbringing and personal strength, while the struggling working class can be defined as victims of parental incompetence. This reasoning has proved politically potent, inspiring a broad cross-party consensus and shaping the new coalition government's agenda.

From child poverty to poverty of parenting

The change of government in 2010 to the Conservative-led coalition has been marked by strong continuities as well as significant differences in relation to the foregrounding of parenting as a policy solution. Rhetoric positioning family as the primary driver of inequality has remained strong, but policy solutions have been modified to fit the broader Big Society commitment of shrinking the state and enforcing personal responsibility. Under New Labour, the conviction that family relationships were at the core of persistent social problems and could be harnessed to promote a more meritocratic society underpinned a huge expansion of state and third sector services aiming to support parenting. In contrast, the coalition's rise to power was driven by a very different austerity agenda in the context of a global financial crisis. Plans to slash welfare and state spending were announced in the new government's first budget as part of a fiscal tightening package. Much of the previous government's investments were dismissed as wasteful, ineffective and symptomatic of a 'nanny state' ideology degrading personal responsibility.

This divergence is particularly evident in relation to the issue of child poverty. For New Labour, reducing the number of children living in poverty was a core objective associated with tackling perceived cycles of deprivation. This was enacted through direct cash support (tax credit schemes, improvements to social assistance payments to children, Educational Maintenance Allowances for post-16s remaining at school and a universal child trust fund) as well as an expansion of services designed to 'support' and regulate parenting. The dying days of the last government also saw the introduction of the Child Poverty

Act with specific targets for reducing the numbers of children living in low-income families. Less than a year after coming to power, the coalition government released the strategy document *A New Approach to Child Poverty: Tackling the Causes of Disadvantage and Transforming Families' Lives*, signalling a discrete shift in direction. Emphasis in this document is firmly placed on the need to look beyond the issue of household income in order to generate a more 'sustainable' solution.

> This Government is committed to eradicating child poverty but recognises that income measures and targets do not tell the full story about the causes and consequences of childhood disadvantage. The previous Government's focus on narrow income targets meant they poured resources into short-term fixes to the symptoms of poverty instead of focusing on the causes. We plan to tackle head-on the causes of poverty which underpin low achievement, aspiration and opportunity across generations. Our radical programme of reform to deliver social justice will focus on combating worklessness and educational failure and preventing family and relationship breakdown with the aim of supporting the most disadvantaged groups struggling at the bottom of society.[25]

Much of the impetus and justification for this 'new approach to child poverty' was derived from two independent reviews commissioned by the Prime Minister, David Cameron, shortly after he came to power in 2010. The first was conducted by Labour MP Frank Field and examined poverty and life chances, while the second was produced by the Labour MP Graham Allen and centred on the role of early intervention in preventing cycles of deprivation. Both reports present a similar case, tightly tying children's future outcomes to the efforts and proficiency of their parents while downplaying the relevance of structural disadvantage and income poverty. Significantly, the reports also pave the way for new policy narratives around family and child development, taking concepts of parental determinism to ever more reductive extremes.

Frank Field's report on poverty echoes the assertions made by the previous government about a perceived transmission of deprivation through the generations, but offers a distinctly different analysis of root causes. As Beverly Skeggs noted, New Labour policy discourse was saturated with representations of the working classes as old-fashioned, backward and an atavistic block to progress.[26] Social ills were explained in terms of the personal inability of the working classes to adapt to contemporary society and seize available opportunities ensuring policy interventions were oriented towards nurturing competent selves at the level of the family. Frank Field offers a contrasting explanation that sits more comfortably with conservative sensibilities, outlining a more familiar account of progressive decline in parental responsibility and personal values. Claiming that 'Britain is witnessing a rupturing in its once strong parenting tradition',[27] he cites a weakening of 'tough love' style discipline as a result of greater questioning of hierarchies. Also implicated are post-war housing policies, deindustrialisation, as well as a reduction in male employment, a linked rise in lone motherhood and a lack of will among governments to enforce the financial responsibilities of fathers. This account rehearses many contentions of the 1980s underclass debate, but crucially the main direction of expressed concern is shifted away from crime and the burden on the public purse and instead centres on the emotionally-potent vision of children as perceived victims of neglect:

I no longer believe that the poverty endured by all too many children can simply be measured by their lack of income. Something more fundamental than the scarcity of money is adversely dominating the lives of these children. Since 1969 I have witnessed a growing indifference from some parents to meeting the most basic needs of children, and particularly younger children, those who are least able to fend for themselves. I have also observed how the home life of a minority but, worryingly, a growing minority of children, fails to express an unconditional commitment to the successful nurturing of children.[28]

Field's report resonates with abiding preoccupations of those on the political right, particularly in its invocation of a 'golden age' of parenting and family in the 1950s and 60s. Yet, such claims have no basis in evidence and fail to engage with the dramatic change in understandings of children's capacities and welfare needs over the last 50 years. Historical comparative analysis highlights how childrearing practices that were taken for granted in the 1960s would be viewed by today's standards in terms of serious neglect and abuse. For example, young children were commonly left home alone, babies and toddlers were often cared for by very young siblings and serious accidents were more common because children were left to roam free without adult supervision.[29] Moreover, many of the 'basic needs' outlined in Field's report and other recent family policy and practice documents would simply not have been recognised in times gone by. In particular, expectations that parents should cultivate cognitive and emotional skills and actively involve themselves in their children's education reflect uniquely contemporary preoccupations.

Nevertheless, Field's report was welcomed as contributing to a more general Conservative-led exposition on the progressive social and moray decay embodying 'Broken Britain'. On a practical level, the government adopted the report's key recommendation to broaden understandings of poverty and develop new indicators to assess progress in improving children's future life chances (including measures of child development). In addition, the Child Poverty Commission, set up as a requirement of the Child Poverty Act, was amended to the 'Social Mobility and Child Poverty Commission' to emphasise this focus on the 'causes and not just the symptoms of poverty'.[30] The implications of this new approach are conveyed more explicitly in recent political rhetoric. In a speech in 2010 on social mobility, the Deputy Prime Minister, Nick Clegg, has unequivocally stated that 'parenting not poverty shapes a child's destiny' declaring 'we must not remain silent on what is an enormously important issue. Parents hold the fortunes of the children they bring into this world in their hands. All parents have a responsibility to nurture the potential in their children'.[31] Similarly, in making reference to a dubious and under-detailed research claim by the think-tank Demos, the Prime Minister, David Cameron, concluded:

> Differences in child outcomes between a child born in poverty and a child born in wealth are no longer statistically significant when both have been raised by 'confident and able' parents. For those who care about fairness and inequality, this is one of the most important findings in a generation. It would be over the top to say that it is to social science what $E=MC^2$ was to physics, but I think it is a real 'sit up and think' moment. That discovery defined the laws of relativity; this one is the new law for social mobility: What matters most to a child's life chances is not the wealth of their upbringing but the warmth of their parenting.[32]

Early intervention and the rise of 'parenting science'

As the above quote demonstrates, the citing of an 'evidence base' to support claims about the role of parenting in determining life chances has been a prominent characteristic of the turn towards family as a policy panacea. Previous New Labour governments were keen to apply a veneer of science in reclaiming the cycle of deprivation theory, drawing on copious studies to prove that those from poorer families do less well in life and then attributing this to parenting practice. In an effort to gather more robust evidence, research was also commissioned to establish links between parenting interventions and improved child outcomes, pursued through numerous evaluation projects and longitudinal cohort studies. This research itself has been the subject of sustained criticism for flawed methodology and misrepresentation of the evidence. For example, Michael Rutter[33] has cited poor design and weak validity in his assessment of the Sure Start evaluation, while David Gregg[34] has drawn out the selective sampling behind the 'ambiguous and misleading' claims made about the efficacy of Family Intervention Projects. Despite these serious methodological shortcomings and very mixed results on their own terms[35] such studies have been selectively drawn on to enforce a political shibboleth around the power of parenting to overcome disadvantage.

The concept of parenting science appears to have assumed even greater importance in shaping the policy agendas and funding structures of the coalition government. Greater targeting of public funds and better value for money have been pledged through a more intensive focus on the 'neediest families' and a move towards determining and demonstrating social returns on investments.[36] Policy documents promise a 'ruthlessly evidence-based approach, channelling effort and finance in the ways most likely to impact positively on social mobility'.[37] In practice this has involved substantial cuts in services. Most notoriously, the Sure Start initiative has lost any protected funding, with individual services dependent on the budget-making decisions of financially challenged local councils. The government has also introduced a trial 'payment by results' system in selected Children's Centres in an attempt to concentrate and maximise the impact of parenting interventions. This move reflects a broader interest in the potential of 'social impact bonds' to secure upfront investment from non-government sources such as businesses, charitable foundations and private benefactors on the basis of future returns tied to service outcomes and public savings.[38]

Graham Allen's independent review into the role of early childhood intervention has played a formative role in promoting this narrow results-focused evaluation of family services.[39] In a series of two reports Allen details near miraculous social and economic benefits that he claims are achievable through targeting the families of socially disadvantaged children under five. A discourse of science features heavily in this account, with Allen positing simple cause and effect mechanisms and drawing on an eclectic mix of theories and concepts in the process. Behind the report's emphatic conclusions lie contentions and assertions that bear very little scientific scrutiny.[40] Attachment theory, neurodevelopment, neurochemistry and cognitive science are welded together to present an apparently watertight case for what Ellie Lee has described as a new 'phrenology of parenting'.[41]

To the fore of Allen's account is a claim that children develop faulty 'brain architecture' if they receive suboptimal nurturing. This point is conveyed graphically, with the front cover of both his reports featuring brain scan images of three-year-old children. An image branded 'normal' is placed next to a smaller, atrophied brain that has been labelled 'extreme neglect'. The origins of this illustration are testament to the unreliable and overdetermined content that lies within. The images are taken from an article in the journal *Brain and Mind* which considers the impact of the severe physical neglect and sensory deprivation experienced by Romanian orphans after the fall of the Communist government in the late 80s. Allen does not explain where the continuity might lie between infants experiencing malnourishment, disease and minimal human contact and mothers failing to properly 'attune' to children's emotional needs.[42] Instead he details how variations in childrearing proficiency explain away differences in outcomes and, ultimately, social class:

> Success or failure in early childhood also has profound economic consequences. Socially and emotionally capable people are more productive, better educated, tax-paying citizens helping our nation to compete in the global economy, and make fewer demands on public expenditure. Socially and emotionally incapable people are far less likely to be productive taxpayers and far more likely to be a cost to public funds in benefits, health care, social work and policing and criminal justice.[43]

Allen's biologised, pseudoscientific treatise bares a notable resemblance to the eugenic-inspired caricatures informing the thinking and practices of pre- and post-war welfare and public health workers. While brain development has replaced the concept of genetic weakness, the alleged consequences of a lack of timely intervention are almost as immutable. The 'prime window' for development is estimated at 18 months (plus the prenatal period), beyond which deficits are portrayed as increasingly harder to overcome:

> One of the key concepts used when we are looking at the problems of dysfunction is through that cold business phrase – stock and flow.

Remedial or late intervention policies address the stock of people already suffering from deep-rooted problems. Early Intervention seeks to block, reduce or filter the flow of new people (babies, children and young people) entering the stock.[44]

Such overblown, unfounded and highly contentious claims form the evidence base that springboards into Allen's second report, *Early Interventions: Smart Investments, Massive Savings*, detailing how greater intervention can be implemented at a time of straitened public investment primarily through attracting funding from the private, voluntary and community sectors. Chiming with the Big Society agenda, localism is presented as the natural enabler and commissioner of early intervention, coordinating and delivering on outcomes-based contracts to stem the costly 'tsunami of dysfunction' associated with inaction.[45]

Shortly after the publication of Allen's second report the coalition set out to raise £40m from private investors in the form of social impact bonds, specifically to fund family intervention projects. Against the broader context of cuts to children's services this attempt to secure alternative, 'innovative' sources of finance marks a noticeable shift away from New Labour rhetoric about social justice and inclusion towards a more instrumental cost benefit analysis. Policy discussions have centred on how to incentivise and reward organisations prepared to invest in curing troublesome families by introducing a market in social investment. Providers able to construct an appealing 'evidence base' for investors are to be awarded contracts, while investors are promised future dividends. Meanwhile, practical and financial support relied on by poor families is further eroded in line with narratives around austerity, personal responsibility and the mantra of 'big society, small state'.

Contradictions and implications

Despite attempts to promote the Big Society as a core political vision, the family policy it has spawned is strikingly incoherent and self-contradictory, particularly in relation to the most disadvantaged in society. The large-scale withdrawal of state support ill fits the government's broader contention that significant parts of Britain are broken, dysfunctional and in need of urgent repair. Calls for the charitable and voluntary sector (itself largely dependant on ever-decreasing government grants) to fill the gaps in provision are widely regarded as unrealistic, exposing the gulf between ideological aspirations and real-world challenges.[46] Even more questionable is the attempt to create a private market in early intervention in the form of investment bonds. As the *Guardian* columnist Polly Tonybee pointed out, the government would have to offer virtually guaranteed returns to make such financial products attractive in the first place.[47] This, combined with costly involvement from City financiers, accounts, lawyers and project evaluators in drawing up marketable bonds, would result in considerably greater public expense compared to direct state investment.

Such issues have come increasingly to the fore in the context of a worsening financial climate and after rioting and looting spread across English towns and cities in the summer of 2011. Commentators and politicians widely blamed the disorder on a crisis in parenting skills, with this theme forming a centrepiece of the government's 'social fightback' initiative. Urgent action was promised to tackle the families that 'everyone in their neighbourhood knows and often avoids', through a specific promise to 'turn around the lives of the 120,000 most troubled families in the country'.[48] Returning to this theme later in 2011 the Prime Minister stressed his passionate mission to 'fix the responsibility deficit' and address 'a culture of disruption and irresponsibility that cascades through generations....Our heart tells us we can't just stand by while people live these lives and cause others so much misery. Our head tells us we can't afford to keep footing the monumental bills for social failure'.[49]

As Jonathon Portes has established, the estimated figure of 120,000 troubled families has been calculated on the basis that at least five out of a possible seven criteria are met.[50] These are: a) no parent in work, b) poor quality housing, c) no parent with qualifications, d) mother with mental health problems, e) one parent with long-standing disability/illness, f) family has low income, g) the family cannot afford some food/clothing items.[51] As Portes highlights, this amounts to a shockingly direct and unmediated equation of disadvantage with criminality. As has also been noted, any serious attempt to address such issues would require a massive reversal of cuts to family support services and an estimated government spend of £1.5bn.[52] Instead the government have ordered cash-strapped local councils to establish and partially fund networks of 'trouble-shooters' to tackle the problems facing such families, further redirecting scarce funds away from universal services and resources.

At a more fundamental level there is a marked tendency to focus on either end of the social spectrum, side-lining wider issues of discrimination and injustice. Paragons of Big Society create and consume opportunities for their children, while troubled and troublesome pariahs merely reproduce their poverty. Inequalities structuring the lives of those in between are normalised, with both the privileges of the rich and the struggles of the poor rationalised through reference to an inclusive, meritocratic society. The differential impact on families of withdrawing state services and resources for children and parents is largely obscured through the public and political reframing of childrearing as a classless and gender-neutral activity able to transcend socio-economic realities. A reverse logic that holds class-specific parenting practices to account for the inequality they reflect ensures little effort is made to engage with the diverse resources and constraints contextualising family and parenting practices.[53]

The gendered implications of this approach cut across and compound the class inequality they perpetuate with mothers disproportionately bearing both blame and the brunt of cuts to support services. New Labour were careful to construct their family policy around inclusive references to parenting, concealing the extent to which initiatives were targeted towards poor and disadvantaged mothers. However, coalition policy is more explicit in directing early intervention at mothers, depicting them as the core mediators of children's development. Old and highly contentious tenets of attachment theory are reinvoked to emphasise the primacy of mother-child relationships in the early years. For example, the following quote from Allan Schore is drawn on in the Allen Review to highlight the importance of maternal 'attunement':

> The child's first relationship, the one with the mother, acts as a template that permanently moulds the individual's capacity to enter into all later emotional relationships.[54]

Gendered connotations are particularly evident in a current policy focus on pre- and post-natal care provision in poor communities. Following the recommendations of the Allen Review the government have pledged to increase the numbers of Health Visitors and to expand their role to include targeted parenting education for disadvantaged pregnant women and new mothers. This strategy is also viewed as an opportunistic method of inculcating particular values and practices: 'Health visitors are there when a new mum needs a bit of help and she's open to that support when she may not be at other times in her life'.[55]

Concerns about fathers have tended to centre on more traditional themes of financial maintenance and discipline, articulated through references to feckless 'runaway dads' and the consequences of father absence for crime and disorder.[56] This was particularly evident in the aftermath of the English riots with David Cameron declaring in his 'fightback' speech:

> I don't doubt that many of the rioters out last week have no father at home. Perhaps they come from one of the neighbourhoods where it's standard for children to have a mum and not a dad, where it's normal for young men to grow up without a male role model, looking to the streets for their father figures, filled up with rage and anger.[57]

Meanwhile mothers are allocated primary responsibility for childrearing against a backdrop of increasing expectations and decreasing state support. The ideal model of parenting promoted at the level of policy and practice intervention demands intensive labour to ensure constant cognitive stimulation, monitoring of development and liaison with relevant professionals.

The central role the government currently accords mothering is further contextualised by rising female unemployment and soaring childcare costs. Women make up the largest proportion of the public sector workforce and as a consequence have been most vulnerable to cost cutting redundancies. At the same time, reduced childcare subsidies and changes to tax credit benefits are forcing working mothers on low incomes back into the home.[58] This impact appears to be regarded by the government as problematic only for lone mothers dependent on the welfare state with those on Income Support now compelled (on the threat of losing 40 per cent of their benefit) to demonstrate they are actively seeking work once their children turn five. Reflecting the re-traditionalisation instincts of those on the political right, the Big Society policy agenda fits neatly with an old-fashioned male breadwinner/female carer binary in which unpaid female labour plugs the holes as the state retreats.

In conclusion, parental determinism has come to infuse contemporary policy agendas as yet another manifestation of long-standing efforts to personalise and normalise experiences of inequality. Unlike previous attempts to explain away inequality through eugenic genealogies or subcultures of deprivation, a focus on the minutiae of parenting practice has lent itself to simple policy solutions marketed as 'evidence based'. Deserving poor families must demonstrate competence and commitment to save their children, while undeserving parents who fail to invest appropriately in their children must be compelled and coerced to change their practices in the name of social justice and social order. From this perspective, state support for parents is a measure of last resort, consisting of highly contingent interventions designed to re-shape the intimate family relationships of the very poorest in society. Financial and practical family support (subsidised childcare, tax credits, child trust funds etc.) can be removed on the basis that strength of will and parenting proficiency are all that is needed to sustain a fair society. While a Big Society narrative aims to paper over the many dis-crepancies and inconsistencies inherent in neoliberal approaches to family, there will be no hiding the severe hardship inflicted on the most vulnerable in society.

Notes

1 N. Rose (1999) *Powers of Freedom: Reframing Political Thought*. Cambridge: Cambridge University Press; V. Gillies (2005) 'Meeting Parents' Needs? Discourses of "Support" and "Inclusion"', *Critical Social Policy*, 25(1): 70–91.

2 L. Wacquant (1993) 'On the Tracks of Symbolic Power: Preparatory Notes to Bourdieu's State Nobility', *Theory, Culture and Society*, 10: 1–17.

3 A. Coote (2010) *Cutting It: Big Society and the New Austerity*. London: NEF.

4 CACI and *The Guardian* (2011) 'What Type of Children Go to Free Schools?', available at http://www.guardian.co.uk/news/datablog/2011/aug/31/education-free-school-admissions.

5 P. Brown (1990) 'The "Third Wave": Education and the Ideology of Parento-cracy', *British Journal of Sociology of Education*, 11(1): 65–86.

6 S. Ball (2008) *The Education Debate*. Bristol: Policy Press.

7 R. Edwards and V. Gillies (2011) 'Clients or Consumers, Commonplace or Pioneers? Navigating the Contemporary Class Politics of Family, Parenting Skills and Education', *Ethics and Education*, 6(2): 141–54.

8 See B. Jordan (1974) *Poor Parents: Social Policy and the Cycle of Deprivation*. London: Routledge; P. Townsend (1979) *Poverty in the United Kingdom*. Harmonds-worth: Penguin; J. Welshman (2006) *Underclass: A History of the Excluded, 1880–2000*. London: Hambledon Continuum; A. Walker (1990) 'Blaming the Victims' in C. Murray (ed.) *The Emerging British Underclass*. London: Institute of Economic Affairs, pp. 66–75.

9 Rose (1999) *op. cit.*

10 Welshman (2006) *op. cit.*

11 Townsend (1979) *op. cit.*

12 L. Morris (1994) *Dangerous Classes. The Underclass and Social Citizenship*. London: Routledge.

13 Walker (1990) *op. cit.*

14 C. Murray (1994) *Underclass: The Crisis Deepens*. London: Institute of Economic Affairs.

15 R. Edwards and S. Duncan (1997) 'Supporting the Family: Lone Mothers, Paid Work and the Underclass Debate', *Critical Social Policy*, 17(4): 29–49;

K. Mann (1994) 'Watching the Defectives: Observers of the Underclass in the USA, Britain and Australia', *Critical Social Policy*, 41: 79–99.

16 J. Rodger (1995) 'Family Policy or Moral Regulation?', *Critical Social Policy*, 15: 5–25.

17 V. Gillies (2005) 'Raising the Meritocracy: Parenting and the Individualisation of Social Class', *Sociology*, 39(5): 835–52.

18 Ibid.; V. Gillies (2011) 'From Function to Competence: Engaging with the New Politics of Family', *Sociological Research Online*, 16(4): http://www.socresonline.org.uk/16/4/11.html.

19 V. Gillies (2008) 'Perspectives on Parenting Responsibility: Contextualising Values and Practices', *Law and Society*, 35(1): 95–112.

20 See Welshman (2006), *op. cit.*

21 Ibid.

22 S. Ramaekers and J. Suissa (2011) *The Claims of Parenting; Reasons, Responsibility and Society.* New York: Springer; V. Gillies (2007) *Marginalised Mothers: Exploring Working Class Experiences of Parenting.* Abingdon: Routledge; C. Lind and H. Keating (2008) *Children, Family Relationships and the State.* Oxford: Wiley Blackwell.

23 Figures released by the Ministry of Justice following a freedom of information request in 2011 see truancy laws caught 12,000 parents last year: *The Guardian*, Tuesday 8 November 2011, available at http://www.guardian.co.uk/education/2011/nov/08/truancy-parents-12000-prosecutions.

24 Gillies (2011) 'From Function to Competence', *op. cit.*

25 Department for Work and Pensions and Department of Education (2011) *A New Approach to Child Poverty: Tackling the Causes of Disadvantage.* London: HMSO, p. 8.

26 B. Skeggs (2004) *Class, Self, Culture.* London: Routledge.

27 F. Field (2010) *The Foundation Years: Preventing Poor Children Becoming Poor Adults.* London: HMSO, p. 20.

28 Ibid., p. 18.

29 See V. Gillies and R. Edwards (2011) *An Historical Comparative Analysis of Family and Parenting: A Feasibility Study Across Sources and Timeframes.* Families and Social Capital Research Group Working Paper No. 29, available at http://www.lsbu.ac.uk/ahs/research/familiespub.shtml.

30 Department for Work and Pensions and Department of Education, *op. cit.*, p. 11.

31 Nick Clegg, Speech on Social Mobility, 18 Aug 2010. Transcript available at www.libdems.org.uk/press_releases_detail.aspx?title=Nick_Clegg_delivers_speech_on_social_mobility&pPK=38cf9a88-0577-403e-9dcb-50b8e30-ed119.

32 David Cameron, Supporting Families Speech, available at http://www.conservatives.com/News/Speeches/2010/01/David_Cameron_Supporting_parents.aspx.

33 M. Rutter (2006) 'Is Sure Start an Effective Preventive Intervention?', *Child and Adolescent Mental Health*, 11(3): 135–41.

34 D. Gregg (2010) *Family Intervention Projects: A Classic Case of Policy-Based Evidence.* London: Centre for Crime and Justice Studies.

35 See also D. Hartas (2011) 'Inequality and the Home Learning Environment', *British Educational Research Journal*, iFirst article; M. Rutter (2007) 'Sure Start

Local Programmes: An Outsider's Perspective' in J. Belsky, J. Barnes and E. Melhuish (eds) *The National Evaluation of Sure Start: Does Area Based Early Intervention Work?* Bristol: Policy Press.

36 Department for Education and Department of Health (2011) 'Supporting Families in the Foundation Years', available at http://www.parliament.uk/deposits/depositedpapers/ 2011/DEP2011-1250.pdf.

37 Cabinet Office (2010) *The Coalition: Our Programme for Government*, available at http://webarchive.nationalarchives.gov.uk/20100526084809/http://programmeforgovernment.hmg.gov.uk.

38 Coote (2010) *op. cit.*

39 G. Allen (2011) *Early Intervention: The Next Step*. London: HMSO; G. Allen (2011) *Early Intervention: Smart Investment, Massive Savings*. London: HMSO.

40 See for example the keynote papers given at the conference Monitoring Parents: Science, Evidence, Experts and the New Parenting Culture, University of Kent 14th September 2011, including J. Bruer, 'The Myth of the First Three Years', S. Derbyshire, 'The Problem of Infant Determinism' and R. Tallis, 'Aping Mankind: Neuromania, Darwinitis and the Misrepresentation of Mankind'.

41 E. Lee (2011) 'Parenting and the New "Phrenology"', paper presented at Monitoring Parents: Science, Evidence, Experts and the New Parenting Culture, University of Kent 13th September.

42 Allen, *Early Intervention: The Next Step, op. cit*, p. 40.

43 Ibid., p. 24.

44 Ibid., p. xv.

45 Allen, *Early Intervention: Smart Investment, Massive Savings, op. cit.*, p. 3.

46 Coote (2010) *op. cit.*

47 P. Tonybee (2011) 'Who's in the Market for Sub-Prime Behaviour Bonds?', *The Guardian*, Monday 4 July 2011, available at http://www.guardian.co.uk/commentisfree/2011/jul/04/sub-prime-behaviour-bonds-fools-gold.

48 David Cameron's 'Social Fightback' speech, 15th August 2011, available at http://www.politics.co.uk/comment-analysis/2011/08/15/cameron-fightback-speech-in-full.

49 David Cameron's 'Troubled Families' Speech, Thursday 15 December 2011, available at http://www.number10.gov.uk/news/troubled-families-speech/.

50 J. Portes (2012) '"Neighbours from Hell": Who is the Prime Minister Talking About?', available at http://notthetreasuryview.blogspot.com/2012/02/families-from-hell-who-is-prime.html?m=1.

51 See Explanatory Note, Department for Communities and Local Government, available at http://www.communities.gov.uk/documents/newsroom/pdf/2053538.pdf.

52 See Channel 4's FactCheck, 'Why Cameron's Problem Families Vow Will Cost Billions', available at http://blogs.channel4.com/factcheck/factcheck-why-camerons-problem-families-vow-will-cost-billions/8210.

53 Gillies (2011) 'Perspectives on Parenting Responsibility', *op. cit.*

54 Cited in Allen, *Early Intervention: The Next Step, op. cit.*, p. 40.

55 http://www.communitycare.co.uk/Articles/26/11/2010/115901/health-visitors-and-social-workers-to-work-more-closely-in-early-intervention.htm.

56 See for example, D. Cameron (2011) 'Dad's Gift to Me was His Optimism', *Daily Telegraph*, 19 June 2011, available at www.telegraph.co.uk/news/politics/david-cameron/8584238/David-Cameron-Dads-gift-to-me-was-his-optimism.html.
57 See Cameron's 'Fight-Back' speech, *op. cit.*
58 Daycare Trust/Save the Children (2011) *Making Work Pay: The Childcare Trap*, available at http://www.savethechildren.org.uk/en/docs/Making_Work_Pay_UK_briefing.pdf.

7
The Urban Outcasts of the British City

Matt Clement

> Though the number of the poor do daily increase, all things yet worketh for the worst in their behalf...many of these parishes turneth forth their poor, yea, and their lusty labourers that will not work...to beg, filch, and steal for their maintenance, so that the country is pitifully pestered with them.
>
> Thomas Dekker (1622) *Grievous Groan for the Poor*

Dekker's outburst at the worsening condition of those people mired in poverty and embittered by inequality appears timely nearly 400 years on. It is argued by Foucault in *Madness and Civilization* to have 'constituted one of the answers the seventeenth century gave to an economic crisis that affected the entire Western world'.[1] In words that seem prescient of the fate of the twenty-first century's urban outcasts he talks not only of 'a class rejected or rendered mobile by the new economic developments' but of the very same solutions to their existence mobilised today – 'the unemployed person was no longer driven away or punished, he was taken in charge, at the expense of the nation but at the cost of his individual liberty'.[2] Hence the prison population continues its inexorable rise, with the recent spike caused by the overnight trials in the wake of the 2011 London riots just the latest twist of a long-term trend: in 1993 the UK prison population was 45,000; by March 2012 the figure had almost doubled to a staggering 88,434.[3]

This chapter will unravel some of the processes underlying this scenario by examining the conditions and experiences of young people whose exclusion from school and inclusion in the institutions of the criminal justice system are intensely interwoven. It will trace and critique nationwide developments and policy before moving on to two more refined case studies to put flesh on the argument's bones: the

London riots of August 2011 and the changes occurring in Bristol, a provincial city in the South West of the UK which, incidentally, Foucault identified as the first British conurbation to introduce the workhouse, in 1697,[4] and where, just a few months before London's summer disturbances, two riots occurred – demonstrating in both cases its curious capacity to set national precedents. The context of the argument is the mutations that have occurred in Britain's working-class neighbourhoods in the post-war years, characterised at first by 'thirty glorious years' (1945–75) of the welfare state, before a neoliberal phase of free market capitalism took hold from the mid-seventies. Looking across the cities of the Western world, Loic Wacquant outlined the existence of 'a new regime of urban poverty, distinct from the Fordist-Keynesian regime that had prevailed until the 1970s. I call it *advanced marginality* because it is neither residual or cyclical, but lies ahead of us'. It is, he continues, 'superseding the ghetto on the American side and the traditional working-class territory on the European side' creating a 'new government of social insecurity'.[5] The degree to which deindustrialisation separates metropolises from their previous Fordist-Keynesian structures and institutions will, therefore, be examined to explore whether neoliberalism has advanced the condition of marginality and precariousness more deeply into patterns of urban living. By separating out the Fordist-Keynesian regime from its neoliberal successor, Wacquant's periodisation of capitalism, it will be seen, helps to capture changes in its character which partially explain the rise of marginality. It grasps how policy shifts involving combined elements of state authoritarianism and abandonment have created not only the toxic mix of alienation and unemployment that has scarred America's 'new black ghettos',[6] but a milder, multicultural variant form in the marginalised 'neighbourhoods of relegation' in Europe.

Obviously the notion that we are witnessing a novel form of capitalism characterised by a precarious economy and labour market has to be balanced against an emphasis on the evident continuities of the economic system.[7] In other words, yes, things look bad, but we have been here before: capitalism has always relied upon a combination of more or less precariously employed sections within the working class, often utilising short-term contracts and flexible hiring practices to maximise the rate of exploitation, especially in its newer industries, so its existence today is more a sign of the endurance and intensification of working conditions rather than the invention of new ones. Nevertheless, the advanced marginality outlined by Wacquant, rooted in the scaling back of welfare and public sector jobs and the opting for a censorious 'new punitiveness'[8] to deal with marginalised elements, is a growing European phenomenon.

The specific thesis is that the practice of not attending school – and therefore of being unattached from a socialising institution – could be described as *decivilising* in the sense given to that term by Norbert Elias. Though this German thinker applied it to his home nation's painful descent into fascism, the concept has since been deployed to analyse various contemporary phenomena such as the onset of US inner city anomie,[9] anti-social behaviour[10] and knife crime amongst UK teenagers.[11] It occurs when the civilising process – the pressure, identified by Elias[12] in his detailed history of European society since the Middle Ages, to self-regulate behaviour born of intense networks of interdependence – breaks down for a group stigmatised and shut out of society. 'The suffusive spatial stigma that discredits people trapped in neighbourhoods of relegation'[13] can, in such instances, lead to what Elias called 'decivilising spurts'.[14] Lacking strong interdependent relations with others in work, education and/or their community obtained through stable inclusion in the educational system and labour market, in other words, these groups experience their norms breaking down and a form of anti-social crisis of identity and self-worth. The typical consequence of this phenomenon appears to be a 'deadly symbiosis', in Wacquant's phrase, of factors for those excluded from education and stigmatised by association with crime and its 'civilising' institution, the prison.[15]

From learning to labour to fear for the future

The starting point is the transformation in transitions from school to work brought by 30 years of neoliberalism. Before the end of the 1970s the process was secure and relatively predictable, albeit hierarchical and rigidly reflecting differences in life expectations mediated by social class.[16] Many working-class boys were destined for factory apprenticeships, several joined the armed forces or the police, while girls from similar backgrounds trained as hairdressers, nurses and shop assistants. The more academically able, mostly sons and daughters of those with professional positions, generally attended further education and destined for university. In short, young people were following pre-defined avenues of vocational development consistent with the paths of previous generations. Even those sections of the cohort deemed to be 'failing', such as the 'lads' in Paul Willis's path-breaking *Learning to Labour*,[17] were aware of their likely occupational future and created a semi-deviant subculture within the school allowing them to adjust to their low-waged, low-status future careers by appearing not to care about their academic achievements and reputations.

The 1980s changed all of these certainties, as mass deindustrialisation destroyed the objective basis of apprenticeships and obliterated job opportunities. The trauma of mass unemployment undermined the idea of a 'job for life' in industry and consequently placed a higher premium on the value of (higher) educational achievements. Education systems could no longer be judged as satisfactory if they merely reproduced the old patterns of social inequality, so a National Curriculum was introduced aiming to guarantee 'higher standards' for all, accompanied by both an emphasis on self-help and a climate of greater competition within and between schools whereby each would be judged by their results and funded directly from central coffers rather than locally. New forms of financial management would transform schools, consequently spreading greater inequality through the education system as a whole by giving headteachers the power over and responsibility for their schools' 'output'.[18]

From then up to now the pressure upon school leavers has steadily increased, with qualification levels required for even entry-level jobs soaring at the same time as the labour market for those fresh out of school or college at 16 or 18 has shrunk. Competition has inevitably bred institutional winners and losers: some schools find themselves endlessly oversubscribed while others are flatly judged 'failing', usually due to their constant difficulties attracting pupils with a reasonable chance of educational success, leading inexorably to an invidious self-fulfilling prophecy whereby parental choice amongst the privileged bypasses them completely and undermines their budgets and sustainability.[19] Now the old regulated system of schools run by the local authority has been broken up, furthermore, the recipe for educational success has become increasingly uniform – represented above all by the (in)famous 'league tables' which rank all local institutions according to the numbers of pupils achieving the standard expectation of five GCSE exams at grade C or above at 16. Whilst this experiment has been deemed a success for some, with exam grades rising each year and the percentage of young people going on to further study, and often later into university, growing from around 10 per cent at the end of the 1970s to between 35 and 45 per cent today,[20] there has also emerged a rising tide of marginalised youth who fail to reach these standards and struggle to catch up through further post-16 study. For instance, taking figures from 2010, before the current government's controversial hike in tuition fees, many commentators noted the class contrast in higher education uptake, with a lofty 57 per cent of those from more affluent areas entering university straight from school compared to a mere 19 per cent from the most deprived.[21] Even allowing for some later entry, this means the vast majority of young people in poorer communities are shut out from the higher education experience increasingly becoming the norm for the privileged, and it can only be the case that the coalition government's decision to remove the Educational Maintenance Allowance (EMA) for students in further education will exacerbate the problem.

Out of this wretched landscape of deindustrialisation and educational inequality has emerged a cluster of young people often labelled the 'NEETs', the acronym coined by New Labour's Social Exclusion Unit for those 18 to 24 year-olds not in education, employment or training, a subsection of which, dropping out of school before they reach the age of 16 – often well beforehand – and facing far higher barriers to reaching the degree of social inclusion attained by their peers, turn, instead, to crime as a mode of securing income and recognition.[22] A recent Home Office Report on *Ending Gang and Youth Violence* has firmly committed, with the thin gloss of respectability gained from citing valuable academic research, to solve this pressing problem by pressuring schools to act faster on truancy by dropping threshold levels of acceptability and threatening to publish pupil absence data for all to see.[23] It fails to recognise that the problem of rising school exclusion was initiated by the previous Tory government's programme of 'education reform', which institutionalised a competitive educational meritocracy and compelled headteachers to exclude disruptive pupils in order to compete in the league tables by which they are judged[24] – a policy maintained and exacerbated by New Labour and their concern with expanding school autonomy and introducing City Academies. Now the coalition government led by David Cameron has extended the market model still further by not only fervently pushing primary schools to deregulate and embrace Academy status too but introducing so-called 'Free' schools which can effectively retain state subsidies but control who they admit – a model imported from Sweden where it has hardly been deemed a success.

The extra autonomy that schools gain from attaining Academy status reduces the required level of reporting on pupils' progress to the local authority, but national government has aimed to encourage retention of pupils by introducing fines for schools that permanently exclude pupils, which will no doubt act as an incentive to school management to devise creative ways of keeping young people attached to the institution. The Home Office rationale is explicitly outlined as maintaining attachment and social inclusion:

> If the education he [an excluded young person] received after his exclusion from school had succeeded in reengaging him, he might have been encouraged to stay on at 16 rather than sinking ever more rapidly into the illegal economy.[25]

There is clearly a critical contradiction between the warm government messages to schools about enhancing their autonomy from the overall responsibilities of the local education authority as a whole and the cold directive to improve levels of attachment to educational institutions amongst this most marginalised section of the school-age population.

The effect of school non-attendance in its various forms on broader social exclusion and juvenile delinquency has long been demonstrated in sociology, from the Chicago school on. Most recently, Jean Kane's research has uncovered that 'the young people most vulnerable to social exclusion were also those most likely to be excluded from school',[26] noting:

> The apparent paradox between policy which emphasises inclusion but continues to exclude begins to look false: social inclusion policies are not at odds with exclusion. Rather, they have helped to solidify the economic identity of one group as needy and different from other groups, set apart by virtue of their reliance upon government welfare.[27]

So 'inclusive' policies have achieved their opposite, potentially *decivilising* sections of the UK populace by removing them from stable networks of interdependence and unambiguously *pathologising* them by placing an anti-social stigma upon them through arrests, curfews and anti-social behaviour orders (ASBOs).[28] Many young people excluded from school, for instance, end up receiving education 'other than at school', sequestering them from mainstream provision. The Department for Education recently reported rather bluntly that:

> In 2009/10, 5020 pupils were permanently excluded from their secondary school. Most were sent to alternative provision such as Pupil Referral Units. Latest statistics show that only 1.4 per cent of pupils in alternative provision achieved five good GCSEs including

maths and English. The Government believes this is not good enough.[29]

This statement was part of a press release announcing a new initiative whereby 'headteachers will be responsible for ensuring that the pupils they exclude continue to receive a decent education' in a trial involving 'around 300 schools'. Such initiatives are welcome of course, but risk understating the scale of the problem by only turning the lens on those pupils *officially* permanently excluded, missing out those who never appear on the rolls or end up out of school without being registered as formally excluded by any institution.

In any case, the crucial point is that lack of education and social integration severs youth from the job market and self-regulatory pressures and creates what John Pitts has dubbed 'reluctant gangsters': small-scale drug dealers earning very little from their trade for want of a more sustainable option.[30] As Mike Davis put it, gangs 'mint power for the otherwise powerless from their control of small urban spaces…these informal spatial monopolies equal entrepreneurial opportunity'.[31] Violence is often a vital tool in this quest, fostering a casual attitude towards the use of physical force, and weapons, as part of daily life. Indeed, the contemporary decivilising process could be said to create a mindscape similar to those of the 'pre-civilised' societies that pre-dated welfare state capitalism in the world's advanced economies – figurations such as the knightly warrior caste, the nineteenth century 'gangs of New York' or prohibition-era gangsters, where an aggressive mentality is an instrumental survival goal. Norbert Elias liked to counsel his readers not to normalise their own (implicit) educated and 'civilised' standards as applicable to all situations or all sections of society, reminding us that:

> The armour of civilized conduct would crumble very rapidly if…the danger of insecurity…were to break in upon us again, and if danger became as incalculable as once it was. Corresponding fears would soon burst the limits set to them today.[32]

This is increasingly the fate of today's urban outcasts, in this instance the teenagers turned out of mainstream school. Nature abhors a vacuum, and in their case the potentially integrative effects of school attendance and resultant full-time work are replaced with a form of what Edwin Sutherland described as 'differential association' – *the socialisation of the street*, where 'violence is pandemic because of the dominance of the informal economy over the wage-labour sector'.[33] One cannot but be reminded of Marx's assertion that:

> [...] crime must not be punished in the individual, but the anti-social sources of crime must be destroyed to give everyone social scope for the essential assertion of this vitality. If man is formed by circumstances, then his circumstances must be made human.[34]

We do create our own life-world, but not in circumstances of our own choosing. The reality of 'choice' is that it is perennially reflected through class prisms delimiting one's 'options', with the dominated being 'guided by the material pressures, limited capital and classed dispositions inscribed in their situation'.[35] This is why it is fruitless to condemn anti-social behaviour, for it is the inevitable product of attitudes bred in decidedly anti-social circumstances.

The London riots

Many young people will have had little or no attachment to the formal labour market thanks to their educational exclusion, then, yet may well have earned cash for their labour in the informal economy or through illegal activities. An example of this was broadcast in August 2011, when Sky Television interviewed three incognito London rioters on the banks of the Thames. Police helicopters hovered overhead and pursued them as they ran off, reinforcing their outlaw status, but the stories these young men told of their exploits, their own perceptions and rationalisations of their situations, are instructive, even if the peculiarities of the situation eliciting their vocabularies of motive have to be taken into account. Of course the catalyst was the disgraceful treatment of Mark Duggan's family and friends after the police had killed him, which provoked the people of Tottenham, feeling as if they had little emotional alternative to venting their frustration, to protest at the local police station the following Saturday afternoon. Tottenham youth, interviewed for the 'Reel News'[36] citizen-journalism DVD, described how the lack of explanation from the police about the circumstances of Mark Duggan's shooting bred an atmosphere of alienation from the police due to the disrespectful manner in which they justified their actions to the grieving family and the local community. But the young men interviewed by Sky Television revealed that underlying the rioting and looting that continued for days afterwards were not simply the alternative values of a 'deviant subculture', as many commentators and popular criminologists would have it, but *a wish to be socially included* in the values and norms of UK society and a reaction against their existence as 'urban outcasts'.

The first young person, his face masked by a red bandana to conceal his identity, as there is no exemption from prosecution for the interviewees, explained his situation over the hum of the police helicopter above: 'They're not giving us the opportunity to work hard and show them – yeah, we can do this. We can be as wealthy as you, we can do exactly what you can do.' He went on to explain how his efforts to 'do the right thing' by canvassing for work have led him nowhere, breeding a sense of anomie:

> All the time I feel like I'm not being noticed. Every time I go out, I'll go Bromley, West End, I'll dress smart, the smartest I can. I even begged my mum for a new pair of trainers, a pair of shoes, smart shoes. Go out, hand out my CV, you know, talk the politest I can: But nah, they ain't noticin' me, so obviously, if they ain't noticin' me from that, I'm gonna have to start doin' it a different way.[37]

So, for this 'looter', his actions seem to have been driven less by the destructive urge to smash up a shop and damage someone else's job prospects than resistance against a system which fails to offer him a legitimate way into the labour market – he even admitted in the interview that he had made a point of going across town on the night of the riots to target a shop where he felt the employer had simply ignored him when he asked about work. Not only that, but, faced with a lack of legitimate opportunities to accrue economic capital and the consumer goods it affords, they seize upon an illegitimate one, as his 'colleague' next to him put it: 'Everything's expensive…we have a free opportunity. We can take whatever we want.' At first this could be read as an apolitical statement – grist to the mill of those who have wanted to label the protests as 'alienated consumerism' – manifesting the rioters' ensnarement within an iron cage of addiction to the goals of a consumer society, a theme all too popular amongst sociologists and criminologists alike.[38] Yet he goes on to make a more explicitly political announcement: 'The government, they don't care for us. They just leave us on the block – to do whatever we do'. This leads the first rioter to specify the root of his concerns in what could be described as unmistakably class-conscious terms: 'The government, they're not thinking about us. They're thinking about that pocket' – he gestures across the river to the towers of Canary Wharf – 'one pocket that's up there'.

This comment inspires his 'colleague' to launch into an outburst that is little short of a political manifesto, noteworthy because it stresses how these young men identify with the aspirations of their more 'included' peers and clearly relate to how current austerity measures are contributing to their sense of alienation:

> They should put back on EMA. Help all those single mothers that are struggling. Uni, cuts, everythin' – we're not doin' this for the fun of it. We're doing it for money – to survive in this *world*. But until we get that, or a little bit of support from the government, then it's not gonna stop. That's what I think innit.

Perhaps the most interesting parts of these 'looters' accounts, however, are those which demonstrate that making money as an urban outcast in UK society involves being willing to take on a job whenever it appears, however unexpectedly. The way they went on to describe their activities – getting hold of a transit van, seizing and transporting goods to a pre-arranged 'lock-up' for storage prior to later distribution – certainly demonstrated their commitment to entrepreneurialism and a notable work-ethic: this was, after all, their route to gainful employment. The teenagers boasted of making £500 each from their labour, possibly an exaggerated figure, but testament to their adherence to conventional values of work and reward. Rather than being caught up in a 'consumer culture', then, and seeing themselves as simply 'flawed consumers', their actions could be described as those of *frustrated workers*. They do not merely value the material goods they have looted, but desire the opportunity to acquire them legitimately, with the accompanying status conferred as a reward for their labours. These London rioters, even if they cannot be said to represent all those who took part in the events of August 2011, articulate something of the character of marginalised UK youth – something expressed long ago by Martin Luther King in his description of riots as 'the voice of the unheard' and in the eloquent words of his fellow activist Kenneth Clark on the rioting outcasts of Harlem in 1963 shut out of the 'American dream':

> They know consciously or unconsciously that their fate is not the common fate of mankind. They tend to regard their predicament as a personal disability or as an inherent and imposed powerlessness...This persistent and agonising conflict dominates their lives.[39]

Civilising and decivilising processes in the South West

The 2011 riots were a product of the need to express collective anger at the way the new austerity was ratcheting up the degree of alienation felt in Britain's poorer quarters. Many commentators saw in them a sign of decivilisation – 'a slow motion moral collapse' as Cameron put it in the House of Commons at the time. But Britain has a long history of riots, or at least events demonised as 'riots' by the authorities, and, historically, they often do engender reform and/or reaction. The role of the police is often central to their occurrence, for as Robert van Krieken explains, updating Elias's thesis, 'civilization and decivilization can occur simultaneously...the monopolization of physical force by the state, through the military and the police, cuts in two direction and has a Janus-faced character'.[40] The city of Bristol, in the South West of the UK, can claim a founding role in this tradition of resistance.

The riots in St Paul's – a deprived neighbourhood within the city with a large black community – in April 1980 echoed the wave of US ghetto riots starting in Harlem in 1964 and Watts, Los Angeles, in 1965.[41] It is now widely acknowledged that the police sparked off the process with a large-scale raid on the Black and White Café, encountering resistance and outrage at the military style of the operation. Like Young's description of the Harlem rioters, the St Paul's mutineers 'seemed deliberately to be prodding the police to behave openly as the barbarians that they felt they actually were'.[42] The police, for their part, saw their mission as 'civilising' a dangerous racial 'other' – an orientation forged at the national rather than local level as various police actions contributed significantly to the wave of riots across no less than 13 UK cities the following summer.[43] By the early 2000s, the old 'front line' of urban conflict had been converted into a regular residential street with the demolition of the Black and White Café and the building of two replacement mock-Georgian terraced houses to fill the gap. A learning centre and local library have been built opposite and the area finally has its own publicly-funded community and sports centres. New arrivals would never know that this spot was for two decades Bristol's principal area for street dealing of illegal drugs.

This record of capital investment was, however, driven by the rising inner city property values dramatically called into question during the 2008 bank quake, and the steady advance of austerity is already undermining the sustainability of those communities closest to the economic margins of Bristol. Furthermore, Maggie Atkinson, the Children's Commissioner, recently highlighted the significant degree of illegal exclusion from school that is occurring nationwide, noting the various ways that headteachers can persuade parents not to appeal against their child's removal from school and turn a blind eye to the persistent absence of those pupils they believe will undermine the school's overall standard of academic achievement.[44] The research underpinning Atkinson's report highlighted that over half of those young people with a criminal record had experienced exclusion from school, and it was made clear that simply maintaining this brutal status quo will only reinforce the divide between the mainstream majority and their other – the growing and embittered marginalised minority. My own research in Bristol conducted over 2011–12 has confirmed Atkinson's findings in this city, establishing that over one-third of those young people involved in Bristol's criminal justice system have had their education disrupted by school non-attendance.[45]

The numbers thus compelled to enter the informal economy are already provoking a rising tide of gang-involved criminality in the inner city over recent years, with points of contact between St Paul's and neighbouring Easton being scenes of increasing animosity and small-scale turf wars between gangs from the two areas. Yet one Bristol youth aged 16 was stabbed to death, in a case of mistaken identity and territorial rivalry at the World's End pub in summer 2009, not in an inner city zone or one of the 'sink estates' dotted around Bristol's topography but in the solid working-class suburb of St George in the East of the city. It appears that the conditions breeding these symptoms of advancing marginality in the modern city are spreading, and the inhabitants of many more affluent working-class areas are at risk. In large provincial cities like Bristol, the numbers of areas designated in need of 'neighbourhood renewal' due to embedded patterns of long-term unemployment and reliance upon a growing unregulated, and often illegal, informal economy are growing. During the 2003 boom period Bristol identified ten such wards within its boundaries, but this did not include St George, nor the neighbouring Hillfields estate. Now these once 'respectable' working-class neighbourhoods are being increasingly ravaged by unemployment and underemployment and may soon see greater attachment to the informal economy.[46] The increasing stresses of maintaining work amongst a climate of austerity and rising living costs, and greater risk of becoming less securely employed, in other words, threaten to generate advancing anomie.

The current public sector cuts infamously closed most of Tottenham's youth clubs in the build-up to the 2011 riots.[47] Similar scale cuts are occurring in Bristol, with city councilors clearly fretting over the potentially devastating losses in local services and initiatives supporting young people and community safety, not least the Connexions Career Service.[48] The shrunken local economy, moreover, offers very little chance of acquiring legitimate unskilled work, with what little there is tending to go to better-qualified groups such as the multitude of FE and HE students within the city, and social housing has been cut nationally 'from £8.4 billion in 2007–10 to just £4.4 billion in 2011–14'.[49] For the most marginalised youth, particularly young offenders, then, the prospect is one of no jobs, no cash to attend college, no chance of independent housing and rising living costs. No wonder the rate of recidivism is over 70 per cent,[50] and little surprise that in these circumstances a group of people can end up ganging together in a joint enterprise that society labels a riot.

Nor is it shocking, therefore, that, just as Bristol in 1980 set the trend for the events of 1981, 31 years later events in the city, less than 500 metres from the where the Black and White Café stood, were the first of a national wave of riots. Bristol's 'Tesco riots', so-named because they initially focused on opposition to the siting of a new supermarket in St Paul's, occurred at the end of April 2011. There were two riots, on consecutive weeks, the second being bigger and rather more socially inclusive than the first.[51] Although the media and politicians were keen to demonise those taking part and trivialise their motives, it is possible to see these events as collective reaction against the disrespectful treatment most often meted out by the police, but present in the attitude and behaviour of society's other principal institutions such as the courts and the system of housing and educational provision, towards the marginalised, foreshadowing the actions and explicit accounts of those London youth standing on the banks of the Thames in front of national television cameras just four months later.

Conclusion: Past and present

For the 'teenagers under the knife'[52] described in this chapter, the process of marginalisation is already having a decivilising impact, and deepening austerity could widen the ranks of those exposed to this level of insecurity, heightening fears of loss of status. The best chance of success is for measures to be taken that *prevent* the tendency towards committing crime in this group. As Joan Moore put it, 'one of the most destructive things that can be done is to allow the criminal justice approach to gangs to prevail...[based on] a "moral panic" without much foundation'.[53] The Home Office report on ending gang violence mentioned above has made a welcome concession to the value of analysing those 'root causes' so disparaged by contemporary social control theorists and popular criminologists. Rather than merely upholding measures of 'deterrence', such as school exclusion and the ASBO, the report acknowledges the need to achieve greater attachment and inclusion of marginalised youth in mainstream secondary schools. It is true that the institutionalised school culture can itself promote social exclusion and stigmatise certain groups – especially those least likely to provide the higher grade exam passes by which schools are measured and graded by both government and local communities – yet young peoples' effective removal from their legal entitlement to schooling creates still greater stigma and shame amongst those affected. Whether the government follows through on the report's recommendations given their rhetoric and taste for market solutions, however, is another question.

Those neoliberal politicians who only believe free markets will solve social problems can look back to the 'old liberalism' of *laissez faire* to learn where things may be leading. In his epic denunciation of early Victorian capitalism, Thomas Carlyle railed against 'world-wide entanglements of Landlord interests, Manufacturing interests, Tory-Whig interests',[54] and reminds his audience that:

> The world has retrograded in its talent of apportioning wages to work...Time was when the mere hand-worker needed not announce his claim to the world by Manchester insurrection.[55]

He refers here to the mass 'turn out', or general strike, in Manchester in 1842. Events have not yet run so far in Britain, although their spectre can be seen in Mediterranean Europe as austerity prioritises profits and squeezes living standards. David Cameron may not have set up workhouses to discipline the poor, but his (un)employment policy has alienated those now threatened with compulsory work experience programmes to remain eligible for welfare payments. In place of the dreaded beadles and the boards that maintained and profited from the Victorian workhouses, we now have the heads of A4E, one of the companies that run schemes for the unemployed, enriching themselves through claiming payments from government for jobs that never existed. As inflation rises, minimum wage levels are frozen for young people, pensions are shrunk and indirect taxes are maintained at ever-higher levels across more and more goods, the vast majority feel their incomes squeezed whilst those at the top expand further still. Anomie, the slow and steady strain upon individuals resulting from real exclusion from expected entitlements, is slowly generalising a condition once only felt by the most marginalised minorities, namely the 'endless pressure' that generated the 1980s riots.[56]

Notes

1 M. Foucault (2001) *Madness and Civilization*. London: Routledge, pp. 49–50.
2 Ibid., p. 48.
3 Figures obtained by the Ministry of Justice website (www.justice.gov.uk) 2nd March 2012, which states that this is dangerously near to the current capacity of 89,302.
4 Foucault (2001) *op. cit.*, p. 51.
5 L. Wacquant (2009) 'The Body, the Ghetto and the Penal State', *Qualitative Sociology*, 32: 101–29, 112–13.
6 D. Wilson (2007) *Cities and Race: America's New Black Ghetto*. Abingdon: Routledge.
7 K. Doogan (2009) *New Capitalism?* Cambridge: Polity.
8 J. Pratt (2005) 'Elias, Punishment and Civilisation' in J. Pratt, D. Brown, S. Hallsworth, M. Brown and W. Morrison (eds) *The New Punitiveness*. Cullompton: Willan, pp. 256–71.
9 L. Wacquant (2004) 'Decivilizing and Demonizing' in S. Loyal and S. Quilley (eds) *The Sociology of Norbert Elias*. Cambridge: Cambridge University Press, pp. 95–121.
10 J. Rodger (2008) *Criminalising Social Policy*. Cullompton: Willan.
11 M. Clement (2010) 'Teenagers Under the Knife: Decivilising Processes in a Western City', *Journal of Youth Studies*, 13(4): 439–51.
12 N. Elias (2000) *The Civilizing Process*. Oxford: Blackwell.
13 L. Wacquant (2008) *Urban Outcasts: A Comparative Sociology of Advanced Marginality*. Cambridge: Polity, p. 116.
14 N. Elias (1996) *The Germans: Power Struggles and the Development of Habitus in the 19th and 20th Centuries*. Cambridge: Polity.
15 L. Wacquant (2009) *Punishing the Poor: The Neoliberal Government of Social Insecurity*. Durham: Duke University Press.
16 See A. H. Halsey, A. F. Heath and J. M. Ridge (1980) *Origins and Destinations: Family, Class and Education in Modern Britain*. Oxford: Clarendon Press; cf. also J. Goodwin and H. O'Connor (2005) 'Exploring Complex Transitions: Looking Back at the "Golden Age" of From School to Work', *Sociology*, 39(2): 201–20.
17 P. Willis (1977) *Learning to Labour: How Working Class Kids Get Working Class Jobs*. Farnborough: Saxon House.
18 S. Ranson (1989) 'Education Reform' in J. Stewart and G. Stoker (eds) *The Future of Local Government*. London: Macmillan.
19 S. Ball (2008) *The Education Debate*. Bristol: Policy Press.

20   G. Paton 'Gap Between Rich and Poor Students Widens', *Daily Telegraph*, 28th January 2010.
21   Ibid.
22   See, amongst others, A. Furlong and F. Cartmel (2009) *Higher Education and Social Justice*. Buckingham: Open University Press.
23   Home Office (2011) *Ending Gang Violence: Cross Government Report*. London: HMSO.
24   Ball (2008) *op. cit.*
25   Home Office (2011) *op. cit.*
26   J. Kane (2011) *Social Class, Gender and Exclusion from School*. Abingdon: Routledge, p. 16.
27   Ibid., p. 18.
28   For an overview of the research demonstrating the link between networks of interdependence gained from school and stable work, as well as family, see A. Furlong and F. Cartmel (2007) *Young People and Social Change* (2nd Ed). Buckingham: Open University Press, pp. 110ff.
29   Department for Education, Press Notice, 17/10/11.
30   J. Pitts (2008) *Reluctant Gangsters: The Changing Face of Youth Crime*. Cullompton: Willan.
31   M. Davis (2008) 'Foreword: Reading John Hagedorn' in J. Hagedorn, *A World of Gangs*. Minneapolis: University of Minnesota Press, p. vi.
32   Elias (2000) *op. cit.*, p. 253.
33   Wacquant (2008) *op. cit.*, p. 213.
34   K. Marx (1843) 'The Holy Family' in D. McLellan (ed.) (1971) *The Thought of Karl Marx*. London: Macmillan, pp. 32–3.
35   W. Atkinson (2010) *Class, Individualization and Late Modernity*. Basingstoke: Palgrave Macmillan, p. 132.
36   Reel News DVD, *Tottenham Rebellion*, September 2011.
37   The events were reported in a Sky Television news feature entitled 'Looters' on 12th August 2011.
38   S. Hall, S. Winlow and C. Ancrum (2008) *Criminal Identities and Consumer Culture*. Cullompton: Willan; Z. Bauman (2011) 'Interview: Zygmunt Bauman on the UK Riots', *Social Europe Journal*, 15 August 2011, available online at: http://www.social-europe.eu/2011/08/interview-zygmunt-bauman-on-the-uk-riots/>. There are also echoes here of the classical strain theory proposed by Robert Merton and its radical reinterpretation by I. Taylor, P. Walton and J. Young (1973) *The New Criminology: For a Social Theory of Deviance*. London: Routledge and Kegan Paul.
39   K. Clark (1965) *Dark Ghetto*. London: Gollancz, p. 12.
40   R. van Krieken (1999) *Governance, Law and Civilization*. Sydney: University of Sydney, pp. 8–9.
41   A. Kopkind (1969) *America: The Mixed Curse*. Harmondsworth: Penguin.
42   Clark (1965) *op. cit.*, p. 16.
43   M. Kettle and L. Hodges (1982) *Uprising! The Police, the People and the Riots in Britain's Cities*. London: Pan.
44   M. Atkinson (2012) *They Never Give Up on You*. London: Office of the Children's Commissioner.
45   M. Clement (forthcoming) 'Deadly Symbiosis: How School Exclusion and Juvenile Crime Interweave' in M. Koegeler and R. Parncutt (eds) *Interculturality: Practice Meets Research*. Cambridge: Cambridge Scholars Publishing.

46 The South West Observatory (www.swo.org.uk) maps the areas of Bristol suffering from multiple measures of deprivation, including unemployment, crime, low income, educational attainment and so on. From 2004 to 2007 it charted a growth in the number of areas within not only the most deprived 20 per cent of the country, but the most deprived 10 per cent, with 19 neighbourhoods in the most deprived 5 per cent. There was, it is true, a reduction in the number of these areas between 2007 and the next report in 2010, but the measures, on close inspection, gave a mixed picture, revealing that whilst some indicators had improved, measures of un(der)-employment had increased.

47 J. Jones (2011) 'August 2011: A Riot of Our Own', *International Socialism*, 132: 35–58.

48 Bristol City Council (2012) *Equalities Consultation on Budget Proposals for 2011–12*, available at www.bristol.gov.uk (accessed 26th April 2012).

49 M. Raco and J. Flint (2012) 'Characterising the "New" Politics of Sustainability: From Managing Growth to Coping with Crisis' in J. Flint and M. Raco (eds) *The Future of Sustainable Cities*. Bristol: Policy Press.

50 Clement (2010) *op. cit.*

51 M. Clement (2012) 'Rage Against the Market: Bristol's Tesco Riot', *Race and Class*, 53(3): 81–90.

52 Clement (2010) *op. cit.*

53 J. Moore (1988) 'Introduction' to J. Hagedorn, *People and Folks: Gangs, Crime and the Underclass in a Rustbelt City*. Chicago: Lake View Press, p. 8.

54 T. Carlyle (1912[1842]) *Past and Present*. London: Dent, p. 18.

55 Ibid., p. 21.

56 K. Pryce (1979) *Endless Pressure: A Study of West Indian Life-styles in Bristol*. Harmondsworth: Penguin.

8
The Stigmatised and De-valued Working Class: The State of a Council Estate

Lisa McKenzie

This chapter will explore the experiences of those living on a council estate in Nottingham, called St Ann's, as a means to understanding the causes of the riots in the UK's major cities in August 2011. These people are amongst the most disadvantaged in Britain, with families who have not known regular or stable paid employment since the deindustrialisation of the 1980s and social housing and public services being necessary to, as they say, 'keep their heads above water'. Some still do work in what is left of the traditional industries – factory work, warehousing, low-level engineering – and many also work in the new low-pay service sector or public authority jobs, such as teaching assistance, youth assistance, social work and retail, but a significant group, due to changes in social housing policy,[1] remain unemployed through sickness, disability or lack of jobs. There is also, however, a distinct cultural dynamic to being working class in the UK today as significant as the economic, material forces. Working-classness has, in short, been negatively re-branded and stigmatised over the last 30 years under successive Conservative and New Labour governments,[2] such that being a resident of a council estate in the UK in the twenty-first century has a very different meaning compared to the last century, when social housing was connected to the employed working class, keeping extended families close together and allowing communities to grow around work and local services.[3] Skeggs argues that the consequences of this stigmatisation, this re-branding of the working class as valueless, are central in producing new modes of exploitation through the cultural and media fields and new forms of class differentiation operating through what Pierre Bourdieu called *symbolic violence*.[4] Engels recognised in 1844 that class inequality was linked to living space – to be precise, that the restriction of space at home or work produces unsanitary conditions and poor health.[5] In 2012 we can add that 'limited space' is also *social,* or *symbolic,* that is, linked to value: who has the space to be valued, to become a person of value, and who is limited through class prejudice and class inequality and consequently de-valued? The research I have undertaken over the last seven years in St Ann's has allowed me to pursue these questions in a community suffering the consequences of increasing class inequality, class prejudice and the harshest of austerity measures.

Researching St Ann's

The St Ann's estate is one of the poorest 10 per cent of neighbourhoods in the UK[6] and has a long history with social research. Ken Coates and Bill Silburn first brought to light the poor conditions in which the people of St Ann's were living, working and raising their children in their 1960s study *Poverty: The Forgotten Englishmen,* conducted largely in response to Peter Townsend's doubts, published in the *British Journal of Sociology* in 1954, over the government assurances at the time that poverty had been eliminated in the UK thanks to full employment for men and the welfare state.[7] Instead of poverty being eliminated, argued Townsend and the two Nottingham researchers, it was taking on new forms created through the tensions between increased demands of the individual consumer and the need for basic public amenities, and this was as visible in St Ann's as any other working-class neighbourhood.

Over the decades since, the area has witnessed a number of harsh social realities, particularly the loss of manufacturing jobs in the city, leading to unemployment and insecure low-paid work, and the lack of decent housing and education for a changing workforce. Locally it has become stigmatised as a 'place to avoid' supposedly full of crime, drugs, single mothers and benefit claimants, not least through media reporting on gun- and gang-related crime on the estate in recent years and the perception nationally that council estates have become holding pens for the undeserving poor.[8] The neighbourhood also has a long history as the place where the poorest migrant workers have resided in Nottingham – people from Ireland, the West Indies, Italy, Poland, and South East Asia have been documented as living in St Ann's since the early 1950s.[9] The area has thus always been in flux, with people moving in and then, as they become more financially secure, often moving out. However, the West Indian and, especially, Jamaican populations who arrived in the 1950s have stayed constant, creating long-standing homes, families, and communities alongside a large population of migrants from Ireland and existing English working-class residents. The estate today is thus mostly made up of families who have been St Ann's residents for several generations, and there is a high percentage of mixing of white and black families on the estate – a fact which, seven years ago, spurred the research on which this chapter is based.[10]

The initial ESRC-funded project in 2005 focused upon a group of 35 white women who are mothers to mixed-race children living on the estate. The study examined how these women find value for themselves and their families when the place where they live, and they themselves, are often represented as of little or no value. The first four years were spent following them and their families ethnographically, spending time with them on the estate in the local community centres and cafes. I interviewed the women in their family and friendship groups, but also one-to-one in their homes, and I took part in local community activities, and public meetings, as a community member. Significantly, I have lived on this estate myself for over 20 years, and I am also a white mother with mixed-race children, meaning my integration with the women was not difficult. There was commonality between us: we shared the same interests and fears regarding the neighbourhood, all our children were growing up in St Ann's and we all had stories about how we had felt 'looked down on' because of our council estate status and the fact that we were white mothers with mixed-race children.

Although the initial study focused upon women, however, the last two years, funded by the Leverhulme Trust, concentrated upon men. They were absent from the first four years of the ethnography simply because they had little involvement in either the community activities revolving around youth clubs, cafes and local schools or the daily lives of the women I was engaged with. There were many reasons for their absence, some of which I knew at the time. Mostly, the men did not live with the women they had relationships with on a full-time basis simply because it made no economic sense to the family to have a man 'officially' living at the address who was unemployed or employed in very low-pay work. Sometimes the men were involved in the underground criminal economy which thrives in this neighbourhood, handling stolen goods and drug dealing at various levels, such that having them full time in the home carried too much risk – the women told me they did not want the police 'kicking down the door' looking for whoever, or whatever, with the added risk of losing their tenancy, never mind the occupational hazard of them going to jail and thus being unreliable as full-time partners. Initially, then, I was unsure as to where I might find the 'missing men'. Yet the older sons, brothers, partners, and baby fathers of the women I had previously engaged with, even if rarely present in the spaces on the estate the women occupied, often 'passed by' – a term used by men to describe their plans for the day. It has origins in the Jamaican community, where 'pass-by' means to visit, but 'passing by' in St Ann's described a lifestyle and a transient identity on the estate for men. Searching for the missing men was not as difficult as it might seem, therefore, as they were never actually far away but always on and around the estate, just in specific spaces seldom frequented by women and children. Thus I joined a local boxing gym and started to train alongside the men, while also spending many hours sitting in a barber shop opposite the gym. This is where I made contact with the missing St Ann's men – where they spent most of their time during the day – and where I drew material for my ethnographic diary.

Being valued and being St Ann's

The women's lives were full of risk management, not only through the dilemmas of what to do about the 'missing men' but also because they had an acute understanding of how they were perceived, or 'looked down on', more widely in society because of the fact they lived on a council estate, were single parents and lived on welfare benefits. Bev Skeggs has noted the specific disadvantages regarding women and class, namely, the struggle to be 'respectable' and adopt middle-class values in order to avoid being seen as 'rough'.[11] The young women in Skeggs' study knew their valueless social position, in other words, but were always trying to *leave* it by using culture to dis-identify with being a working-class woman, that is, disengaging with what they thought was 'common' and engaging in the 'respectable'. However, the women in St Ann's never denied where they thought they were positioned, often saying they are 'at the bottom' or 'lower class': they recognised their de-valued position because of where they lived and because of their constant interactions and associations with the welfare system and statutory services.[12] Furthermore, instead of looking for self-worth in what Skeggs described as 'middle-class values', the women in Nottingham found value for themselves and their children *within* the community through engaging in a local culture they described as 'being St Anns'. This local identity was valued and had meaning for the women within the estate at the same time as it was ridiculed, demeaned and feared by those outside of the estate.

Mandy was a mother with three sons whose family had lived on the estate 'a long time', she said. She thus described herself as 'proper

St Anns', yet she recounted how, on many occasions, she had experienced various forms of class prejudice:

> Mandy: it's like people looking in, I mean it's when you've heard it on the telly about the gun crime and everything, I mean my friend she actually made a complaint the other year cos she went to a pantomime at the Nottingham Ice Stadium and one of the people in the pantomime, he turned round and said 'oh I don't want to go into St Ann's cos we'll get shot' and they brought that into the pantomime and my friend actually made a complaint about it.
> Lisa: so they actually made a joke and other local people in the audience could laugh at it?
> Mandy: yeah, but for us that's not funny.

As Mandy makes clear, what happens on the estate in terms of gang-related crime was far from funny for the residents, especially when one's children are living, growing up and playing in the neighbourhood. Another instance is provided by Louise, a woman in her 40s who has been raised on the estate and currently lives with her adult daughter. Her family had originally migrated from Ireland and settled in St Ann's in the fifties, but were given a house immediately after the slum clearance programme in 1970. They were extremely proud of their 'new' house when the council handed the keys over, and Louise told me how her mum had thought that they were 'posh' and tried to keep it immaculate in spite of having five kids. However, Louise also told me that, since the 1980s, she has noticed that 'when you tell people where you come from, yeah you feel like, you know, that they class you like rough and ready'. She expanded on what this meant: not only were you 'rough' because of the notoriety of the estate, you were also seen as 'ready', or a 'council estate slag' as Louise put it, i.e. sexually available – especially if you were a mother of a mixed-race child. This stigmatisation, based upon local perceptions but also wider assumptions about council estates in the UK, was recounted by the women as the most distressing part of life. They talked about 'never being good enough', 'being looked down on' and being 'made to feel ashamed'.

This produces anger, and a certain defensiveness, throughout the estate, with the residents rejecting these de-valued terms and stating they were proud of 'being St Anns' – an identity that signified being 'able to tough it out' and having qualities carrying worth and meaning on the estate and to them as a group. Thus they compensated for the exclusion and disadvantage on offer to them on the outside of the estate by relying upon the local, available and, importantly, demonstrable: what is proven and what works for those who live within this neighbourhood. An example of this is how education, especially higher education, is viewed. With educational attainment within the resident population of St Ann's being low and attendance at university rare, the merits of gaining a university education are unknown and the thought of going through the system carries too much anticipation of being rejected and ridiculed as not good enough.[13] Consequently *local* practices form an autonomous, alternative value system defined in opposition to the norms of wider society. This way those who are marginalised can create feelings of worth, power and status on the inside of their neighbourhood and amongst those who recognise and take part in that system. Just as classical strain theory and its 'community' variant say that the pressures of poverty, discrimination, inequality and lack of social mobility lead to the search for alternative, illegal, sources of opportunity,[14] therefore, so, following Bourdieu, we might say that when there is a lack of status or respect (symbolic capital) suffered by a community there is a search for alternative sources of value within the community to compensate.

Due to the complex nature of the estate, the alternative value system and the elements which make it up take different forms for different constituent groups. For women, a high value is placed on motherhood, and therefore being a mother ranks highly on the estate. Indeed, being a mother and coping with the difficulties of living on the estate are often the only things the women cite as being proud of in their lives, but also there is an emphasis on being a 'sufferer' – another Jamaican term widely used on the estate to describe endured hardships as personal achievements. During a discussion about the drug dealing on the estate with some of the men involved in the research, the conversation turned to how difficult life was for those who are part of the drug and gang culture on the estate. The following is a discussion between Della, a white single mum of five children, her partner 'Dread', a black African-Caribbean man in his 40s who spent his time between Della's council house and a flat he rented in the neighbourhood, and Raphel, Della's eldest son who was mixed-race and 18 years old and lived between his mum's house and his grandmother's house on the estate:

> Raphel: buoy its tough out there, mans killing man, you have to be ready, it's not easy to live in Notts especially when you are Stannz [St Ann's], dem man out there wouldn't survive in here.

Dread: yeah but…if you're gonna die for Nottingham die for Nottingham, not just NG3 [the postcode of St Ann's], die for NG, that would make life a lot easier if that's what you want, just be NG, there's enough crackheads here for all of you to sell drugs to them, let's be honest about it here… there's enough crackheads for all of you to make money rather than dying, let's be honest…killing each other doesn't make sense, life's hard enough here, just do your business and done.

Della: Well I try not to beat myself up about it anymore, I'm proud that my son breathes today, that's it, the way he is he does things which aren't legal but he makes money and he's still alive for now.

This discussion went on to describe the difficulties that Della, Dread, and Raphel had in maintaining a family relationship amidst the problems on the estate. Della could not afford Dread living with her full time, but they wanted to maintain a relationship, and Raphel struggled with his mum's relationship with Dread. There were also four other children living at home and Della could not risk Raphel permanently living at the address because of his involvement with gang-related drug dealing on the estate. However, she was proud of her son as he was independent, he made money and he helped her out sometimes, and importantly he was valued and respected on the estate.

There is a real and acknowledged value in engaging in the local culture, which has been heavily influenced by black Jamaican culture, particularly for the mothers who have mixed-race children. Being authentic to the neighbourhood, being known and fitting in are other elements in becoming a person of value on the estate, but also to whom on the estate and how you are connected to the estate are equally important. In particular, there has been an exchange of culture between residents, noting that they are proud of their success in 'mixing' and 'everyone getting on'. While this type of 'cultural mixing' has often been associated with youth culture, in St Ann's it is not limited to young people only. Instead it has become a hybrid, interchangeable culture that has grown throughout the whole community over 50 years of West Indian and white working-class communities living side by side. Particular ways of speaking, such as using words originating from Jamaica, and of dressing, such as gold jewellery and expensive branded sportswear, are important signifiers of what 'being St Anns' means and value on the estate, as are how one cooks and eats, with rice and peas and chicken cooked and consumed by most families.

Although the importance of 'being St Ann's' presented itself in the initial research with women, a far more comprehensive understanding to what it meant in terms of 'being a person of value' in the neighbourhood emerged in the course of the research with the men living on the estate. During the year prior to the riots across the country in August 2011 – a watershed moment of the research – I spent time with a group of men from the estate. It is hard to say how many because of the transient and fragmented nature of their relationships to the neighbourhood and to the women they are involved with and have family relationships with. There was a core group of 15 men, though there were conversations and informal meetings with many more as they 'passed by'. All of the men are either black African-Caribbean, born in the UK or in Jamaica, or mixed-race and born in the UK.

Consequences of unfair representation and stigmatisation

It had taken me many months to gain the trust of the women I was first involved with, even though I lived on the estate and we had very similar backgrounds. As we usually knew some of the same people and found connections through friends and family, however, this type of local knowledge always situated me as an insider, and allowed the men and women to 'risk assess' me through their and my local connections. They needed to be sure that I would not represent them negatively, as the women in particular are, in their words, used to 'the looks' and the 'snide comments' whenever they come into contact with what they call 'official services'. Gina, for instance, was 21 and pregnant and lived alone with her six-month-old and two-years-old sons who she described as 'quarter caste', their father Jordan being mixed-race and living between the homes of his mum and Gina on the estate. She told me how she felt an acute stigma whenever she went to any of the benefit agencies, as although she was studying at a local college she claimed income support and housing benefit and was therefore in constant contact with 'officials'. She said that every time she gave her address to any of the 'officials' there was often a silence as they mentally processed her single-parent status, the ethnicity of her children, and then her address in St Ann's: 'I know what they're thinking, you can see it ticking over in their brain as you wait for them to think "oh its one of them from there"'.

The men at the gym and the barbers were far less suspicious of me than the women had been and appeared to be less aware of the opinions of others of them. They talked openly about how they made money, their time spent in jail, the problems they had with the police in the neighbourhood and their relationships with their girlfriends and 'baby-mothers'. This frankness was surprising compared to the guardedness of the women, particularly when the men talked about drug dealing and receiving and selling stolen goods. As the women were constantly involved in local schools, Sure Start centres, community projects, housing officers and benefit agencies they knew they were scrutinised and 'looked down on', whereas the men had very little engagement with anyone from outside of the neighbourhood, particularly statutory services or projects, unless it was through the police and judicial system. They had minimum interaction with benefit agencies or housing departments, amounting to signing on every two weeks in order to claim job seekers allowance, and some of the men did not even do this, simply because they did not want to be connected to any address. They told me about the cat and mouse games they played with the police and knowing 'how to get around things': if you have no address the police cannot find you, and they need substantial evidence to search an address you do not live at. The men instead spent most of their time with each other and had strong friendships and family bonds, often introducing new friends to me as their 'cus' or their 'fam'. Sometimes these were blood relatives, but mostly the family relationships were more complicated and interwoven across the estate – and if you had to ask how people were related you were definitely an outsider. The networks, family ties and relationship to the estate were very important for both men and women – 'being St Anns' was the most likely way women would described themselves and their families, whilst the men subscribed to the idea that 'Stannz' was territory that belonged to them. I have met very few people who imagine themselves 'being' or living anywhere else: moving out was not an ambition in this neighbourhood as a means to pursue social mobility and the 'getting on in life' identified by Coates and Silburn nearly 50 years ago.[15]

Slow rioting

Loic Wacquant has noted that the halt in social mobility and the structures of 'new poverty' are far from fully explained, but what is happening within poor neighbourhoods and to working-class people are easy to see: long-term joblessness, the proliferation of low-pay and part-time employment and the build up of multiple deprivations within the same households and neighbourhoods.[16] This has meant there have been difficulties throughout Europe, and fear within the US that established programmes of welfare remedying hardship have caused welfare dependency. There has also been a widening gap between rich and poor, and dissatisfaction and disillusionment with mainstream politics. This level of distrust and disenfranchisement, particularly within working-class neighbourhoods, have lead to undermine the legitimacy of the social order, and, as both Wacquant and Philippe Bourgois argue, that hostility is directed toward the state organisation of power and repressiveness symbolised and represented in local communities first and foremost by the police.[17]

There is, then, anger bubbling under the surface within poor communities because of the disappointments and difficulties working-class families endure. However, over the last six years there has been a definite progressive sense of despair, something which can explode instantly and without warning into outburst of anger and situations of violence within the estate and between residents. The hopelessness and the feelings of constant hard work in order to get through any day have been recounted by both men and women; the women describe their lives as 'fighting brick walls', with no one listening or caring about any of the problems they face. Della, for example, was having problems with her eldest daughter truanting from school – she was trying to keep her daughter in school but said she felt exhausted by what she described as the 'constant process':

> It's like fighting a brick wall, they hide behind policies like now if your child don't go to school you get a fine…I've had a fine for my daughter for not going to school even though she was made to go to school every day. What she does, once she's up there, isn't my fault so why should we get the fine?

The women are also disappointed by service providers coming in and setting up projects offering the 'false hope' of training and jobs usually by supplying voluntary work before retreating as quickly as they entered the community when funding runs out or when they realise the promises they made cannot be realised. The men thus talk about the hopelessness of ever getting a job offering economic stability and respect amongst their friends and family, for they know that getting a low-skilled, low-paid job will not give them the valued identity they need to live on this estate or even the means to live as 'a proper family', which is usually more of an aspiration for the future than a reality in the present. When I spoke to Dread about working and getting a job, his reaction was typical of many of the men on the estate: 'There's no jobs here for anyone, what can I do now? I used to work for the council as a gardener, I liked that but that's gone now, I'm not doing no gay job in a call centre.' Macdonald et al have used the term 'displaced masculinities' to describe the disengagement and difficulties young working-class men encounter in the transition from youth to adulthood given the absence of 'masculine employment' offering status and respect.[18] In this neighbourhood status and respect have had to become important resources, and so to look for employment that may diminish them carries far too much risk of too much loss. Moreover, there is a distrust of anyone who does not live in this neighbourhood, and the people of St Ann's can spot a mile off anyone who does not come from a similar background yet claims to, as many of the visiting service providers tend to. This is mixed with anger, even hatred, towards the police because they are seen as policing the residents rather than the neighbourhood: the women accuse the police of 'doing fuck all', while the men recount stories of being harassed, particularly in their cars, and stopped and searched constantly on the streets.

During the mid-2000s it became clear that most families did not think things might get better: 'just managing' was okay as long as the neighbourhood provided friends, family, and local value. However, since the end of 2010 apathy has been replaced by fear that things are getting worse, that no one cares, and even that it is state policy to purposefully punish council estates and their residents through death, prison or both. The women attempt to work together for safety and support, but the men are disconnected, and further disconnect through their belief that they are 'on their own' and that making as much money as possible and by any means is their only route away from their situation. I say *away* and not *out*, because there is no appetite to 'get out' of the neighbourhood: the goal is to stay within the neighbourhood and be successful according to the rules of the local value system, the logic being that to be somebody on the estate is always preferable to being nobody on the outside. As one of the younger male respondents told me 'it's about money, nothing else matters, if you have got money no one cares who you are'. His father was 'on road' (drug dealing) and this 14-year-old in St Ann's knew and recognised the respect and status that came from this local position.

With the vacuum created by the lack of political connections and the absence of communication between a marginalised and excluded group of people and a society which they feel casts them out, it is no wonder that relations with the police and other officials representing the state have become both important and confrontational. The council, 'the social', and social workers have always been mistrusted, yet when these state representatives are moving out of poorer neighbourhoods either through centralisation of bureaucracy or through redundancy – the latter increasingly being the case as services close down through current austerity measures and cuts – it is the repressive force of the police that becomes the sole representative of the state.[19]

Lynn Curtis introduced the concept of 'slow rioting' in the 1980s to explain the rise in violent crime within urban areas of the USA, especially violent crime committed by members of the local community on members of the local community, which in the USA was framed as black-on-black crime.[20] Slow rioting, argued Curtis, is what happens in a neighbourhood when internal and internalised social decay leads to mass school rejection compensated by street knowledge, when unemployment leads to street work and when devaluation by the wider population leads to locally-valued sources of pride and success. Crime, drug dealing, and teenage pregnancy become accepted and provable ways in becoming successful, and this is, in turn, met with a return to the imagery of the 'underclass', with council estates representing a modern version of Hogarth's Gin Lane and the two main characters being the dangerous and violent gang member and the welfare-absorbing single mother. The underclass discourse decries their lack of common societal values and morality and their self-destructive behaviour as a real threat to British values and national life to be curbed only through punitive measures. Yet it can be argued that street crime is, in many ways, a form of slow rioting: by committing crime on your own streets you are less vulnerable to police intervention than a group of looters, and it is possible that some crime became a safer, private expression of protest against one's social position and powerlessness.[21]

August 2011

August 2011 was a significant moment in this neighbourhood. I had been involved with the group of men on the estate for almost a year and was winding up the ethnographic study. I was focusing upon how disconnected this group of men were from what we might consider everyday society. Employment and work featured little in their lives, yet making money and having money were all encompassing in their practices and discussions with each other. Premiership footballers and what they owned, for instance, were a constant source of discussion, especially those players who had come from Nottingham and had similar backgrounds to the men. So too, however, were the rules of boxing and cage fighting, along with substantial and heated debates regarding conspiracy theories, usually relating to the relationship between the Freemasons, racism, and rap music, which they had watched on YouTube and believed explained their situation of 'being kept down' and unable to prosper. The right to carry weapons, protect their territory, grow weed in their 'yards' and not pay taxes to a corrupt and racist elite – some of these ideas being bound up with a movement called 'Freeman' which appears to be in line with American survivalist ways of thinking – plus a strong anti-Semitism, with the men coming to believe that it was predominantly the Jews who were to blame for their powerlessness as black men through their time spent in jail and internet surfing, ran through their exchanges. This is when I began to understand just how disconnected these men were, and how their inability to situate themselves within society in both economic and conceptual terms had produced frustration, anger and slow rioting.

Events took a fateful turn in the first week of August when a 29-year-old man, Mark Duggan, was shot and killed by a police officer in Tottenham, London. The police had been attempting to carry out an arrest under the Trident operational command unit which deals with gun crime in the black community.[22] Following the shooting there was a demonstration and march against the police in London followed by almost a week of civil unrest, looting and rioting in the capital and many other inner-city neighbourhoods in England. For two days, the 8th and 9th of August 2011, there was disorder and rioting within the inner city of Nottingham, but unlike other cities experiencing similar levels of disorder the focus of the anger here was specifically the police, with several inner-city police stations being firebombed and police cars being attacked as they drove through the estates. I found out the next day in the gym that some of the men I had been researching had been caught up in the disturbances and arrested – and they have now been remanded in jail for the last eight months awaiting trial. They have not yet been convicted, although they have been judged by most of the English media, and by almost all of our mainstream politicians and the general public, as morally bankrupt or feral, with Max Hastings of the *Daily Mail* claiming 'their behavior on the streets resembled that of the polar bear which attacked a Norwegian tourist camp last week. They were doing what came naturally and, unlike the bear, no one even shot them for it'.[23] The Prime Minister David Cameron argued in his speech a week after the riots that they were not about race, government cuts or poverty, they were about 'behaviour', and that, although England had seen some 'sickening acts', the 'Big Society' was then in action with the 'Best of British' involved in the cleanup operation in Tottenham as the local community came out and cleared the streets with their own brooms.[24] These comments from the media and politicians are neither surprising nor shocking, and neither were the levels of crime, anger and violence on the streets during that first week of the riots. There has been a gradual exclusion, de-valuing and stigmatisation of sections of the British working class for several generations, and I have noted over seven years the narratives of those who live in St Ann's, the feelings of powerlessness, the rage which comes out of this level of despair and consequently the ways the community turns in on itself. The residents of poor communities are looking inwards for sanctuary; they find it locally, but with the unintended consequence of causing damage to themselves and their own communities.

Conclusion

This chapter has attempted to illuminate the lives of working-class people living in one council estate through a period of adversity caused by 30 years of neoliberal policy. Unemployment, stigmatisation, anger, feelings of utter powerlessness alongside a strong sense of identity and community are some of the outcomes. Over several generations there have been some well-intentioned politicians, and some not so well-intentioned, who have treated the disadvantages and inequalities found within council estates as a matter of morality, blaming the poor for their poverty and inflicting terrible levels of symbolic violence on deprived neighbourhoods and people who are already suffering economic disadvantage. For decades in the UK there have been symbolic boundaries drawn around certain territories: places where the poor live, places one should avoid going if at all possible not because of the poverty in that particular place but because of the behaviour of those who live there. The boundaries drawn around council estates have lead to limited space for those who live there, and that space can be physical but also symbolic, linked to value. Consequently, for this section of the working class – those who are the least skilled and least educated – their lives are very much centred upon where they live, their family and local networks become important, they turn their adversity into a meaningful identity, they become recognised and recognisable, yet at the same time they have been re-branded from working class to underclass.

Wacquant and Curtis have argued that the concept of slow rioting seems an appropriate explanation for the anger and apathy, violence and passivity of a group who have been rejected by the wider population. Yet slow rioting gave way in August 2011 to actual rioting: an opportunity had arisen for this marginalised group in the UK to display their frustration and anger with the state as represented by the police. For almost a week in England people from these marginalised communities attacked, looted, and firebombed places that symbolised their powerlessness. There was also destruction of property and looting from people within their own neighbourhoods which seemed unfathomable to the media, and to wider society. It would also have been to me had I not have spent a year with a group of men who displayed their disconnect to society, whose existences were so fragmented and fragile that employment and stable family life were beyond their expectations and became aspirations for the future, and whose worth, self-respect and dignity came from a local value system born of stigmatisation, joblessness and the lack of space and mobility.

David Cameron's vision of the 'Big Society' as a remedy to the UK's problems is flawed. It appeals to social cohesion and localism, something the people who live in St Ann's in Nottingham would have no disagreement with – there is a community spirit and a clear value system in operation already. Yet they argue that the problem is the lack of opportunities for the paid work which enables people to have respect for themselves by offering a living wage allowing families to live together – offering, in other words, hope in a place where people fear what will happen to them next. This puts the coalition government in a tight spot. Will they invest in employment, a living wage, and security for those who live within council estates, or will they continue the rhetoric of the 'Big Society', expecting the least powerful and the most disadvantaged to create social enterprises and get themselves out of a situation over which they have little power?

Notes

1   P. Malpass and A. Murie (1999) *Housing Policy and Practice*. Basingstoke: Palgrave, pp. 82–6.
2   C. Haylett (2000) 'Modernisation, Welfare and "Third Way" Politics: Limits to Theorising in "Thirds"?', *Transactions of the Institute of British Geographers*, 26(1): 43–56; C. Haylett (2001) 'Illegitimate Subjects? Abject Whites, Neo-Liberal Modernisation and Middle Class Multiculturalism', *Environment and*

*Planning D: Society and Spac*e, 19(3): 351–70; Haylett (2003) *Culture, Class and Urban Policy: Reconsidering Inequality.* Oxford: Blackwell Publishing; B. Skeggs (2004) *Class, Self, Culture.* London: Routledge; B. Skeggs (2005) 'The Re-branding of Class: Propertising Culture' in F. Devine, M. Savage, J. Scott and R. Crompton (eds) *Rethinking Class: Culture, Identities and Lifestyle.* Basingstoke: Palgrave, pp. 46–68; S. Lawler (2008) *Identity: Sociological Perspectives.* Cambridge: Polity.

3 J. Welshman (2006) *Underclass: A History of the Excluded, 1880–2000.* London: Hambledon Continuum.

4 Skeggs (2005) *op. cit.*

5 F. Engels (1845/1987) *The Condition of The Working Class in England.* London: Penguin.

6 Office for National Statistics (2010) *The English Indices of Deprivation 2010.* London: HMSO Communities and Local Government Publication.

7 K. Coates and R. Silburn (1970) *Poverty: The Forgotten Englishmen.* London: Penguin; P. Townsend (1954) 'Measuring Poverty', *British Journal of Sociology,* 5(2): 130–7.

8 B. Rogaly and B. Taylor (2009) *Moving Histories of Class and Community.* Basingstoke: Palgrave Macmillan.

9 Coates and Silburn (1970) *op. cit.*, pp. 25–8; J. Solomos (2003) *Race and Racism in Britain* (3ʳᵈ ed). Basingstoke: Palgrave; R. Johns (2002) *St Ann's: Inner City Voices.* Warwick: Plowright Press.

10 See also L. McKenzie (2012) 'Finding Value on a Council Estate: Voices of White Working Class Women' in R. Edwards, S. Ali, C. Caballero and M. Song (eds) *International Perspectives on Racial and Ethnic Mixed-ness and Mixing.* London: Routledge; C. Caballero and R. Edwards (2010) *Lone Mothers of Mixed Racial and Ethnic Children: Then and Now.* London: Runnymede.

11 B. Skeggs (1997) *Formations of Class and Gender.* London: Sage.

12 Cf. V. Gillies (2007) *Marginalised Mothers: Exploring Working-Class Experiences of Parenting.* London: Routledge; Welshman (2006) *op. cit.*

13 Cf. D. Reay (2001) 'Finding or Losing Yourself? Working Class Relation-ships to Education', *Journal of Education Policy,* 16(4): 333–46; Skeggs (1997) *op. cit.*; S. Duncan (2007) 'What's the Problem with Teenage Parents? And What's the Problem with Policy?', *Critical Social Policy,* 27(3): 307–34.

14 E. Anderson (1990) *Streetwise.* Chicago: University of Chicago Press; R. Agnew (1999) 'A General Strain Theory of Community Differences in Crime Rates', *Journal of Research in Crime and Delinquency,* 36: 123–55.

15 Coates and Silburn (1970) *op. cit.*, pp. 105–30.

16 L. Wacquant (1994) 'The New Urban Colour Line: The State and Fate of the Ghetto in Post-Fordist America' in C. Calhoun (ed.) *Social Theory and the Politics of Identity.* Blackwell: Oxford, pp. 231–76; L. Wacquant (2008) *Urban Outcasts: A Comparative Sociology of Advanced Marginality.* Cambridge: Polity, pp. 30–3.

17 Wacquant (2008) *op. cit.*; P. Bourgois (2009) 'Recognizing Invisible Violence: A Thirty Year Ethnographic Retrospective' in B. Rylko-Bauer, L. Whiteford and P. Farmer (eds) *Global Health and Violence.* Santa Fe, New Mexico: School of Advanced Research Press, pp. 18–40.

18 R. Macdonald, T. Shildrick, C. Webster and D. Simpson (2005) 'Growing Up in Poor Neighbourhoods: The Significance of Class and Place in the Extended Transitions of "Socially Excluded" Young Adults', *Sociology*, 39(5): 873–91.

19 Wacquant (2008) *op. cit.*

20 L. A. Curtis (1985) *American Violence and Public Policy*. New Haven: Yale University Press.

21 Wacquant (2008) *op. cit.*; Curtis (1985) *op. cit.*, p. 8.

22 G. Morrell, S. Scott, D. McNeish and S. Webster (2011) *The August Riots in England: Understanding the Involvement of Young People*. London: National Centre for Social Research; Home Office (2011) *Ending Gang and Youth Violence*. London: Home Office.

23 M. Hastings (2011) 'Years of Liberal Dogma have Spawned a Generation of Amoral, Un-educated, Welfare Dependent, Brutalised Youngsters', *Daily Mail*, 12th August 2011.

24 David Cameron (2011) 'The Fightback After the Riots', speech delivered on 15th August, available at http://www.number10.gov.uk/news/pms-speech-on-the-fightback-after-the-riots/.

9
Broken Communities?

Mike Savage

> *Tackling Broken Britain: building a stronger society* will follow the report of the Communities and Victims Panel, getting to grips with the fundamental issues of our society, and establishing how to build strong, socially and economically resilient communities. Covering areas such as youth services, education, welfare, health and social care and criminal justice, and examining potential solutions such as community budgets and early intervention initiatives, this timely and high-profile seminar is a must-attend event for professionals from across the public sector and beyond.[1]

Experts of all kinds are now being inveigled to 'tackle Broken Britain'. We are surrounded by pessimistic accounts of the 'slow-motion moral collapse' of Britain[2] and by the invocation to fashion something called the 'Big Society' to respond to the challenge of encouraging ordinary people to take back responsibility for their lives and destinies. As the above quote designed to publicise a major conference reveals, exhortation proliferates. Such hyperbole was undoubtedly a major plank of Conservative Party policy in its 2010 election campaign. The official Cabinet Office statement proudly boasts that the 'Big Society is about helping people to come together to improve their own lives. It's about putting more power in people's hands – a massive transfer of power from Whitehall to local communities'.[3] And in a very short time the tentacles of the 'Big Society' have reached far: there is a 'Big Society Network' which 'exists to develop talent, innovation and enterprise to deliver social impact' and has begun to build links between businesses and third sector organisations. Although the idea of the 'Big Society' has no intellectual warrant whatsoever, the Arts and

Humanities Research Council emphasises in its 'Delivery plan' that its work on 'Connected communities' will 'enable the AHRC to contribute to the government's initiatives on localism and the "Big Society"',[4] even though many respected academics resigned from its ranks in protest at what they saw as government interference in academic research.

It would be wrong to assume that this concern is only the product of febrile Conservative party 'wonk machines'. It is in many respects a reworking of a familiar nostalgic trope regarding the weakening social bonds of contemporary society. Influential sociologists such as Zygmunt Bauman and Anthony Giddens have marched to the same drum for two decades and more.[5] The previous Labour government's concern with 'Sustainable Communities' in a programme launched in 2003 shares many of the same assumptions. Using a similar jarring fusion of apocalyptic pessimism and banal policy prescription, Deputy Prime Minister John Prescott wrote that:

> For more than 30 years this country lost its way. All governments failed to meet housing need. We built housing in a way that failed to put the needs of communities first. We did not invest for the long term.[6]

These concerns to link physical development with social renewal were intellectually underpinned by arguments about the problems of social exclusion and the need to recover 'social capital', which became internationally celebrated in arguments by Robert Putnam and associated scholars working within a loosely communitarian frame.[7]

The aim of my chapter is to contest the problematic behind this concern with 'broken communities' and the associated implication that some kind of 'Big Society' is the answer. My argument will be that this perspective misunderstands communal social relations in two ways. Firstly, there is no simple moral breakdown or loss of social support in poor and deprived working-class areas. Rather, a range of powerful and pervasive support mechanisms are in evidence, but although these are generally robust, they are not those which articulate with formal institutional devices and policy circles and hence are largely invisible to more privileged writers. I will reflect specifically on issues of cultural participation as a focus here.

Secondly, if we are concerned with moral breakdown, it is to the practices of the very wealthy that we should turn. In their lives and practices, notably those associated with what I term 'elective belonging', they do not conform to the assumptions about good communal life which underpin notions of the 'Big Society'. To seek to 'foist' communal attachments which they would not personally adopt on poorer communities is therefore a form of calculated hypocrisy, or what Bourdieu might term 'symbolic violence'.

In making these arguments I rework long-term themes in the study of social and communal relations.[8] The argument that poorer populations are passive and thereby complicit in their misfortunes has surfaced not only in the influential 'culture of poverty' argument, but also more recently in Pierre Bourdieu's emphasis on the pragmatic 'culture of necessity' which he sees as characteristic of the limited horizons of a working class excluded from cultural capital.[9] I wish to take my distance from both these perspectives, however, my aim is not to romanticise the vitality of working-class cultural life,[10] but to offer a worked-through evaluation of its strengths and limitations. I am especially interested in noting how its institutional detachment from the Labour movement has reduced its visibility and affected the capacity of its social capital to be recognised and legitimated.

In pursuing these aims, I will argue that the popularity of the moral breakdown discourse is indeed telling – so long as we read it not as a literal statement about recent social trends, but rather as a covert indicator of social malaise. In my book *Class Analysis and Social Transformation* I elaborated what I termed the 'paradox of class' – that at the very moment that structural class divisions appear to become more acute, so overt popular awareness of class identities appears more muted.[11] This apparent paradox, I argued, was linked to a neoliberal hegemony in which the marketisation of services and amenities allows – generally privileged – rational consumers to gain advantages over those less well equipped to 'play' the market. These advantages, however, are not deemed to be the product of class division so much as the individual aptitudes and qualities of the discerning consumer, and are hence naturalised. Accentuating class advantages are thus associated with the apparent decline of *overt* class and status hierarchies.

In this chapter I unravel this 'paradox of class' further to explore how popular identities are being further re-configured in an age of austerity. Here, concerns about moral breakdown and a sense of malaise can be read as a form of recognition of the inequities of contemporary British society, but without using an overt discourse of class. The challenge posed, therefore, is to recognise that the moral breakdown discourse is saying something important, but to read it in a different register. In pursuing this argument, I firstly examine the social and cultural engagement of the working class before going on in the second section to consider how the lack of overt class consciousness in popular identities can be seen as evidence of a fundamental fracture between reflexive middle-class identities and marginalised popular ones. In the final section I then explore how the fortunes of the popular classes need to be placed in the context of emerging forms of upper- and middle-class power.

1: The social and cultural engagement of the popular classes

Just how 'broken' are the communal social ties of working-class communities? Certainly, as already mentioned, there is extensive moral panic over the breakdown of social cohesion at the most deprived parts of the social structure. The urban riots of 2011 in many parts of the UK were seen as evidence for young people's preparedness to break the law given the opportunity in order to loot for 'free stuff'. Deploying familiar tropes, Christine Odone saw the riots as the product of family breakdown and the absence of fathers.[12] Similarly, high teenage pregnancy rates in the UK are sometimes held up as an indicator of moral decline. As the *Sunday Times* put it in 2009:

> Britain is doing low life better than almost all other developed countries...as each generation moves further away from family stability, we lumber ourselves with the enormous cost of propping up failed families and living with the social consequences. It is a grim prospect, especially as the country moves into deeper recession.[13]

Yet the existing evidence suggests that such apocalyptic visions are completely unwarranted. Let us review a few – relatively accessible – pieces of evidence. According to the British Crime Survey (BCS), crime rates in 2010–11 were lower than at any time since the introduction of the BCS in 1981, being roughly half the level of 1996. Violent crimes had declined by 44 per cent from 1994 to 2010–11. This hardly seems evidence for moral breakdown. Yet the interesting point here is that the same data source reveals that the proportion of the population *feeling* that crime is rising actually increased from the late 1990s – from around 60 per cent to nearly 80 per cent.[14] It is this increasing mismatch between popular perceptions and underlying trends which requires pondering.

Similar trends are evident as regards family structure and practices. Teenage pregnancy rates, for example, have fallen strikingly in recent years, now being at their lowest since 1969,[15] while divorce rates in 2010 were at their lowest level for 29 years. There is also no evidence that the 'family meal' has been undermined in favour of solitary or lazy 'grazing' in front of the TV screen.[16] In fact, the rise of the internet and 'screen culture' seem to have impacted very little on other forms of 'moral engagement', such as literary cultures. There has been no trend towards people reading less – indeed, in the UK the mean number of minutes spent reading books per day *doubled* from three in 1975 to seven in 2000 and the proportion of people reading books on any one day rose from 13 to 17 per cent. Finally, it also appears that the amount of altruistic volunteering has increased somewhat, from about 39 per cent of adults volunteering at least once a year in 2001 to 41 per cent by 2008–09.[17] Of course, I am only using these indicators for rhetorical jousting purposes. Nonetheless, it seems that the 'moral decline' discourse floats free of any obvious empirical reference point. It is surely incumbent on proponents of this argument to identify some concrete changes which might be related to it.

There is, however, one area often flagged where the data is more mixed: the extent of popular engagement with civic and voluntary associations, politics, and the public sphere in general. Electoral turn-out fell from 77.4 per cent in 1992 to 59.4 per cent in 2001 and rose only slightly thereafter back to 65.1 per cent in 2010.[18] This concern with political withdrawal extends into numerous studies of participation in voluntary associations and 'civil society'. Inspired in part by Putnam's claims that Americans are increasingly 'bowling alone' and are markedly less likely to join civil associations, British research shows that there are no comparable trends towards declining memberships amongst the population as a whole, but that the major shifts are caused by the working class being much less likely to be active.[19] However, detailed scrutiny of which organisations are especially marked by this decline indicate that it mainly affects trade unions and working men's or social clubs and that, leaving aside these cases, there is no marked trend for the working classes to be less likely to join.[20] In addition, it is also clear that informal modes of political engagement are increasing and that large proportions of the population are politically involved, for instance through signing petitions, boycotts, and the like.[21]

There does, on the other hand, appear to be an important shift in the culture of popular mobilisation. As late as the 1960s, working-class towns and communities were marked by considerable formal institutional mobilisation, at least by adult men. The most obvious case here is trade union membership, but this fell from over 13 million members at its peak in the late 1970s to just over seven million by 2007. It is important not to glamorise or romanticise such involvements in the past. They were very much oriented to skilled white male workers and were often deferential to elite figures. As Brian Jackson's study of the Yorkshire town of Huddersfield points out, extensive popular involvement in bowling clubs, brass bands, and trade unions was nonetheless consistent with the co-option of prestigious patrons.[22] As Ross McKibbin has explored, it suited Conservative Party interests during the middle years of the twentieth century to recognise the labour interest as a means of frightening diverse middle-class groups into accepting the Conservative writ.[23]

The point here, then, is that, rather than a general 'moral breakdown', we might be seeing a more specific kind of institutional demobilisation in which the male working classes are much less involved in formal political channels than used to be the case. I need to make it clear that I am not claiming that there ever was a homogenous or collective working class with a uniform political manifestation. Gender, ethnic, and local divisions were always marked. Indeed, such divisions were actively implicated in the organisational capacities of the working classes.[24] It is now clear, however, that even 'labour' organisations have been radically re-made. Union density is now much higher in professional than manual working-class occupations: 43 per cent of professionals are unionised, compared to 21 per cent of skilled manual workers and 29 per cent of process, plant and machine workers.[25]

It would be quite erroneous to read this trend as indicative of a wider breakdown of social connectivity and affiliation. Women, for instance, are now more likely to be trade union members than men and have also shown more likelihood to join voluntary organisations – they are by these measures more 'engaged' than they used to be. More generally, as I and my colleagues have shown in previous research, membership of a voluntary association should not be seen to be a wider proxy for other kinds of social connection. Voluntary associations tend to be highly visible, to attract more educated members, and are also easier to articulate with formal political apparatuses, but this does not mean that they convey wider social contacts. It is evident that forms of *friendship* and *neighbourhood sociability* are largely autonomous from it. Working-class respondents tend to report higher amounts of neighbourhood interaction than do other kinds of residents.[26] Indeed, Platt shows that only 10 per cent of White British people are socially isolated (which rises to 17 per cent for some ethnic minorities), that it is to say, neither belong to clubs, go out regularly, nor visit or are visited by friends. Some of the more dystopian accounts of social isolation hardly seem borne out.[27]

It is therefore important to distinguish different dimensions or forms of social capital rather than focus on formal access to civic organisations alone. Civic participation, so vaunted by recent governments, are just one out of a range of channels of social capital generation and has been amply shown to favour the middle class who, among other things, tend to be more likely than the working class to have the skills, resources and interests for civic engagement. Informal social networks both with neighbours, with acquaintances and with intimate friends beyond one's immediate neighbourhood also play an important role and affect people's attitudes, values, preferences and key aspects of their life-chances, such as health conditions, in ways which convey considerable benefits yet figure not one jot in the prevailing definitions of good citizenship and strong communities. These forms of social engagement are less socially unequal.

We can draw similar lessons from the now extensive research on the organisation of cultural tastes and practices in contemporary Britain.[28] There is ample evidence showing that formal cultural practices, especially those associated with what Bourdieu defines as 'legitimate' or highbrow culture such as a liking for classical music, opera, modern literature, attending art galleries and museums, eating in French restaurants, etc., are highly socially skewed towards the educated middle classes. But rather than the working classes simply partaking of popular culture – such as football, bowls, or bingo, which were singled out in the 1960s – they appear to abstain from nearly all of the cultural activities specifically asked about on surveys.

The Cultural Capital and Social Exclusion survey, conducted in the UK in 2004–5, offers the most comprehensive account here, and asked about a wide range of cultural tastes covering the area of music, eating out, visual arts, reading, TV and film, and sport, yet only a very small minority of these were predominantly associated with the popular classes, namely watching the television, eating fish and chips, liking Western films, enjoying social sports and watching soap operas. Although this list includes many of the activities which one might associate with popular taste, others such as a liking for football, for rock music or heavy metal music are now associated with the more educated middle classes. The same kind of finding was revealed by the BBC's Great

British Class Survey conducted in 2011, which also indicated that many of new kinds of digital social communication such as the use of networking sites and computer games are also predominantly associated with educated young people, as is enthusiasm for contemporary music and all kinds of sport and physical exercise.[29]

On the face of it, these arguments support the idea that the major cultural divide is now between a culturally omnivorous or 'voracious' middle class and a largely disengaged working class. Certainly, the association of the popular classes with watching TV is striking given the arguments of Putnam, who attributes the decline of social capital partly to this, and feeds into the view that the 'white working class' is now largely disengaged and isolated. However, as Bennett et al emphasise, this would be a problematic reading, insufficiently attentive to the way that survey measures are not innocent tools which reveal patterns but themselves help construct certain understandings. Three important points are pertinent here.

Firstly, the apparent lack of engagement of popular groups with formal leisure and cultural activities is not necessarily a sign of more general social withdrawal. Face-to-face interviews with some of those who completed the Cultural Capital and Social Exclusion questionnaire indicated that many who appear culturally disengaged according to their survey responses are actually living close to kin and friends who they have grown up with.[30] They thus often draw on a wide ranging informal social network located close by. In contrast, middle-class residents are much more likely to have migrated during their careers, are more likely to lack such routine contacts, and are more predisposed to use formal cultural activities as part of their social life. From this perspective, then, it is the middle classes who might be more *socially* disengaged from their immediate peers, family and neighbours, with the result that they have therefore to compensate by seeking some kind of formal cultural engagement.

Secondly, we need a more nuanced recognition of the importance of television in popular culture than simply assuming that its consumption is a sign of detachment and isolation. As is widely recognised in audience research studies, the watching of television is not necessarily a sign of isolation but can be a *collective* act which provides common talking and reference points, not only to those living in the same house but also family members and neighbours living in the proximity who gather round the electronic 'hearth'.[31]

Thirdly, at least in some cases, it seems that the questions which are asked in surveys are not pre-disposed to reveal the subtle patterns of engagement evident in working-class communities. Detailed ethnographic studies of working-class areas invariably detect sophisticated patterns of engagement which require subtle understanding. McKenzie in this volume, for example, demonstrates that to characterise working-class residents in St Ann's, Nottingham, simply in terms of their 'deficit' culture is to underestimate the more positive features of their friendship and family ties.[32] This point is especially apparent with respect to interviews with some ethnic minorities, whose interests could be too specific to have been revealed through general responses regarding their liking of musical genres, for instance. Thus, an interview with an apparently (according to his survey responses) disengaged Indian business man actually revealed that when he had the chance to talk in his own words he actually had a great liking for Indian literature and films.

In short, we need to be wary of assuming a large group of disengaged and atomised individuals at the lower reaches of the social structure. This is not to jump to the opposite perspective of assuming that there are necessarily wide ranging communal attachments. In fact, in some urban areas marked by de-industrialisation, public disinvestment and high crime rates, there is evidence of certain kinds of withdrawal.[33] My point, however, is that we should not over-generalise from these specific cases. Amongst ethnic minorities, for instance, there can be considerable social engagement based on religious as well as ethnic identities.

Reflections on the character of political mobilisation are also revealing here. Despite considerable media concern, there is little clear evidence that the white working class has become politically detached or isolated. If we consider the far right, although the British National Party (BNP) has enjoyed some political success in some parts of England, it is not clear that its demographic support comes specifically from the popular classes. Although Ford and Goodwin argue that support comes from older, poorly educated working-class men, they also note that these tend to be found in particular locations in Northern England, and, furthermore, are not especially deprived or poor. The electoral setbacks experienced by the BNP in working-class areas of London in 2010 indicate strongly that there is no direct relationship between support for the extreme right and working-class voters.[34] Furthermore, Biggs and Knauss show there is little direct relationship between working-class areas of residence and membership in the BNP, and rather that 'the social class most strongly associated with membership is small employers and the self-employed'.[35] The evidence points much more to the idea that the working class are largely disengaged from formal politics – including that of the far right – and can be mobilised to support a variety of political platforms in specific local circumstances. However, this is a sign not of general social breakdown but of the lack of articulation between their values and practices and those which are mobilised through formal politics.

To characterise popular social and cultural engagement as somehow 'broken' is, therefore, at best a wild exaggeration and at worst deliberately misleading. What does appear fractured, on the other hand, is the kind of articulation between forms of popular culture and formal institutional involvement of the kind which partially existed when the Labour movement was stronger and more embedded in popular culture. Of course, this is not to claim there was ever a moment when such links were ever straightforward. Extensive historical research has revealed that it was predominantly skilled male manual workers who were associated with these institutional forms. Nonetheless, if we extend our focus to include the Co-operative movement, which was the largest multiple retailer in the UK down to the 1960s, then we should not assume that such institutional forms had no wider resonance either.

The point here is that, given this organisation of popular cultural life, to seek to 'fix' it with formal intervention from government agencies and third sector organisations will only reinforce the tendencies to see such bodies as institutions of governance rather than as 'belonging' to a wider public. At best they are likely only to mobilise popular groups instrumentally and for contingent purposes, and for this reason will only exacerbate the problems identified above.

2: The paradox of popular identities

Notwithstanding all this, the widespread sense of malaise – which the 'Big Society' seeks to respond to – does touch an important nerve. To be sure, many of the most widely heralded views claiming epochal shifts in identities have also proved to be simplistic. Thus, the popular view that people are less trusting than they used to be, as argued by Peter Hall, has shown to be problematic. A question used in 1959 to measure trust included an option for 'it depends', which throws the results when compared with more recent questions which do not include this option.[36] Similarly, Ronald Inglehart's view that there is a shift from 'materialist' to 'post-materialist' values appears difficult to sustain since the attitude questions which are used to operationalise these two values systems are historically dependent.[37]

But there are some areas where changes in popular identities can be identified more consistently. Explicit working-class identities, for instance, are not as marked or as manifest as they used to be, even if the extent of decline should not be overestimated. The most careful study here, by Anthony Heath and his colleagues, shows that whereas 34 per cent of Britons identified themselves as working class without any prompting in 1964, this fell to 25 per cent by 2005. If one includes those who are prompted into naming a class identity, the drop off is from 65 per cent to 57 per cent. Heath et al show, furthermore, that these working-class identities are much less politically salient and appear to carry less cultural meaning than they used to.[38]

This finding is closely consistent with studies demonstrating a rapid decline of class allegiances over the last 30 years, to the extent that examinations of the 2010 General Election, when the Labour Party received the second lowest number of votes ever, indicate that class was not a significant factor in structuring political choice. Once 'pre-eminent among the factors used to explain party allegiance in Britain', since the 1960s class has thus lost much of its ability to condition electoral behaviour to the extent that even proponents of the 'trendless fluctuation' interpretation of class voting patterns, advocated by Heath et al in the 1980s and taken to characterise the period from the 1960s to the early 1990s, concede that by the late 1990s there had indeed been a decline.[39] Heath et al thus show a striking weakening in the association between class consciousness and party affiliation between 1964 and 2005. However, this point largely reinforces the previous discussion of the dis-articulation between the popular classes and formal political organisation. In other ways, class-specific beliefs and practices remain marked. Surridge, for example, shows that there has actually been a growing divergence between working- and middle-class respondents in their political attitudes. In the 1990s there was an association between the left-leaning middle classes and having liberal attitudes, but by 2007 this had broken down. However, amongst the working classes there is an increasing association between having left-wing political views, including a persistent support for redistributive politics, and authoritarian outlooks.[40]

Qualitative studies demonstrate similar themes. The values and practices of the popular classes are clearly oriented by a strong emphasis on 'getting by' and graft, often through working long hours. These values are often associated with a commitment to the local neighbourhood, to personal contacts and, in certain areas, to the values of being 'born and bred'.[41] One aspect of this, which recurs in much recent research, are the strong feelings towards 'ordinary' identities, where people feel a certain pride in emphasising that they are nothing 'special', but that they are 'normal' individuals who act naturally and responsibly. These kinds of ordinary identities overlap with claims to be working class, and in some cases, middle class.[42]

This point chimes with Bourdieu's claims about the role of the 'culture of the necessary' amongst the working classes. Yet care needs to be taken to recognise the sophistication and wide ranging cultural reference points of these repertoires. As Walkerdine explores, they also retain a strong concern with aesthetic elements, linked to a concern to 'escape'. Qualitative data from the Cultural Capital and Social Exclusion project suggests that working-class respondents seek to define a bounded arena in which they can forget daily constraints and 'find time to themselves'. This is an area that Walkerdine, with Helen Lucey, has examined with considerable subtlety in an account of how working-class mothers seek to find 'treats' and define bounded parts of their children's lives which are not constrained by school regimes. In her more recent work, moreover, she explores the powerful affectual relations associated with de-industrialising industrial areas, where intensities and passions remain marked.[43]

To summarise: the practices and values of the popular classes are not marked by a simple fatalism or a breakdown of morality or social cohesion requiring policy intervention. Rather, the values of ordinariness, endurance, graft, and getting by have considerable resonance. At times, to be sure, these can slide into a sense of frustration, even despair, when the daily reality of people's lives appears to make it impossible to live up to these values. Antagonism can also be directed towards those groups who might appear to violate these values – such as welfare claimants – but such feelings can also be directed against wealthy upper- and middle-class individuals who appear to live by different rules.

3: Elective belonging

Let me now turn to the politics of 'elective belonging'. This form of attachment to place, increasingly evident amongst the middle classes, articulates a very different kind of communal ethic to that which is propagated in the 'Big Society' rhetoric.[44] It denotes that the middle classes have not become rootless cosmopolitans – readily upping sticks to advance their career – but are, on the contrary, passionately invested in place and location. However, their orientations to place are not premised on any historical attachments which they or their family might have but are linked to a concern with whether their residence is right for 'someone like me'.[45] In assessing whether a locale feels right, and hence whether one belongs, then, a number of considerations are important. These certainly include its instrumental suitability in terms of its access to work, and amenities such as schools. However, they also stretch out to include a concern with the 'feel' of the place, and whether it has the right 'tone'. This perception frequently draws on aesthetic cues, such as associated with architectural features or the neighbouring landscape, as well as the characteristics of local residents.

The concept of elective belonging thus draws upon Bourdieu's conception of choice, namely that it is when one feels one is making a real choice, which seems intensely personal to the person concerned, that one is actually following a highly socially predictable path. Realising one's destiny involves both a conscious choice, passionately made, but also a kind of social contract. The result is that commodified housing markets, seeking to appeal to discerning consumers, generate a process of sorting and sifting in which similar kinds of people self-select themselves into equivalent kinds of locations, without even knowing most of the time the specific identities of their future neighbours. It follows that the ties one has with fellow residents are often relatively restricted and that the actual social connections with neighbours can be rather muted.

My research with residents in different middle-class areas of Manchester, as well as across the UK using contacts from the Cultural Capital and Social Exclusion Survey and the National Child Development Study, thus reveal that it is possible for people to feel they passionately belong to a place even when they have little day-to-day contact with neighbours or local amenities. This is a form of 'community in the mind' hardly conforming to the preconceptions of the 'Big Society' with its invocation for formal joint activities and support services. Nonetheless, it is meaningful to, indeed highly valued by many more privileged residents. This is not to say that social interaction in these areas does not exist, but it often takes the form of friendship with 'like-minded' local residents and a degree of selectivity in which certain residents are often ignored or neglected. In this respect, neighbouring and local residence tends not to bring strangers together in a communitarian way but creates more isolated 'lifestyle enclaves'.

Two further features of this 'elective belonging' are important. Firstly, it is, ultimately, premised on a form of consumerist ethic of belonging and attachment in which places to live are actively chosen by the discerning individual. This lends itself to a politics which discriminates between discerning consumers and those who are prepared to 'put up with things' as well as an ethic of the individual as rational and strategic, able to operate effectively within market systems to decide what is of maximum value, which implicitly endorses those with a more educated and privileged habitus.[46] This is especially marked with respect to concerns about schooling, which, as Stephen Ball, Diane Reay and Tim Butler have shown, are now key issues in the way that middle-class parents assess the qualities of their residential location.[47] The important point, however, is that rather than drawing attention to the differences between the values and priorities of different social groups, so leading to a sense of class differences, this kind of orientation differentiates between 'good' and 'bad' consumers (or in Bauman's terms 'flawed' consumers), and hence lends itself to a moralising discourse around the capacity to be capable individuals.

Secondly, whilst elective belonging endorses a consumerist ethic in which places can be possessed by those with no historic ties but with appropriate amounts of economic and cultural capital, there are also strong moral concerns at work. In particular, having chosen to move to a location, there is a belief that one should 'put down roots' and take some interest in the local area, often associated with bringing up children in the local environment. But this also then shades into the view that it is those who have chosen to move to an area who better understand its distinctiveness than those who 'happen' to have been brought up there. This therefore amounts to a form of moral claim over belonging by those who chose to move to an area which can be strongly normalising and, by implication pathologising of those who do not share it – including those 'born and bred' in that locality. This kind of elective belonging is, ultimately, contingent, in the sense that any particular place can be abandoned in preference for another.

My point, then, is that the search for the 'Big Society' is not one which preoccupies the affluent middle classes in their own lives. They are largely content with an attachment to community which is relatively contingent, often secluded, and which is not policed by strong formal organisational ties. The mobilisation of the 'Big Society' discourse therefore carries with it a moralistic and pathologising overtone, where community ties are seen as in need of encouragement for some (poor, deprived, etc) people whereas the privileged middle classes are left to conduct life in their own way.

Conclusion

I have argued that in a period of extensive moral mobilisation around place and community, in which there is strong endorsement for the view that we need to reduce state intervention in favour of the 'Big Society', we need to recognise the fundamental nature of social inequalities in Britain today. I have emphasised that there is actually considerable resilience in the everyday lives of the popular classes, and little obvious sign of large-scale social breakdown warranting major public panic. To this extent, we need to recognise the creativity and ingenuity of most 'ordinary' citizens as they go about their daily life. This is not to deny the existence of intense areas and poverty and deprivation, such as those discussed by Clement and McKenzie in this book, but it is to argue that we should be careful not to proliferate the kinds of moralising discourses which so easily attach themselves to such problems.

What has happened, I have argued, is a marked disengagement of ordinary people's lives from formal institutional articulation, other than through a use of state services and amenities. This leads to a withdrawal of popular interest in formal political or civic activity experienced as belonging to other kinds of people and not the kind of thing which 'ordinary' people might be interested in. Hence, to seek to animate voluntary organisations or civic society through the so called 'Big Society' will only reproduce the existing paternalistic relationships of domination between social classes, while prized popular values of autonomy and self-reliance are seen to be more compatible with consumer-oriented market activity.

I have also argued that the 'Big Society' idea is profoundly hypocritical insofar as it fails to recognise that the ethics of belonging and attachment of the affluent middle classes are very different from those seen as desirable in policy circles. As writers such as Tim Butler have shown, the affluent middle classes increasingly seek to live in environments with relatively restricted social networks and neighbouring relations and make sure they live with 'people like themselves', thus helping, unwittingly, to generate forms of social segregation and inequality. It is this routine and unremarked reproduction and accentuation of social inequalities that should be the subject of public concern in this age of austerity.

Notes

1 Unsolicited email sent to me 2nd April 2012, by PS Events.
2 David Cameron, quoted in *The Guardian*, 16th April 2011.
3 See www.cabinet.office.gov.uk/big-society (accessed 12th April 2012).

4   AHRC Delivery Plan, 2011–2015, paragraph 2.4.4. Though the AHRC plan does also note that many of the evaluative concepts used in the 'Big Society' 'can be difficult to pin down'.

5   See A. Giddens (1994) *Beyond Left and Right*. Cambridge: Polity; Z. Bauman (1989) *Freedom*. Milton Keynes: Open University Press.

6   *Sustainable Communities: Building for the Future* (2003) HMSO: Office of the Deputy Prime Minister, p. 3.

7   On social exclusion see R. Levitas (2005) *The Inclusive Society?* (2nd ed.) Palgrave Macmillan; R. Putnam (2000) *Bowling Alone*. New York: Simon and Shuster; also see the useful overviews in D. Halpern (2000) *Social Capital*. Cambridge: Polity; R. Edwards, J. Franklin and J. Holland (eds) (2007) *Assessing Social Capital: Concept, Policy and Practice*. Cambridge: Scholars Press.

8   The culture of poverty idea originates in Oscar Lewis's (1960) *The Children of Sanchez*. London: Penguin, and emphasised the fatalism and lack of initiative in poor cultures.

9   P. Bourdieu (1984) *Distinction*. London: Routledge; P. Bourdieu et al (1999) *The Weight of the World*. Cambridge: Polity.

10 I should note here that in this paper I use 'working class' and 'popular classes' indistinguishably. This is deliberate because I wish to escape from a form of sociological logic which reduces forms of identity and practice to specific occupational groups – such as those of the 'working class'. Yet, given the prominent role of 'working class' identities in British society, I do not want to entirely abandon the term: this slippage between the populist and class-specific identities is important to retain.

11 M. Savage (2000) *Class Analysis and Social Transformation*. Milton Keynes: Open University Press.

12 C. Odone, *Sunday Times*, August 11th 2011.

13 Quoted in S. Duncan, R. Edwards and C. Alexander (eds) (2009) *Teenage Parenthood: What's the Problem?* London: Tufnell Press.

14 *British Crime Survey*, 2nd edition, 2010–11.

15 See BBC News, 28th February 2012.

16 See A. Warde, D. Southerton, W. Olsen and S. Cheung (n.d.) 'Deviating from the Norm: The Uneven Diffusion of Cultures of Consumption', mimeo.

17 S. Howlett (2009) 'Setting the Scene: Volunteering Trends and Issues', Roehampton University, mimeo.

18 H. Clarke, D. Sanders, M. Stewart and P. Whiteley (2006) 'Taking the Bloom off New Labour's Rose: Party Choice and Voter Turnout in Britain', *Journal of Elections, Public Opinion and Parties*, 16(1): 3–36.

19 P. Hall (1998) 'Social Capital in Britain', *British Journal of Politics*, 29: 417–61.

20 See A. Warde, G. Tampubolon, B. Longhurst, K. Ray, M. Savage and M. Tomlinson (2003) 'Trends in Social Capital: Membership of Associations in Great Britain', *British Journal of Political Science*, 33: 515–25.

21 See C. Pattie, P. Syed and P. Whiteley (2004) *Citizenship in Britain: Values, Participation and Democracy*. Cambridge: Cambridge University Press.

22 B. Jackson (1968) *Working Class Community*. London: Penguin.

23 R. McKibbin (1998) *Classes and Cultures in Britain*. Oxford: Oxford University Press.

24 See M. Savage (1987) *The Dynamics of Working Class Politics: The Labour Movement in Preston, 1880–1940*. Cambridge: Cambridge University Press;

M. Savage and A. Miles (1993) *The Remaking of the British Working Classes 1880–1940*. London: Routledge.

25 All details taken from J. Achur (2011) *Trade Union Membership 2010*. HMSO: Department for Business, Information and Skills.

26 Y. Li, M. Savage and A. Pickles (2003) 'Social Capital and Social Exclusion in England and Wales, 1972–1999', *British Journal of Sociology*, 54: 497–526.

27 L. Platt (2009) 'Social Participation, Social Isolation and Ethnicity', *The Sociological Review*, 57(4): 670–702.

28 See T. Bennett, M. Savage, E. Silva, A. Warde, M. Gayo-Cal and D. Wright (2009) *Culture, Class Distinction*. London: Routledge. See also B. LeRoux, H. Rouanet, M. Savage and A. Warde (2008) 'Class and Cultural Division in the UK', *Sociology*, 42(6): 1049–71; Y. Li, M. Savage and A. Warde (2008) 'Social Mobility and Social Capital in Contemporary Britain', *British Journal of Sociology*, 59(3): 391–411.

29 See F. Devine, M. Savage et al (2011) *Britain's New Class Structure*, mimeo, report to the BBC.

30 I have developed this argument at length in M. Savage (2010) 'The Politics of Elective Belonging', *Housing, Theory and Society*, 26(1): 115–61, where I argue that working-class households display a concern to 'dwell', characterised by extensive informal engagement with kin and acquaintances living nearby and a relatively weak set of interests in formal cultural engagement. This is in direct contrast to middle-class forms of 'elective belonging' discussed later in this chapter.

31 See R. Silverstone (1995) *Media and Everyday Life*. London: Routledge; D. Morley (2005) 'The Domestication of the Media and the Dis-location of Domesticity' in T. Berker, M. Hartmann, Y. Purie and K. Ward (eds) *The Domestication of Media and Technology*. Milton Keynes: Open University Press.

32 See McKenzie, this volume.

33 See A. Miles and M. Savage (2011) 'Telling a Modest Story: Accounts of Men's Upward Mobility from the National Child Development Study', *British Journal of Sociology*, 62(3): 418–41. V. Walkerdine and L. Jiminez (2012) *Gender, Work and Community After De-industrialisation*. Basingstoke: Palgrave.

34 R. Ford and M. Goodwin (2008) 'Angry White Men: Individual and Contextual Predictors of Support for the British National Party', *Political Studies*, 58: 1–25.

35 M. Biggs, and S. Knauss (forthcoming) 'Explaining Membership in the British National Party: A Multilevel Analysis of Contact and Threat', *European Sociological Review*.

36 See notably Hall (1998) *op. cit.*

37 See S. Majima and M. Savage (2007) 'Have There Been Culture Shifts in Britain?', *Cultural Sociology*, 1(3): 293–315. The specific problem here is that Inglehart argues that materialist values have declined in part because fewer people see fighting inflation as a national priority. However, given that inflation rates have fallen in most nations since the 1970s, the fact that fewer respondents identify this as a problem may simply reflect these economic trends.

38 A. Heath, J. Curtice and G. Elgenius (2009) 'Individualisation and the Decline of Class Identity' in M. Wetherell (ed.) *Identity in the 21ˢᵗ Century*. Basingstoke: Palgrave. See also P. Surridge (2007) 'Class Belonging: A Quantitative Exploration of Identity and Consciousness', *British Journal of Sociology*, 58(2): 207–27.

39   G. Evans and J. Tilley (2012) 'How Parties Shape Class Politics: Explaining the Decline of the Class Basis of Party Support', *British Journal of Political Science*, 42: 137–61.

40   P. Surridge (2012) 'A Reactive Core? The Configuration of Values in the British Electorate, 1986–2007', *Journal of Elections, Public Opinion and Parties*, 22(1): 51–76; A. Heath, D. Fisher, D. Sanders and M. Sobolewska (2011) 'Ethnic Heterogeneity in the Social Bases of Voting at the 2010 British General Election', *Journal of Elections, Public Opinion and Parties*, 21(2): 255–77.

41   G. Evans (2007) *Educational Failure and the White Working Class*. Basingstoke: Palgrave; J. Edwards (2000) *Born and Bred*. Oxford: Clarendon; McKenzie, this volume.

42   M. Savage, G. Bagnall and B. Longhurst (2001) 'Ordinary, Ambivalent and Defensive: Class Identities in the North-West of England', *Sociology*, 35(4): 875–92.

43   M. Savage (2007) 'Changing Social Class Identities in Post-War Britain: Perspectives from Mass-Observation', *Sociological Research Online*, 12(3); V. Walkerdine, H. Lucey and J. Melody (2002) *Growing Up Girl: Psychosocial Explorations of Gender and Class*. London: Palgrave.

44   See M. Savage, G. Bagnall and B. Longhurst (2005) *Globalization and Belonging*. London: Sage; M. Savage (2010) *Identities and Social Change in Britain Since 1940*. Oxford: Oxford University Press.

45   See more generally, T. Butler and G. Robson (2003) *London Calling*. Aldershot: Ashgate; S. Parker, E. Uprichard and R. Burrows (2007) 'Class Places and Place Classes: Geodemographics and the Spatialisation of Class', *Information, Communication and Society*, 10(6): 902–21; R. Atkinson (2006) 'Padding the Bunker: Strategies of Middle Class Disaffiliation and Colonization in the City', *Urban Studies*, 43(3): 819–32.

46   B. Skeggs (2004) *Class, Self, Culture*. London: Routledge.

47   S. Ball (2003) *Educational Strategies and the Middle Classes*. London: Falmer; D. Reay, G. Crozier and D. James (2011) *White Middle Class Identities and Urban Schooling*. Basingstoke: Palgrave.

10

Facing the Challenge of the Return of the Rich

Andrew Sayer

> There's class war, all right, but it's my class, the rich class, that's making war, and we're winning.
>
> Warren Buffett, *New York Times*, 26.11.2006

The last 15 years have seen a growth of sociological studies of the lived experience of class – studies of suffering, low self-esteem, hopelessness, sense of inferiority, but also pride, sense of entitlement and self-congratulation, snobbery and contempt for others. Many of them have been inspired by Bourdieu's work on symbolic domination and capitals, and lifestyles and tastes. These have rescued class analysis from sterile classification exercises and explored how deeply class affects people and the quality of their lives. In addition, the concept of recognition – initially associated with non-class inequalities and differences, such as those of ethnicity and sexuality – was soon used to argue that class was not merely a matter of unequal distribution of economic resources but of unequal recognition. Far from being a minor consideration, recognition often matters to people more than their economic standing, as it affects their sense of self-worth and position in the eyes of others. Yet despite the importance of these aspects of how class is lived, they are more a response to class inequalities than their cause; if people of different classes treated one another with respect, instead of suspicion and contempt, class inequalities would remain. There would still be major differences in life chances, strongly though far from exclusively shaped by economic processes. The economic inequalities derive not only from minority ownership of assets (particularly land, means of production, money and other financial assets), or indeed unequal pay, but also from the unequal division of labour which consigns people to extraordinarily different qualities of work and the recognition that goes with it.[1] Although research on class benefitted from the broader cultural turn through the awakening of interest in identity, symbolic domination and recognition, it was unfortunately accompanied by a neglect of the changing economic influences on class.

In turning away from political economy, sociological research on class largely ignored the biggest change in class structure over the last 30–40 years: the return of the rich. One can only agree with Savage and Williams that it is strange that sociology has taken so little interest in this and the rise of neoliberal plutocracy.[2] It was not merely that it simply wasn't noticed or considered interesting, or that class analysis had become uncritical – far from it – but that theoretical developments in the shape of the cultural turn, together with the post-structuralist emphasis on capillary power, also helped to draw attention away from the arterial economic power of the rich, so that 'elite studies' became 'deeply unfashionable'.[3] Insofar as Bourdieu himself and followers studied elites,[4] it was more in relation to their social capital than the sources of their economic capital.[5] It hasn't escaped the notice of the British public that the government that claimed 'we're all in it together' while implementing an austerity policy hugely skewed against people on low incomes, was itself packed with members of the resurgent upper classes. The rise of the Occupy movement in 2011, which has high-lighted the growing gulf between the top 1 per cent and the remaining 99 per cent, has caught sociology looking the other way, predominantly downwards, and taking little interest in the economic determinants of class.

While I endorse Savage and Williams' critique of sociology's neglect of the rich, I want to argue here that it is important to look at them not only in terms of their wealth and plutocratic power but to understand the sources of their income, their functional position in economic life – in other words, the nature of the economic social relations on which they depend. This requires us to take a critical look at property rights and above all to revive the classical distinction between earned and unearned income. This distinction has been fundamental in the histories of political economy, socialist thought and taxation, but interestingly has been largely forgotten during the last 30 years – precisely the period in which the rich have expanded their unearned income at an extraordinary pace. Sociologists are accustomed to leaving the analysis of the determinants of people's income and other economic capital to economists and political economists, but this would mean merely taking the return of the rich and super-rich as a given, rather than as something requiring explanation. More specifically I argue that the extraordinary expansion of financial services has enabled a new rentier class to gain power. If we are to comprehend these changes we need to link the sociology of class to literature in political economy; further, if we are to adopt a critical approach we need to assess the legitimations of the return of the rich offered in popular and academic discourse. This takes us outside the comfort zone of the sociology of class, but as so often happens, disciplinary parochialism is a barrier to understanding. The resulting focus might be termed 'the moral economy of class'.

The return of the rich

From 1920 to the 1970s, the top 1 per cent of earners' share of national income in the UK fell dramatically from nearly 20 per cent to 6 per cent, but since then, the rich have made an extraordinary comeback, so that in 2010 their share was back to 15 per cent.[6] Even after the credit crunch of 2007, the super-rich have continued to get even richer. Similar U-shaped curves can be found in other industrialised societies: the curve is particularly pronounced in English-speaking countries, slightly less so in Nordic and Southern European countries, and some major developing countries including India and China; it is only very shallow in Japan and some continental European countries including Germany, France and the Netherlands.[7] Meanwhile, for most of the bottom 90 per cent if not 99 per cent, which did relatively well in the post-war boom and saw their incomes rise steadily up to the 1970s, wages and salaries have stagnated in the last three decades. This was temporarily masked by a huge expansion of consumer credit and also by an increase in the participation of women in paid work.

Yet this slow growth of wages and salaries has not been the result of declining labour productivity, for this has continued to grow apace, only it is clear that the rich have been the primary beneficiaries of this. In the US, between 2002 and 2007, the income of the top 1 per cent grew 10.1 per cent annually, enabling them to capture 65 per cent of income growth, while the bottom 99 per cent grew only 1.3 per cent per year.[8] Whereas prior to 1970, wages and salaries had risen in tandem with labour productivity, since then workers have ceased to share much the benefit they have produced.[9]

Historical data on income shares produced by Thomas Piketty and Emmanuel Saez reveals a highly embarrassing fact for neoliberalism:

the most successful period of capitalist development – the post-war boom, at the bottom of the U-shaped curves – was the most equal.[10] It was also the most highly taxed, with top rates of income tax exceeding 80 per cent for much of the period.[11] With the end of the post-war boom, top rates of taxation have decreased dramatically, and it now scarcely seems credible that as recently as 1980 they exceeded 60 per cent in many countries (Table 10.1). It therefore makes less sense than ever to ignore the upper class.

Table 10.1   Top rates of taxation in selected countries 1980–2004 (%)

	1980	2004
UK	83	40
France	60	48
Germany	65	46
Ireland	60	42
Japan	75	50
Spain	66	35
Sweden	87	54
USA	70	35

Source: G. Irvin (2008) *Super Rich*. Cambridge: Polity, p. 21.

But it is not just a quantitative change, for it is associated with changes in the *kinds* of economic social relations through which income and other kinds of economic capital are acquired too. In the post-war boom, there was a strong relation between wealth and investment in the production of goods and services, but since that time there has been a shift to wealth extraction from existing assets via rent, interest, dividends and speculation. This has been the era of the return of the rentier. Since it reflects a change in economic social relations, it warrants the attention of sociologists of class.

While these social relations are functional in the sense that economic processes are organised and reproduced through them, like any institutionalised social relations they also imply particular norms regarding rights, entitlements and responsibilities that pertain to them. These both regulate the particular functions and legitimise them. Justifications of the different economic positions people occupy and of the rewards that they receive or should receive tend to appeal to several criteria. 'Need' as a criterion is especially important for those deemed unable to work and hence provide for themselves, such as the young, the old and the ill. 'Desert' is a particularly important criterion in popular thought insofar as people believe individuals should get what they deserve, and that hard work and valuable contributions should be rewarded while laziness and poor work should not. Finally, there are consequentialist justifications which appeal to the ultimate economic benefits of particular kinds of role or activity. But while these may serve as justifications, they do not necessarily *explain* economic roles and rewards. What people are able to get is largely dependent on what they *have*, relative to others,[12] be it merely labour power, or means of production, land, savings and access to cash, or, like private banks, the right to create credit money.

The issue of desert is complex and fraught in political theory, not least because how one might measure it is highly contested (for example, labour time, effort, merit, or usefulness and quality of the work). However, there is another way of approaching the issue of whether incomes are deserved or warranted, and that is via a distinction which figured prominently in classical political economy and political thought and policy until the end of the post-war boom: the distinction between earned and unearned income. Associated with it as an almost forgotten moral economic vocabulary – of *'rentiers'*, *'illth'*, *'impropery'*, *'functionless investors'* and *'the class of parasites'*.

The earned-unearned income distinction and its application

This distinction is fundamental both for understanding economic functions and how distribution is determined, and for evaluating such distributions in ethical terms. Interestingly, it has fallen out of use just when unearned income has expanded. Roughly speaking, earned income is what waged and salaried employees and self-employed people get from contributing to the production of goods and services. I don't mean to suggest that the size of their pay reflects what they deserve or contribute, but rather that their pay is at least conditional on providing goods and services that others can use. The relation between what we might think people deserve for their work – however we might want to measure that – and the income they actually get is pretty loose, not least because pay levels are influenced by power and scarcity rather than such considerations. The goods or services they produce and deliver have 'use-value', that is, qualities that make them useful or desirable, such as the nutritious and tasty quality of a meal, or the educational qualities of a maths lesson. Many of these products and services are sold in exchange for money in markets, and so have not only use-value but 'exchange-value' and hence are commodities. But many are funded by taxes, providing income for state sector workers, such as police officers and school teachers. Public sector workers, no less than private sector workers, can produce wealth – useful goods and services. These goods and services have costs of production – the labour itself, the care, education, training and support that enables people to work, and the costs of producing the materials used in the process. Some work has a more indirect relation to the production and distribution of goods and services, but is nevertheless necessary for efficient provisioning. For example, accounting is needed to monitor and manage the use of money and other resources in organisations; an insurance industry is important for providing security; and a legal system and police force are needed to protect people and property.

By contrast, unearned income derives not from providing goods or services that would not otherwise exist and hence incur costs of production, but from controlling an already-existing asset, such as land or buildings or spare money, that others lack but need or want, and who can therefore be charged for its use. If the asset already exists, then there are no costs of production apart from any maintenance costs, such as those for repainting a house. Those who receive unearned income from existing assets do so not because they are in any sense 'deserving' – they have not contributed anything that did not previously exist – but because they *can*. It is a reflection of power deriving from unequal control over existing assets. They use their property not as means of production or 'means of work but as an instrument for the acquisition of gain'.[13] This is what Ruskin called 'illth', deriving from what J. A. Hobson later called 'improperty'.[14] In most cases they have this power of control by virtue of property rights that legally entitle them to control it and dispose of it as they wish. Whereas earned income is work-based, unearned income is *asset-based*. In political economy, a person who derives unearned income from ownership of existing assets is known as a *rentier*.

Insofar as owners can extract money from others and hence be able to buy goods and services without producing goods and services in exchange, then those who are producing goods and services must be producing more than they themselves consume. In other words, they must be producing a surplus. The rentier is essentially siphoning off wealth produced by others. In turn, it implies that those who rely on earned income are generally paid less than the value of what they produce.

The rentiers are not the only ones living off unearned income, however. Children, the elderly and sick and those unable to work also get unearned income, whether provided by families or the state. But in these cases the unearned income is likely to be accepted as *warranted on the basis of needs*: producers are unlikely to object to having to produce a bit more than they themselves consume in order to support them. In practice, just who is deemed entitled to this income varies between societies, but it's generally based on a mixture of moral commitment and sense of duty, as in the case of parents providing for their children, and political decisions regarding state benefits. In both cases, the prime justification is usually that the recipients are needy and cannot reasonably be expected to work for an income, or that there are insufficient jobs for them.

But while the unearned income that they get is relatively easy to justify, the unearned income of adult, able-bodied rentiers is unwarranted and undeserved. They free-ride on the labour of others. The term 'free-riding' both denotes a particular kind of economic social relation and raises ethical objections to it. This relation between rentiers and producers is indisputably a social relation, one that is exploitative and an important generator of inequality in its own right. Yet sociology, the discipline that claims social relations as its field, has taken little interest in it. It is a relation that has become increasingly complex and globalised, so that British rentiers, for example, siphon off wealth produced by workers not only in Britain but in many other countries. Let us now examine the main sources of unwarranted unearned income, starting with the classical trio of rent, interest and profit.

The clearest case of the rentier is the landowner. The mere ownership of land or buildings does not make it any more productive, and while it can be claimed that improvements to them should be paid for because they involve production costs and produce enhanced goods, pure rent is not payment for production but merely for access; as Tawney observed, rent is like a private tax on the industry of others.[15]

Interest on loans is also a charge for the use an existing asset – savings – which, as money, is a claim on the labour and products of others. However, banks do not merely act as intermediaries between savers and borrowers by lending their existing deposits, but create new credit money, simply by writing deposits into the accounts of borrowers; the interest they charge far exceeds any production costs in creating the credit money.[16] Lending that fuelled asset price bubbles was a major component of the 2007 credit crunch,[17] and has had an important effect on economic inequalities. For Marx, it was primarily those who made money out of money – 'interest-bearing capital' – who made up 'the class of parasites'.[18]

In classical political economy, profit is the third member of this trio of sources of unearned income. The profits of private (productive) employers derive from their ownership of the means of production and the product, and the dependency of non-owners of means of production on them for employment. Pure capitalists – that is ones who just own their firms and delegate management to others – are not contributing to wealth creation, but merely using their power relative to those of propertyless workers to appropriate the difference between costs and the value of what the workers (and managers) produce. Their income is unearned.

Dividends on shares provide another major source of unearned income. Since over 95 per cent of share transactions are in the secondary market, only in less than 5 per cent of cases does the money paid for them go to the company, and thus might be claimed to be a payment for contributing to any objective productive investment. The extraordinary feature of share ownership is not so much limited liability (for losses made by the company) but that it provides a potentially indefinite source of unearned income – an unlimited asset. Trading in shares serves as a further source of unearned income. Since the growth of share-ownership has exceeded growth of the number of shares in recent decades, average prices have tended to rise too, creating a bubble, so this source has proved lucrative.[19] The development over the last 30 years of the shareholder value movement – a highly successful rentier campaign – has made share prices the primary concern of the management of companies. Firms that fail to deliver rising share prices – for example, by ploughing most of their profits into productive investment instead of distributing them as dividends – are disciplined by the market for companies as they become vulnerable to takeover by managements that will deliver shareholder value.

Banking and speculation are not the only activities in the financial sector that have enabled some to become incredibly rich. Some have done it by arranging major transactions such as mergers and takeovers, involving many millions of pounds, and taking a small percentage commission. In effect, they are standing 'close to a big till',[20] and it is easy for them to put their hands in it without breaking any laws; the income reflects position rather than contribution. It is in their interest to promote as many transactions as possible. Erturk et al call this 'value-skimming' and argue that the financial intermediaries have been a major but hidden beneficiary of financialisation, overlooked by those who limit their gaze to bankers or CEOs. High-income but largely anonymous financial intermediaries far outnumber the much-publicised

CEOs; Savage and Williams estimate that in the City of London there are circa 15,000 senior intermediaries employed at a principal or partner level in investment banking, hedge funds and other kinds of trading and private equity (as well as those providing support services in law and accounting).[21]

Contemporary mainstream economists are of course likely to object to this account. One of the things financial systems, whether privately or publicly run, are supposed to do is move underused or idle resources, particularly savings, to where they can be used more productively, thereby promoting 'allocational efficiency'. The money made by those who do this is supposedly a reward for enabling this. However, this definition is frequently used as a cover for a quite different version of allocational efficiency that is specific to capitalism, in which the allocation of resources among competing ends is according to where expected rates of financial return are highest. This could be where labour is most exploitable, where consumer incomes are highest, where prospects for extracting rent are best, or where asset inflation is highest (for example, the latest bubble), or where taxation is lowest. It could be logging in Sumatra, or mining in Peru, or luxury apartments in Dubai, or buying up land in Africa to rent out, or selling shares.

There is a more fundamental slippage in the use of the word 'investment' itself. This is central to the legitimation of the rich, and their symbolic domination. Investment is invariably understood to be a good thing, and can provide an appealing cover for a vast range of activities, yet the term is used in two radically different senses:

(1) *Use-value/object-oriented definitions* focus on what it is that is invested *in* (e.g. infrastructure, equipment, training)
(2) *Exchange-value/'investor'-oriented definitions* focus on the financial gains from any kind of lending, saving, purchase of financial assets or speculation – regardless of whether they contribute to any objective investment (1), or benefit others.

The standard move is to elide this distinction and pass off the second as based on the first. But it is also perfectly possible for successful investments in the first sense to fail to provide financial benefits to investors in the second sense. The use of my taxes for investing in infrastructure on the other side of the country may benefit others but not me. Conversely, it is equally possible for lucrative investments in the second sense to have neutral or negative effects on productive capacity – through, asset stripping, value-skimming, and rent-seeking.

Such elisions have become so commonplace not so much through a desire to deceive than through ignorance, coupled with the fact that under capitalism individuals have little or no interest in checking whether their 'investments' (2) have positive, neutral or negative effects on the production of goods and services; to the rentier-'investor', £1million from rent is no different from £1million from new productive capacity.

The return of the rentier

So far we have provided empirical evidence of the return of the rich in recent decades, and identified the sources of unearned income that rentiers and capitalists draw upon, but we have not shown that the rise of the rich is very much a product of the rise of rentier, as opposed to a result of increased productive investment, and thus implies a qualitative change in the nature of the economic ruling class. Here we briefly summarise how these sources of income have grown in the context of a long-term crisis of over-accumulation associated with the rapid development of financialisation. There are many accounts of this crisis, of course, but the following sketch identifies some key elements common to the more well-founded ones.

The return of the rentier is a feature – part cause and part consequence – of the crisis of over-accumulation that has been developing for the past 30 years. As we saw earlier, while labour productivity has continued to grow, wages and salaries have on the whole grown much more slowly since the 1970s, partly because of the rise of cheap-labour producers, particularly China, and partly because of the associated weakening of organised labour, which Thatcher and Reagan took advantage of. By the end of the 1970s rates of profit from productive investment were declining. Slow growth in real incomes for the majority meant slow growth in aggregate demand for goods and services so competition among producers intensified, squeezing profits. Neoliberal prioritisation of keeping inflation low meant increased real rates of interest for rentiers. In this context the shareholder value movement gathered momentum, demanding double figure rates of return on investments and continual rises in share prices. The growth of financial securities – including most notoriously Collateralised Debt Obligations based on mortgages – greatly expanded the creation of debt, which, extraordinarily, was seen as a source of wealth creation rather than as a deadweight cost on the economy.[22] As David Harvey put it, capital switched increasingly from the 'primary circuit of capital', where it was invested in the production of goods and services, to the 'secondary circuit' where it was invested in property and other financial assets, as means of extracting wealth via rent, interest, dividends or speculation.[23] In the last 30 years the 'value of financial assets and finance-based income as a percent of GDP has risen dramatically in many countries'.[24] Epstein and Jayadev also show that rentier income has made a spectacular comeback since the 1970s in many OECD countries, especially in countries with limited unionisation, and hence where there was limited resistance to appropriation of economic rents by financial interests.[25] Increased amounts of fictitious capital, involving claims on the value of future production – that is, on labour and what it produces – outstripped credible forecasts of production growth. Yet this diversion of investment (2) into ways of extracting wealth from existing assets was (mis)represented as 'wealth creation' by the financial sector. The expansion of consumer credit initially helped to offset the stagnation of consumer demand, but in the longer run the rising burden of consumer debt has depressed it further.

Financialisation is reflected not only in the growth of the rich and super-rich, whether CEOs, hedge fund owners, bankers or intermediaries, but in a changed economic social relation of the top 40 per cent of households in the UK to other classes. Froud et al estimate that this 'fortunate 40 per cent' have been able to benefit from savings 'invested' via pensions and life assurance in the stock market, accentuating inequalities in retirement.[26] In Britain and the US, they own the majority of shares, mostly through the medium of pension and insurance funds. This flow from household savings to a largely parasitic stock market, accounting for 75 per cent of corporate equity, equalled productive investment in Britain in the 1990s. Most of this 'fortunate 40 per cent' rely mainly on wages and salaries for their income; they are only rentiers in part, and then largely in a passive role, relying on pension funds and insurance companies to seek out returns. Such saving and indirect rentier income is beyond the reach of the remaining 60 per cent of households on lower incomes, many of whom have major debts. The majority of the top 40 per cent thus have a dual and indeed 'contradictory class location',[27] in which they both create wealth and extract it from elsewhere via securities, though this does not happen simply within the national space, but in a much less determinate and increasingly globalised network of flows. The composition of the rich and super-rich above them has shifted since the end of the post-war boom from production-oriented managers and owners to finance-dependent rentiers.

In the nineteenth century, middle-class savings went mostly into productive investment via initial public offerings of shares, whereas now productive investment is mostly financed out of undistributed profits, while most middle-class savings go into the purchase of existing corporate securities on the secondary market.[28] Yet it is the nineteenth-century model of 'productionist capitalism' which provides the basis of popular (mis-) understandings and spurious legitimations of contemporary stock market 'investment'.

Thus, while financialisation has allowed an extraordinary concentration of 'arterial' power in the City of London, Wall Street and the like, this is nevertheless dependent on and supportive of a more dispersed, capillary power of middle-class savers. The latters' mortgage payments also fuelled securitisation, which in turn allowed lenders to create more credit and create a house price bubble – a strategy which, notoriously, extended to sub-prime mortgage markets. The huge expansion of credit for consumers and property owners and pensions dependent on the value of financial securities is symptomatic of a rentier economic imaginary in which wealth extraction through interest and rent on property is mistaken for wealth creation.

The old kind of rentiers attacked by authors such as John Stuart Mill were passive: they simply waited for rents or interest to roll in from their property, shares or other assets. But the new rentiers associated with financialisation are much more active, for they compete with others to seek out the biggest speculative gains and the assets with the highest returns from all around the world. They may actually have to work hard to do this. But one can work hard at using existing assets to milk rent or interest, or gain arbitrage profits, without producing any goods and services that have use-value. So, even though they work, unless their activities contribute at least indirectly to the production of goods and services, their income is still unearned. The key issue is whether one just uses existing assets to prise payments out of others, or adds to the output of new goods and services. The income of the so-called working rich is still mostly unearned.

So is there a rentier class? The vast majority of the rich and super-rich's wealth comes from unearned income, so we can say they are clear members of this class. The shift in power from productive capitalists to rentiers is a major feature of the neoliberal period and the growth of financialisation. The fortunate 40 per cent are only bit-players in the rentier game and their involvement is largely passive. Their main economic role is productive. They are ideologically significant as the main targets of 'the financialisation of everyday life',[29] which encourages them to see everything as having a price, and to use their property and savings as a basis for getting unearned income, legitimised as 'investment'. Instead of seeing themselves as members of a common society with common institutions, contributing what they can, sharing in its growth and pooling risks with others, they are encouraged to see themselves as competing individuals operating in markets with no responsibility towards anyone else. The money pages of the newspapers encourage them to think of this as merely being prudent and smart, a means by which they could have 'a stake in the wealth of the country'. By implication, the bottom 60 per cent, who cannot afford to save significant amounts and share in this income, lack the prudence, self-reliance and 'enterprise' to do this. Furthermore, at a material level – in terms of the value of their houses and pensions – it locks the fortunes of millions into those of the financial sector, so that, as we have seen in the recent credit crisis, however much they deplore its irresponsibility, they are also dependent on the financial sector. Further, the power of the sector to privatise its gains and socialise its costs, to turn corporate debt into sovereign debt, falls most heavily on the bottom 60 per cent. For them, the 'rate of exploitation' – however it is measured – has clearly increased.

Plutocracy

At a structural level, the financial sector's influence over the economy means that even without any lobbying or funding of political parties or influence over the media, it can dominate political decision-making regarding the economy. But it has not been content to rely on this. Part of its success has been due to sustained campaigning to boost its image and persuade governments of its social value as an economic powerhouse, as the goose that lays the golden egg, provided it is allowed to do what it likes. Wealth extraction from the world economy is passed off as wealth creation. As Brett Christopher has shown, the recent 'growth' in the contribution of the financial sector to leading economies owes much to recategorisations of functions that were formerly considered as merely involving transfers of wealth as actually productive of wealth and therefore contributing to GDP.[30] Engelen et al argue that through a 'distributional coalition' whose membership shifts as different financial instruments and sources of income come to the fore, the financial sector has developed its own stories to help resist ceding power even as it has depended on taxpayers to bail it out.[31] As the documentary 'Inside Job' shows,[32] key rentiers from finance have moved into government and back again to finance (sometimes via academic positions) to ensure that regulation is minimised. Engelen et al allege that both major British political parties, Labour and the Conservatives, have suffered from the Stockholm syndrome – identifying with their capturers in the financial sector. No doubt sociological research on the financial and government elites would show extensive connections too. But it is not enough merely to document new forms of plutocracy. It is also necessary to subject the justificatory narratives of the financial sector to critical scrutiny. Though the sectors' activities are notoriously obscure and arcane, it is not merely a matter of understanding them in the style of an engineer explaining how something works, for there is also something more fundamental but also relatively simple: it is a matter of assessing whether it is productive or parasitic, which is also a matter of economic justice and moral economy.

'The successful' and the belief in a just world

The legitimation of the resurgence of the rich has depended on more than their self-presentation as 'wealth creators'. In 1998 New Labour announced itself 'intensely relaxed about people getting filthy rich'. Having initially claimed not to be concerned about the gap between rich and poor, Tony Blair later said:

> What I meant by that was not that I don't care about the gap, so much as I don't care if there are people who earn a lot of money. They're not my concern. I do care about people who are without opportunity, disadvantaged and poor. We've got to lift those people but we don't necessarily do that by hammering the people who are successful (*Guardian*, 2005).

He thus adroitly evaded the question of whether the rich were exploitative or undeserving. In so doing he was affirming a common set of assumptions in everyday thought, indeed a populist belief in meritocracy, called by Melvin Lerner 'the belief in a just world'.[33] According to this view, we live in world in which not only are merit and effort rewarded and lack of merit penalised, but differences in rewards can be taken as reflections of merit. A recent report from the Joseph Rowntree Foundation on attitudes to income inequality shows a systematic tendency of people to view those 'above' them more favourably than those below, and even to 'invent or exaggerate the virtues (and therefore desert) of those with high incomes in order to justify existing inequalities'.[34] Wishful thinking (who would not want to live in a just world?), coupled with deference, allows the dominated to grant the rich generous approval, and avoid the pain of justified resentment. As Bourdieu argued, symbolic domination is most effective when internalised by the dominated.

Conclusion

One of the peculiarities of the language of class is the terminology of 'working' and 'middle class', which not only avoids the connotations of inferiority in 'lower class', but allows the upper class to hide in the middle, so that for example, the right-wing press can represent proposals to tax the upper class as attacks on the middle class. In numerical terms, the new rentiers may seem hardly worth acknowledging in an overview of class, understood as social stratification. Yet their significance in the great political, economic and social changes of the last few decades far outweighs their numbers. In addition, there has been an extension of limited rentier sources of income to the middle classes via house-price inflation and pensions geared to financial assets. It implies a shift in power from the post-war boom managerial, production-based elite, to new active rentiers whose income is largely unearned and based on hidden social relations to tenants, debtors, savers and other market actors.

The content of this chapter might seem strangely economic for a contribution to a sociology book, but unless the sociology of class does something about its neglect of the determinants of economic capital it will fail to understand some of the most momentous changes in class structure in recent decades. It is not merely a matter of relating recognition back to distribution, but of also looking at the sources of income of different classes and their economic roles within contemporary capitalism, acknowledging that some may be *interdependent* and involve exploitative or parasitic relations. It is also necessary, both for explanation and critique, to assess the role of neoliberal discourse in relation to the development of finance and unearned income. And even though the return of the rentier has been driven by economic change rather than shifts in recognition there is still a place for addressing issues of symbolic domination in relation to the rentier class, its systematic mis-recognition of the sources of its own advantages, its representation in popular culture, and its domination of the media. In addition to critical analysis of symbolic domination within the recognition approach we need to look at the moral economy of class, at the economic relations *between* the elite and the rest; for this the distinction between earned and unearned income is crucial, particularly for demonstrating that we are not all in it together.

Notes

1 A. Sayer (2011) 'Habitus, Work and Contributive Justice', *Sociology*, 45(1): 7–21.
2 M. Savage and K. Williams (2008) 'Elites: Remembered in Capitalism and Forgotten in Social Science', *The Sociological Review*, 56(s1): 1–24.
3 Ibid., p. 4.
4 P. Bourdieu (1996) *The State Nobility*. Cambridge: Polity; P. Bourdieu (2005) *The Social Structures of the Economy*. Cambridge: Polity; F. Denord, J. Hjellbrekke, O. Korsnes, F. Lebaron and B. LeRoux (2011) 'Social Capital in the Field of Power: The Case of Norway', *The Sociological Review*, 59(1): 86–108.
5 'As regards economic capital, I leave it to others; it's not my area' – P. Bourdieu (1993) *Sociology in Question*. London: Sage, p. 32.
6 Source: The World Top Incomes Database: http://g-mond.parisschoolof-economic.eu/topincomes.
7 A. B. Atkinson, T. Picketty and E. Saez (2011) 'Top Incomes in the Long Run of History', *Journal of Economic Literature*, 49(1): 3–71.
8 Ibid.
9 T. I. Palley (2007) *Financialization: What it is and Why it Matters*. Working Paper No. 525, The Levy Economics Institute and Economics for Democratic and Open Societies, Washington, D.C.
10 T. Picketty and E. Saez (2003) 'Income Inequality in the United States, 1913–1998', *Quarterly Journal of Economics*, 118(1): 1–39.
11 Ibid.
12 E. O. Wright (2000) *Class Counts*. Cambridge: Cambridge University Press, p. 28.
13 R. H. Tawney (1921) *The Acquisitive Society*. London: G. Bell and Sons, pp. 65–6.
14 J. A. Hobson (1937) *Property and Improperty*. London: Gollancz.
15 Tawney (1921) *op. cit.*
16 M. Hudson (2011) 'How Economic Theory Came to Ignore the Role of Debt', *Real World Economics Review*, 57, 6th September 2011, www.paecon.net; M. Mellor (2010) *The Future of Money: From Financial Crisis to Public Resource*. London: Pluto Press.
17 E. Engelen, I. Ertürk, J. Froud, S. Johal, A. Leaver, M. Moran, A. Nilsson and K. Williams (2011) *After the Great Complacence: Financial Crisis and the Politics of Reform*. Oxford: Oxford University Press.
18 K. Marx (1972) *Capital, Vol. III*. London: Lawrence and Wishart, p. 545.
19 Engelen et al (2011) *op. cit.*
20 I. Erturk, J. Froud, A. Leaver and K. Williams (2007) 'Agency: A Positional Critique', *Economy and Society*, 36(1): 51–77.
21 Savage and Williams (2011) *op. cit.*
22 Hudson (2011) *op. cit.*
23 D. Harvey (1978) 'The Urban Process Under Capitalism: A Framework for Analysis', *International Journal of Urban and Regional Research*, 2: 101–31.
24 J. Crotty (2005) 'The Neoliberal Paradox: The Impact of Destructive Product Market Competition and "Modern" Financial Markets on Nonfinancial Corporation Performance in the Neoliberal Era' in G. A. Epstein (ed.) *Financialization and the World Economy*. Cheltenham: Edward Elgar, p. 85.

25 G. A. Epstein and A. Jayadev (2005) 'The Rise of Rentier Incomes in OECD Countries: Financialization, Central Bank Policy and Labor Solidarity' in G. A. Epstein (ed.) *Financialization and the World Economy*. Cheltenham: Edward Elgar, p. 65.

26 J. Froud, S. Johal, C. Haslam and K. Williams (2001) 'Accumulation Under Conditions of Inequality', *Review of International Political Economy*, 8(1): 66–95.

27 Wright (2000) *op. cit.*

28 Froud et al (2001) *op. cit.*, p. 79.

29 R. Martin (2002) *The Financialization of Everyday Life*. New Jersey: Temple University Press.

30 B. Christophers (2011) 'Making Finance Productive', *New Political Economy and Society*, 40(1): 112–40.

31 Engelen et al (2011) *op. cit.*

32 *Inside Job*, 2010: http://www.sonyclassics.com/insidejob/.

33 M. Lerner (1980) *The Belief in a Just World: A Fundamental Delusion*. New York: Plenum.

34 Joseph Rowntree Foundation (2009) *Understanding Attitudes to Tackling Economic Inequality*. York: JRF, p. 5. Available at http://www.jrf.org.uk/sites/files/jrf/attitudes-tackling-economic-inequality-full.pdf.

11
Conclusion: Three Challenges to the Exportation of Sociological Knowledge

Will Atkinson, Steven Roberts and Mike Savage

We have seen plenty of evidence in the foregoing pages that the post-crisis politics of austerity, and the longer-term neoliberal orthodoxy from which they spring, hardly meet the criteria of 'fairness' set by those who pursue them. Far from the burden being shared equally amongst the populace or the capital-rich shouldering the greatest weight of government belt-tightening, as claimed, it is those lacking the resources valued within Western societies – the unemployed, the low-paid, those with fewer qualifications, the dominated – who suffer most, who disproportionately endure the agonising material and symbolic privations of economic crises and state retrenchment, who have their only modes of attaining recognition remorselessly devalued and who have their reasonable aspirations and hopes for the future closed down. Whether it is school pupils or parents forced to think of themselves as unconstrained, responsible choosers but without the social conditions to make the 'right' choices, first-generation university students battling the constraints of their inherited capital to attain the educational outcomes vaunted by the dominant, families struggling with the loss of that which once furnished some degree of self-worth or communities and modes of living disregarded or assaulted by the discourse and policies of the 'Big Society', this conclusion – a *collective* conclusion – holds firm.

The contributions to this volume have not simply been personal opinion pieces. Political commitment and concern runs through them, for sure, but they have been underpinned by not only a dedication to the language and logics of social science, the better to grasp the contemporary sources of social suffering and domination, but research programmes or lines of argument developed on the basis of their academic merit rather than direct governmental or other outside commission. On that basis, therefore, they can be said to represent the value of rigorous, critical social science *extricated from external demands* as a vital vantage point from which to better speak out in the name of truth and throw accepted ways of thinking and governing into question, thus furnishing the possibility of being of civic *service* without lapsing into *servility* to any one party, organisation, pressure group etc.[1] Yet the current state of the social scientific field poses a problem. It might be said that it gained its necessary independence, or autonomy, only in the post-war period as it gradually disentangled itself from explicit philanthropic, moralising or labourist political interests and projects (such as those of Rowntree, the early LSE and Michael Young respectively), professionalised, became more populous and established its own languages, methods, journals and mechanisms of cross-control.[2] Of course sections remained strongly bound up with the welfarist interests of the state through the sixties, but direct links into the political and bureaucratic fields slowly attenuated, as did (after the decline of *New Society*) sociology's availability and appeal to the 'well-informed citizen', to use Alfred Schutz's phrase, while the sector of the field producing for restricted, *internal* consumption blossomed, bolstered by the evolution of publishing houses aiming to maximise revenues by developing distribution circuits and pricing practices favourable to interior circulation rather than exportation.[3] Paradoxically, therefore, sociology developed the instruments and stakes necessary for the greater exercise of reason and the pursuit of truth at precisely the same time as it lost its inclination to plough its activity back into wider public debate.

We know, however, that unless the message of this volume is exported beyond the sociological field in which it has been produced into the everyday lifeworlds of a broader audience, whether those within the field of power or those subject to it, our efforts to document the perniciousness of the present political juncture will have been in vain. In this closing piece we want to reflect, in a suggestive fashion, on some of the very real obstacles to any action oriented to this goal, less as a rumination on the over-hyped debate over 'public sociology' so much as a realistic appraisal of the political economy of knowledge production. In particular, a trio of barriers to the effective circulation of critical sociological knowledge rooted in the particular configuration of power in UK society today can be detected.

1. Increased competition in the production of politically-useful knowledge

First of all, the advent of what Nigel Thrift calls 'knowing capitalism' has brought in its wake *growing competition in the production of politically-useful knowledge*. From having the ear and direct funds of political circles, in other words, academic social science has now become merely one among a crowd of providers of information upon which policymakers can draw for their own purposes, and not a particularly highly regarded one at that. We refer here not primarily to the growing trend, explored elsewhere, for in-house research amongst private and public organisations with resources, data, access and ethical clearance far beyond those of sociologists, but interests and orientations alien to the social scientific field, and challenging the perceived need for and value of academic intervention.[4] More significantly, since the seventies there has been an explosion of institutions and organisations – generally dubbed 'think-tanks' – explicitly dedicated to producing politically-pertinent research on this or that particular theme (poverty, foreign affairs, economics, education, etc). Forming a space of contestation of their own,[5] they are far from being all of a piece – some boast their academic and 'independent' orientation, others proudly declare their partisan interests; some are endowed with massive budgets from wealthy donors, a large staff and multiple programmes of activity, others are more modest – yet they are all united by a fundamental feature of the field as a whole: it is thoroughly *heteronomous*, that is, overtly or covertly tied to the idiom and aim of propping up or challenging pre-existing worldviews and policy programmes or, at best, investigating pre-constructed 'social issues', whether attached to the political right or (increasingly in the nineties) the 'left of centre'. Dispensing with mechanisms of cross-control such as peer review and collective reflexivity, vaunting their capacities to simplify and synthesise and using their vast reserves of economic capital to effectively court the media and policymakers, these institutions tell politicians – many of whom circulate in and out of top think-tank personnel (David Willetts, Michael Gove, Iain Duncan Smith, James Purnell, Kitty Ussher, etc.) – only what they already know, or what they want to know, under the façade of 'evidence' and, thus, wield undue influence.

The Policy Exchange, for instance – a free-market pressure group only a decade old – is known to be David Cameron's favoured source of ideas and eagerly pumps out endless reports extolling tax cuts, workforce flexibilisation and reduced public spending as the best means of 'balancing the books' after the crisis, but even those at the lower reaches of the bureaucratic field, tasked with the practical, everyday reality of constructing 'evidence-based policy' and overwhelmed by the volume of (often inconclusive) research findings, favour the clarity and simplicity of think-tank talk over methodological caution and critical capacity in the quest to 'boost the persuasiveness of the narrative', as lucidly demonstrated by Alex Stevens' ethnography of the civil service.[6] Social scientific research breaking with the dominant political categories of thought and identifying complex, deep-rooted problems not amenable to remedy by the kind of superficial policy programmes preferred within the political field is simply dismissed as of little use or relevance in answering the types of questions posed by those in positions of power.

2. Increased dependence of social science on the journalistic field

At a recent training event for social scientists held by a major funding body on how to influence policy-making, one of the overriding messages was that, given the dominance of think-tanks and their mode of communication, academics were best off trying to have an indirect impact by becoming visible and available 'public intellectuals'. Quite apart from the dangers built into such a model of intellectual intervention (whether in the 'total' to 'specific' variety of Sartre and Foucault respectively), in which the individual, separated from a *collective* intellectual enterprise and invested with the authority of charisma, risks detachment from the controls of the sociological field and presenting one perspective as communal reason (the better to be shot down with a 'so much for sociology'), this nugget of advice neglects the extent to which meaningful dissemination of social scientific knowledge is *mediated and controlled by the journalistic field.*[7] Possessing a monopoly on the means of public communication, its players determine who will be interviewed, how it will be framed, who is bestowed the honour of writing a newspaper 'opinion piece' and whose press releases – those tickets for exportation increasingly demanded by publicity-hungry universities and so often dashed out in vein by academics – are worthy, in short, who will be consecrated as a 'public intellectual', in line with their *own* logics and interests.[8]

Whatever the structure of the UK journalistic field and its homologies with the social space of classes – and it does not take a correspondence analysis to deduce that *The Guardian*, the BBC, *The Times*, ITV, *The Sun* etc. have somewhat different staff intakes, interests and audiences – it is, like the space of institutions producing political knowledge, highly heteronomous as a whole, that is, utterly bound to and implicated in economic and political struggles.[9] The first consequence is that, being tied to the battle for viewing figures, audience ratings and readership numbers, not only for purposes of revenue but for indicators of being 'on the ball', 'cutting edge' and so on, depending on the organisations' sources of capital, modes of communication conducive to wide but shallow coverage tend to be favoured in the field, to greater and lesser degrees, and foisted upon those coming into contact with it. Short and simplifying solutions are wanted for complex problems and ill-posed questions; fast talk and wit are required over logic and thorough analysis. Indeed, given that such dispositions are forged and valued in the journalistic field, is it so surprising that those who currently pass in the UK for visible 'public intellectuals' on the left as well as the right are overwhelmingly *journalists themselves*, or at least writers trained in or oriented toward the media game? Meanwhile Zygmunt Bauman and Anthony Giddens, perhaps the two figures of British sociology the most lauded (and lambasted) for their status as 'public intellectuals',[10] are in fact virtual non-entities in the media, the one having their populist tone and prolific output misrecognised by sociologists as wider impact, the other circumventing popular consciousness altogether by entering the political field instead.

Moreover, when social scientists *are* given air time or column inches it tends to be for the purpose of buttressing the interests of the players within the journalistic field (whether openly imposed by proprietors or not). Academics are thus wheeled in for two minutes or a paragraph as 'experts' to back up the narrative, more or less hidden under the guise of 'impartiality', of the broadcaster or writer, even if wholly twisted out of context, or to be dismissed by the apparent wisdom of common sense or personal experience; all else is simply ignored or, more accurately, never even encountered due to its irrelevance to the journalistic libido. Some media figures, of course, are far more attentive to and appreciative of social scientific research and are, in turn, given serious attention by appreciative social scientists, but researchers must be aware that relying on such mediators as their mouthpiece means that their message will always be filtered through a very different lens fashioned in very different circumstances. Rather than speak from their own point of view, in other words, social scientists will forever be spoken through another's.

3. Increased attacks on the relative autonomy of social science

The final challenge to effective intervention by social scientists is undoubtedly the most serious of all. Having steadily won its spaces of autonomy from exogenous interests in the post-war period, even if relative and contested, sociology has, since the 1980s, found that precious property *increasingly under threat from the entity on which it depends for its existence*: the state. Initiated by a government hostile to independent academic endeavour and, particularly, to the social sciences that opposed it, but woven into the broader agenda of 'new public management' foisting market mechanisms on the public sector in the name of efficiency, there are several layers to this assault.[11] The most basic is, quite simply, the unanticipated, yet thoroughly deleterious, transformation of the conditions of intellectual production wrought by the constant obligation for audit, assessment, accountability and measurement and financial reward of performance, manifest most obviously in the recurrent round of pressure and paperwork engendered by the Research Assessment Exercise (now the Research Excellence Framework) and the Quality Assurance Agency. Paradoxically these mechanisms, combined with the expectations of greater teaching contact time to match ballooning student fees, diminish the time necessary to do effectively that which they purport to measure. More importantly, however, they operate to undermine academic independence by favouring the persistent intrusion of non-academic logics into intellectual production, observable not least in the blunt efforts by academic management concerned to maximise scores to actively dictate individual researchers' publication and grant proposal plans. With 'success' measured by benchmarks imposed from without and reducible in essence to quantity over quality, whatever the rhetoric, the result is an orthodoxy encouraging the endless production of rushed, repetitive, trite papers and research grants aiming to advance little more than their probability of acceptance.

The added danger here, of course, is that academics thereby inadvertently sustain the dominant constructions of the world and the political and economic interests encoded in them by conforming to the 'funding priorities' (or 'themes') and definitions of 'impact' imposed by the state on Higher Education Funding Council for England (HEFCE) and the research councils. National security (including through multicultural politics), strengthening global competitiveness by making businesses run better, or even, as is the case with the Arts and Humanities Research Council (AHRC), finding academic justification for the coalition government's Big Society agenda, thus become the problematics toward which academics are increasingly obliged to orient themselves if they want to attain the funds through which their worth is gauged, while concrete processes of feedback to demonstrable stakeholders, preferably in the private as well as public and third sector, are the sanctioned modes of dissemination. A volume such as this one, therefore, and the drive to invest its findings into broad public debate, are increasingly *delegitimised* undertakings according to the measures of value imported from outside, and we undertake them well aware that they fail to tick the right boxes on the multitude of pro formas auditing intellectual production. Of course it would be crude and contradictory not to recognise the multitude of interests and struggles within and around the universes of decision-making regulating academic practice and the spaces still open for support of critical inquiry, seeing as the Economic and Social Research Council (ESRC) has funded much of the research drawn upon within this book. Nevertheless, the creeping intervention and regulation from outside forces, added to the competition and mediation from think-tanks and journalism, is in danger of inducing a broad heteronomisation of social science conducive to conservative and complicit thought rather than critical and contrarian intervention.

These, then, are the daunting tides to be navigated in propagating the message of the volume, and social scientific research more generally, beyond the disciplinary field in which it has been formed and in which it will be readily consumed. Ultimately, it might be said, only with concerted, communal action by sociologists practicing reflexivity, in collaboration with other collectives upholding principles of autonomy, and only after the full and frank dialogue *with* the media necessary for full and frank dialogue *through* the media, could we hope to speak effectively and relentlessly to those not disposed to hear or accept sociological knowledge, to feed the space of political position-takings and induce the revolution in the field of political practice necessary to reverse the damage done by 30 years of neoliberalism. We know this is no mean feat, and that the chances of success are contingent upon a range of intermediary changes to modes of organisation and intervention within sociology, but, as Durkheim put it, 'the important thing is not to draw up in advance a plan anticipating everything, but rather to set resolutely to work'.[12]

Notes

1 L. Wacquant (2011) 'From "Public Criminology" to the Reflexive Sociology of Criminological Production and Consumption', *British Journal of Criminology*, 51(2): 438–48, 445.

2 For two rather different accounts of this same process, see A. H. Halsey (2004) *A History of Sociology in Britain*. Oxford: Oxford University Press; and M. Savage (2010) *Identities and Social Change in Britain Since 1940*. Oxford: Oxford University Press.

3 On the opposition between restricted and popular markets in fields of cultural production, see P. Bourdieu (1993) *The Field of Cultural Production*. Cambridge: Polity. The decline of the Penguin paperback is a signal marker of this, as discussed in Savage (2010) *op. cit.*

4 M. Savage and R. Burrows (2007) 'The Coming Crisis of Empirical Sociology', *Sociology*, 41(5): 885–99.

5 On the structure and dynamics of the field of think-tanks in the US, see T. Medvetz (2008) *Think Tanks as an Emergent Field*. New York: The Social Science Research Foundation; also T. Medvetz (2003) 'Les *Think Tanks* aux États-Unis', *Actes de la Recherche en Sciences Sociales*, 174: 4–13. On the history of think-tanks in the UK, see A. Denham and M. Garnett (1998) *British Think Tanks and the Climate of Opinion*. London: UCL Press.

6 A. Stevens (2011) 'Telling Policy Stories: An Ethnographic Study of the Use of Evidence in Policy-Making in the UK', *Journal of Social Policy*, 40(2): 237–56.

7 See P. Bourdieu (1998) *On Television*. New York: The New Press; and P. Bourdieu (2005) 'The Political Field, the Social Scientific Field and the Journalistic Field' in R. Benson and E. Neveu (eds) *Bourdieu and the Journalistic Field*. Cambridge: Polity, pp. 29–47.

8 It might be argued that social networking cites, especially Twitter, allow the circumvention of the journalistic field in political intervention, but in fact the audience for one's 'tweets' is situated in a whole economy of exchanges (tweeting 'at' interested parties and consecrating 'retweets') heavily dependent upon the avatars of the established media.

9 Bourdieu (2005) *op. cit.* Cf. also the contributions by Patrick Champagne and Dominique Marchetti in Benson and Neveu, *op. cit.* The BBC, with its state funding and peculiar mission and values (including 'objectivity'), clearly operates with a certain *relative* degree of autonomy within the field, but, as a diverse field of forces in itself, its different branches and journalists certainly have their own orientations, interests and prenotions and present to greater or lesser degrees the same pitfalls to academics as other media organisations.

10 Witness the triumphant playing of the hagiographical film *The Trouble with Being Human These Days* to delegates at the British Sociological Association annual conference in 2012.

11 For details see, *inter alia*, A. H. Halsey (1992) *The Decline of Donnish Dominion*. Oxford: Oxford University Press; M. Power (1997) *The Audit Society*. Oxford: Oxford University Press; M. Strathern (ed.) (2000) *Audit Cultures*. London: Routledge; R. Brown (2004) *Quality Assurance in Higher Education*. London: RoutledgeFalmer; L. Lucas (2006) *The Research Game in Academic Life*. Maidenhead: Open University Press; J. Welshman (2009) 'Where Lesser Angels May Have Feared to Tread', *Contemporary British History*, 23(2): 199–219; C. Holligan, M. Wilson and W. Humes (2011) 'Research Cultures in English and Scottish University Education Departments', *British Educational Research Journal*, 37(4): 713–34.

12 E. Durkheim (1952) *Suicide*. London: Routledge and Kegan Paul, p. 392.

Select Bibliography

Agamben, G. (2005) *State of Exception*. Chicago: University of Chicago Press.

Agnew, R. (1999) 'A General Strain Theory of Community Differences in Crime Rates', *Journal of Research in Crime and Delinquency*, 36: 123–55.

Archer, L. and Hutchings, M. (2000) '"Bettering Yourself": Discourses of Risk, Cost and Benefit in Ethnically Diverse, Young Working-Class Non-Participants' Constructions of Higher Education', *British Journal of Sociology of Education*, 21(4): 555–74.

Atkinson, R. (2006) 'Padding the Bunker: Strategies of Middle Class Disaffiliation and Colonization in the City', *Urban Studies*, 43(3): 819–32.

Atkinson, W. (2010) *Class, Individualization and Late Modernity: In Search of the Reflexive Worker*. Basingstoke: Palgrave Macmillan.

Ball, S. (2003) *Class Strategies and the Education Market*. London: RoutledgeFalmer.

Ball, S. (2008) *The Education Debate*. Bristol: Policy Press.

Bauman, Z. (2005) *Work, Consumerism and the New Poor*. Milton Keynes: Open University Press.

Bennett, T., Savage, M., Silva, E., Gayo-Cal, M. and Wright, D. (2009) *Culture, Class, Distinction*. London: Routledge.

Bourdieu, P. (1977) *Outline of a Theory of Practice*. Cambridge: Cambridge University Press.

Bourdieu, P. (1984) *Distinction*. London: Routledge.

Bourdieu, P. (1990) *In Other Words*. Cambridge: Polity.

Bourdieu, P. (1993) *Sociology in Question*. London: Sage.

Bourdieu, P. (1993) *The Field of Cultural Production*. Cambridge: Polity.

Bourdieu, P. (1996) *The State Nobility*. Cambridge: Polity Press.

Bourdieu, P. (1998) *Acts of Resistance*. Cambridge: Polity.

Bourdieu, P. (1998) *On Television*. New York: The New Press.

Bourdieu, P. (2001) *Masculine Domination*. Cambridge: Polity.

Bourdieu, P. (2003) *Firing Back*. New York: The New Press.

Bourdieu, P. (2005) 'The Political Field, the Social Scientific Field and the Journalistic Field' in R. Benson and E. Neveu (eds) *Bourdieu and the Journalistic Field*. Cambridge: Polity, pp. 29–47.

Bourdieu, P. and Passeron, J.-C. (1990) *Reproduction in Education, Society and Culture* (2nd Ed.) London: Sage.

Bourdieu, P. et al (1999) *The Weight of the World*. Cambridge: Polity.

Brown, G. (2011) 'Emotional Geographies of Young People's Aspirations for Adult Life', *Children's Geographies*, 9(1): 7–22.

Brown, P., Lauder, H. and Ashton, D. (2010) *The Global Auction: The Broken Promises of Education, Jobs and Incomes*. Oxford: Oxford University Press.

Caballero, C. and Edwards, R. (2010) *Lone Mothers of Mixed Racial and Ethnic Children: Then and Now*. London: Runnymede.

Calhoun, C. (ed.) (1994) *Social Theory and the Politics of Identity*. Oxford: Blackwell.

Clement, M. (2010) 'Teenagers Under the Knife: Decivilising Processes in a Western City', *Journal of Youth Studies*, 13(4): 439–51.

Clement, M. (2012) 'Rage Against the Market: Bristol's Tesco Riot', *Race and Class*, 53(3): 81–90.

Clement, M. (forthcoming) 'Deadly Symbiosis: How School Exclusion and Juvenile Crime Interweave' in M. Koegeler and R. Parncutt (eds) *Interculturality: Practice Meets Research*. Cambridge: Cambridge Scholars Publishing.

Coates, K. and Silburn, R. (1970) *Poverty: The Forgotten Englishmen*. London: Penguin.

Davidson, E. (2011) *The Burdens of Aspiration: Schools, Youth, and Success in the Divided Social Worlds of Silicon Valley*. London: New York University Press.

Denham, A. and Garnett, M. (1998) *British Think Tanks and the Climate of Opinion*. London: UCL Press.

Devine, F. (2004) *Class Practices: How Parents Help Their Children Get Good Jobs*. Cambridge: Cambridge University Press.

Devine, F., Savage, M., Scott, J. and Crompton, R. (eds) (2005) *Rethinking Class*. Basingstoke: Palgrave Macmillan.

Doogan, K. (2009) *New Capitalism?* Cambridge: Polity.

Dorling, D. (2010) 'New Labour and Inequality', *Local Economy*, 25(5–6): 406–23.

Duncan, S. (2007) 'What's the Problem with Teenage Parents? And What's the Problem with Policy?', *Critical Social Policy*, 27(3): 307–34.

Edwards, R. and Duncan, S. (1997) 'Supporting the Family: Lone Mothers, Paid Work and the Underclass Debate', *Critical Social Policy*, 17(4): 29–49.

Elias, N. (1990) *What is Sociology?* Columbia: Columbia University Press.

Elias, N. (2000) *The Civilizing Process*. Oxford: Blackwell.

Engelen, E., Ertürk, I., Froud, J., Johal, S., Leaver, A., Moran, M., Nilsson, A. and Williams, K. (2011) *After the Great Complacence: Financial Crisis and the Politics of Reform*. Oxford: Oxford University Press.

Epstein, G. A. (ed.) (2005) *Financialization and the World Economy*. Cheltenham: Edward Elgar.

Evans, S. (2009) 'In a Different Place: Working-Class Girls and Higher Education', *Sociology*, 43(2): 340–55.

Foucault, M. (2001) *Madness and Civilization*. London: Routledge.

Froud, J., Johal, S., Haslam, C. and Williams, K. (2001) 'Accumulation Under Conditions of Inequality', *Review of International Political Economy*, 8(1): 66–95.

Furlong, A. and Cartmel, F. (2009) *Higher Education and Social Justice*. Buckingham: Open University Press.

Gillies, V. (2005) 'Meeting Parents' Needs? Discourses of "Support" and "Inclusion"', *Critical Social Policy*, 25(1): 70–91.

Gillies, V. (2005) 'Raising the Meritocracy: Parenting and the Individualisation of Social Class', *Sociology*, 39(5): 835–52.

Gillies, V. (2007) *Marginalised Mothers: Exploring Working Class Experiences of Parenting*. Abingdon: Routledge.

Gillies, V. (2008) 'Perspectives on Parenting Responsibility: Contextualising Values and Practices', *Law and Society*, 35(1): 95–112.

Gillies, V. (2011) 'From Function to Competence: Engaging with the New Politics of Family', *Sociological Research Online*, 16(4): http://www.socresonline.org.uk/16/4/11.html.

Goos, M. and Manning, A. (2007) 'Lousy and Lovely Jobs: The Rising Polarization of Work in Britain', *The Review of Economics and Statistics*, 89(1): 118–33.

Hall, S., Winlow, S. and Ancrum, C. (2008) *Criminal Identities and Consumer Culture*. Cullompton: Willan.

Halsey, A. H., Heath, A. F. and Ridge, J. M. (1980) *Origins and Destinations: Family, Class and Education in Modern Britain*. Oxford: Clarendon Press.

Harvey, D. (2005) *A Brief History of Neoliberalism*. Oxford: Oxford University Press.

Haylett, C. (2003) *Culture, Class and Urban Policy: Reconsidering Inequality*. Oxford: Blackwell.

Hobson, J. A. (1937) *Property and Improperty*. London: Gollancz.

Ingram, N. (2011) 'Within School and Beyond the Gate: The Difficulties of Being Educationally Successful and Working-Class', *Sociology*, 45(7): 287–302.

Jordan, B. (1974) *Poor Parents: Social Policy and the Cycle of Deprivation*. London: Routledge.

Lerner, M. (1980) *The Belief in a Just World: A Fundamental Delusion*. New York: Plenum.

LeRoux, B., Rouanet, H., Savage, M. and Warde, A. (2008) 'Class and Cultural Division in the UK', *Sociology*, 42(6): 1049–71.

Levitas, R. (2005) *The Inclusive Society?* (2nd Ed.). Basingstoke: Palgrave Macmillan.

Li, Y., Savage, M. and Pickles, A. (2003) 'Social Capital and Social Exclusion in England and Wales, 1972–1999', *British Journal of Sociology*, 54: 497–526.

Li, Y., Savage, M. and Warde, A. (2008) 'Social Mobility and Social Capital in Contemporary Britain', *British Journal of Sociology*, 59(3): 391–411.

MacDonald, R. and Marsh, J. (2005) *Disconnected Youth? Growing up in Britain's Poor Neighbourhoods*. London: Palgrave Macmillan.

MacDonald, R., Shildrick, T., Webster, C. and Simpson, D. (2005) 'Growing Up in Poor Neighbourhoods: The Significance of Class and Place in the Extended Transitions of "Socially Excluded" Young Adults', *Sociology*, 39(5): 873–91.

Majima, S. and Savage, M. (2007) 'Have There Been Culture Shifts in Britain?', *Cultural Sociology*, 1(3): 293–315.

Martin, R. (2002) *The Financialization of Everyday Life*. New Jersey: Temple University Press.

Marx, K. (1954) *Capital, Vol. I*. London: Lawrence and Wishart.

Marx, K. (1972) *Capital, Vol. III*. London: Lawrence and Wishart.

McKenzie, L. (2012) 'Finding Value on a Council Estate: Voices of White Working Class Women' in R. Edwards, S. Ali, C. Caballero and M. Song (eds) *International Perspectives on Racial and Ethnic Mixedness and Mixing*. London: Routledge.

McKibbin, R. (1998) *Classes and Cultures in Britain*. Oxford: Oxford University Press.

McLennan, G. (2004) 'Travelling with Vehicular Ideas: The Case of the Third Way', *Economy and Society*, 33(4): 484–99.

Mellor, M. (2010) *The Future of Money: From Financial Crisis to Public Resource*. London: Pluto Press.

Miles, A. and Savage, M. (2011) 'Telling a Modest Story: Accounts of Men's Upward Mobility from the National Child Development Study', *British Journal of Sociology*, 62(3): 418–41.

Peck, J. (2010) *Constructions of Neoliberal Reason*. Oxford: Oxford University Press.

Putnam, R. (2000) *Bowling Alone*. New York: Simon and Shuster.

Raco, M. (2009) 'From Expectations to Aspirations: State Modernisation, Urban Policy, and the Existential Politics of Welfare in the UK', *Political Geography*, 28: 436–54.

Reay, D. (2001) 'Finding or Losing Yourself? Working-Class Relationships to Education', *Journal of Education Policy*, 16: 333–46.

Reay, D. (2004) '"Mostly Roughs and Toughs": Social Class, Race and Representation in Inner City Schooling', *Sociology*, 38(4): 1005–23.

Reay, D. and Ball, S. (1997) 'Spoilt for "Choice": The Working Classes and Education Markets', *Oxford Review of Education*, 23: 89–101.

Reay, D., Crozier, G. and Clayton, D. (2010) '"Fitting In" or "Standing Out": Working-Class Students in UK Higher Education', *British Educational Research Journal*, 32(1): 1–19.

Reay, D., Crozier, G. and James, D. (2011) *White Middle Class Identities and Urban Schooling*. Basingstoke: Palgrave Macmillan.

Reay, D., David, M. and Ball, S. (2005) *Degrees of Choice: Class, Race, Gender and Higher Education*. Stoke-on-Trent: Trentham.

Ribbens McCarthy, J., Edwards, R. and Gillies, V. (2003) *Making Families*. Durham: Sociology Press.

Roberts, S. (2011) 'Beyond NEET and "Tidy" Pathways: Considering the Missing Middle of Youth Transitions Studies', *Journal of Youth Studies*, 14(1): 21–39.

Roberts, S. (2012) 'Gaining Skills or Just Paying the Bills? Workplace Learning in Low-Level Retail Employment', *Journal of Education and Work*, iFirst article.

Rodger, J. (1995) 'Family Policy or Moral Regulation?', *Critical Social Policy*, 15: 5–25.

Savage, M. (1987) *The Dynamics of Working Class Politics: The Labour Movement in Preston, 1880–1940*. Cambridge: Cambridge University Press.

Savage, M. (2000) *Class Analysis and Social Transformation*. Milton Keynes: Open University Press.

Savage, M. (2007) 'Changing Social Class Identities in Post-War Britain: Perspectives from Mass-Observation', *Sociological Research Online*, 12(3).

Savage, M. (2010) *Identities and Social Change in Britain Since 1940*. Oxford: Oxford University Press.

Savage, M. (2010) 'The Politics of Elective Belonging', *Housing, Theory and Society*, 26(1): 115–61.

Savage, M. and Burrows, R. (2007) 'The Coming Crisis of Empirical Sociology', *Sociology*, 41(5): 885–99.

Savage, M. and Miles, A. (1993) *The Remaking of the British Working Classes 1880–1940*. London: Routledge.

Savage, M. and Williams, K. (eds) (2008) *Remembering Elites*. Oxford: Blackwell.

Savage, M., Bagnall, G. and Longhurst, B. (2001) 'Ordinary, Ambivalent and Defensive: Class Identities in the North-West of England', *Sociology*, 35(4): 875–92.

Sayer, A. (2011) 'Habitus, Work and Contributive Justice', *Sociology*, 45(1): 7–21.

Sennett, R. and Cobb, J. (1972) *The Hidden Injuries of Class*. New York: Random House.

Skeggs, B. (1997) *Formations of Class and Gender*. London: Sage.

Skeggs, B. (2004) *Class, Self, Culture*. London: Routledge.

Taylor-Gooby, P. (2012) 'Root and Branch Restructuring to Achieve Major Cuts: The Social Policy Programme of the 2010 UK Coalition Government', *Social Policy & Administration*, 46(1): 61–82.

Wacquant, L. (1993) 'On the Tracks of Symbolic Power: Preparatory Notes to Bourdieu's *State Nobility*', *Theory, Culture and Society*, 10: 1–17.

Wacquant, L. (2004) 'Decivilizing and Demonizing' in S. Loyal and S. Quilley (eds) *The Sociology of Norbert Elias*. Cambridge: Cambridge University Press, pp. 95–121.

Wacquant, L. (2008) *Urban Outcasts: A Comparative Sociology of Advanced Marginality*. Cambridge: Polity.

Wacquant, L. (2009) 'The Body, the Ghetto and the Penal State', *Qualitative Sociology*, 32: 101–29.

Wacquant, L. (2009) *Punishing the Poor*. Durham: Duke University Press.

Wacquant, L. (2011) 'From "Public Criminology" to the Reflexive Sociology of Criminological Production and Consumption', *British Journal of Criminology*, 51(2): 438–48.

Wacquant, L. (2012) 'Three Steps to a Historical Anthropology of Actually Existing Neoliberalism', *Social Anthropology*, 20(1): 66–79.

Walkerdine, V. and Jiminez, L. (2012) *Gender, Work and Community After De-industrialisation*. Basingstoke: Palgrave Macmillan.

Walkerdine, V., Lucey, H. and Melody, J. (2002) *Growing Up Girl: Psychosocial Explorations of Gender and Class*. London: Palgrave Macmillan.

Warde, A., Tampubolon, G., Longhurst, B., Ray, K., Savage, M. and Tomlinson, M. (2003) 'Trends in Social Capital: Membership of Associations in Great Britain', *British Journal of Political Science*, 33: 515–25.

Willis, P. (1977) *Learning to Labour: How Working Class Kids Get Working Class Jobs*. Farnborough: Saxon House.

Wright, E. O. (2000) *Class Counts*. Cambridge: Cambridge University Press.

Wright, E. O. (ed.) (2005) *Approaches to Class Analysis*. Cambridge: Cambridge University Press.

Index